Microsoft® Office XP

plain & simple

Your fast-answers, no-jargon guide to Office XP!

Carol Brown and Resources Online

PUBLISHED BY
Microsoft Press
A Division of Microsoft Corporation
One Microsoft Way
Redmond, Washington 98052-6399

MFS
PO Box 43521
Detroit MI 48243-0521

Library of Congress Cataloging-in-Publication Data
Microsoft Office XP Plain & Simple / Carol Brown, Resources Online.
        p. cm.
    Includes index.
    ISBN 0-7356-1449-0
    1. Microsoft Office.   2. Business--Computer programs.   I. Title: Microsoft Office XP
Plain and Simple.   II. Resources Online.

    HF5548.4.M525 M5385   2001
    005.369--dc21   2001044400

Printed and bound in the United States of America.

7 8 9   QWT   6 5 4

Distributed in Canada by H.B. Fenn and Company Ltd.

A CIP catalogue record for this book is available from the British Library.

Microsoft Press books are available through booksellers and distributors worldwide. For further information about international editions, contact your local Microsoft Corporation office or contact Microsoft Press International directly at fax (425) 936-7329. Visit our Web site at www.microsoft.com/mspress. Send comments to *mspinput@microsoft.com*.

Acquisitions Editor: Kong Cheung
Project Editors: Judith Bloch and Kristen Weatherby

Body Part No. X08-24301

Contents

4 Creating, Editing, and Printing a Word Document 37

5 Formatting a Word Document 61

6) Building Complex Documents Using Word   77

7) Creating an Excel Worksheet   97

14 Creating a PowerPoint Presentation   211

15 Enhancing a PowerPoint Presentation   227

16 Delivering a PowerPoint Presentation   239

17 Getting Started Using an Access Database   251

18 Using FrontPage   265

19 Publishing Web Pages in Office — 281

20 Creating a Publication with Publisher — 297

NEW FEATURE

21 Creating and Working with a SharePoint Team Web Site 319

i Index 333

Acknowledgments

Contributing writers

Nanette J. Eaton, for clean, concise, correct copy, delivered on time, every time

Tycen Hopkins, for practicing technical wizardry while writing three challenging chapters

Erin Page, for condensing years of experience and expertise into the chapters on Excel

Editors

Norreen Holmes, Lead, our Delphic oracle of copy, for interpreting what is correct and what ain't

Nona Allison, for her infusion of energy as a one-person editorial emergency response team

Jan Bultmann, for her keen eye and meticulous attention to the fine points

Jill Carlsen, readers' advocate, for bringing a fresh perspective to technical detail

Cindy Riskin, for her unflagging and conscientious pursuit of technical accuracy

Production

Kat Marriner, Lead, as Ruler of Organization for keeping us on task, and as Monarch of Tight Spaces, for making it all fit

Heidi Hackler, for her speed and versatility as a production crew of one

April Richards, FreeHand jockey extraordinaire, for transforming screenshots into illustrations

Laren Watson, for working up pages and polishing them shiny

Indexer

Luke Celt, for working under deadlines to build an index that is as thoughtful as it is thorough

Microsoft Press

Judith Bloch, for even-handed grace under pressure

Kristen Weatherby, for her hard work and thorough reviews

Kong Cheung, for entrusting us with this title

About This Book

If you want to get the most from your computer and Microsoft Office XP with the least amount of time and effort—and who doesn't?—this book is for you. You'll find *Microsoft Office XP Plain & Simple* to be a straightforward, easy-to-read reference tool. With the premise that your computer should work for you, not you for it, this book's purpose is to help you get your work done quickly and efficiently so that you can get away from the computer and live your life.

No Computerese!

Let's face it—when there's a task you don't know how to do but you need to get it done in a hurry, or when you're stuck in the middle of a task and can't figure out what to do next, there's nothing more frustrating than having to read page after page of technical background material. You want the information you need—nothing more, nothing less—and you want it now! *And* it should be easy to find and understand.

That's what this book is all about. It's written in plain English—no technical jargon and no computerese. There's no single task in the book that takes more than three pages. Just look the task up in the index or the table of contents, turn to the page, and there's the information you need, laid out in an illustrated step-by-step format. You don't get bogged down by the whys and wherefores: just follow the steps and get your work done with a minimum of hassle.

Occasionally you might have to turn to another page if the procedure you're working on is accompanied by a "See Also." That's because there's a lot of overlap among tasks, and we didn't want to keep repeating ourselves. We've scattered some useful "Tips" here and there, and thrown in a "Try This" or a "Caution" once in awhile, but by and large we've tried to remain true to the heart and soul of the book, which is that the information you need should be available to you at a glance.

Useful Tasks...

Whether you use Office XP at home or on the road, we've tried to pack this book with procedures for everything we could think of that you might want to do, from the simplest tasks to some of the more esoteric ones.

...And the Easiest Way to Do Them

Another thing we've tried to do in this book is find and document the easiest way to accomplish a task. Office XP often provides a multitude of methods to accomplish a single end result—which can be daunting or delightful, depending on the way you like to work. If you tend to stick with one favorite and familiar approach, we think the methods described in this book are the way to go. If you like trying out alternative techniques, go ahead! The intuitiveness of Office XP invites exploration, and you're likely to discover ways of doing things that you think are easier or that you like better than ours. If you do, that's great! It's exactly what the developers of Office XP had in mind when they provided so many alternatives.

A Quick Overview

Your computer may have come with Office XP already installed, but if you do have to install it yourself, the Setup Wizard makes installation so simple that you won't need our help. So, unlike many computer books, this one doesn't start with installation instructions and a list of system requirements.

Next, you don't have to read this book in any particular order. It's designed so that you can jump in, get the information you need, and then close the book and keep it near your computer until the next time you need to know how to get something done. But that doesn't mean we scattered the information about with wild abandon.

We've organized the book by Office program, dedicating from one to three sections to each program. We've also included four sections that cover commonalities in all the programs. In each section we arranged procedures within the main task in a loose progression from the simplest to the most complex.

We cover the mainstays of Office—Microsoft Word, Microsoft Excel, Microsoft PowerPoint, and Microsoft Outlook—with three sections devoted to each program. In each case, we start with the basics of building a document, spreadsheet, presentation, or e-mail message, and then, in subsequent sections, build on the basics as appropriate for each program.

There are many features that work in similar ways no matter what program you're using. As a demonstration of the tight integration and consistency in the Office XP suite, two sections describe tasks from the point of view of any Office program.

First, Section 2, "Jumping Into Microsoft Office," introduces the basic commonalities in Office—starting and quitting programs; opening, finding, saving, closing, deleting, and printing files; and getting assistance. There are, however, other features common to all programs. We've put some in the sections where you might encounter them first—for example, formatting text in Section 5, "Formatting a Word Document." Look for others in sections where they are integral to a program. For example, you can send e-mail from most Office programs, but you'll find the details in Section 10, "Using Outlook for E-Mail." These common features are listed in a table in "Common Office XP Tasks and Where to Find Them," on page 22.

Second, Section 3, "Enhancing Documents," describes tools available in virtually every program. Here you'll find out how to add media ranging from clip art and WordArt to sound and video and learn how to embellish pictures by playing with their size, position, color, and the like.

Office XP has greatly enhanced the collaborative experience, so two sections highlight both new and familiar tools to help build cohesive and effective teams. Section 13, "Collaborating Using Office," focuses on Office tools for creating and managing a document in a team environment. Section 21, "Creating and Working with a SharePoint Team Web Site," outlines the ways you can build and manage a team Web site for creating event calendars, storing documents, and other team activities, without any knowledge of HTML (Hypertext Markup Language) or other programming.

We've devoted two sections to Office features for publishing to the Web. Section 19, "Publishing Web Pages in Office," focuses primarily on how to create Web pages based on Word, Excel, PowerPoint, and Microsoft Publisher documents. Section 18, "Using FrontPage," introduces the basic skills you'll need to build and maintain an entire Web site.

To get you going in Microsoft Access and Publisher we offer one section on each. Section 17, "Getting Started Using an Access Database," introduces the practical and simple ways you can take advantage of the powerful data-management tools in Access. Section 20, "Creating a Publication with Publisher," gives you a jump-start on creating a publication and introduces you to Publisher's powerful wizards that help you add text and pictures and embellish your publication in myriad ways.

A Few Assumptions

We had to make a few educated guesses about you, our audience, when we started writing this book. You may work at home, in a small or medium-sized office, or in a large corporation; we also assume that you have a connection to the Internet. Although you may have a system administrator or other technical help available to you, with a few exceptions as noted, the aim of the book is to help you acquire the fundamental (and not-so-fundamental) skills of working productively in Office XP without leaning on these resources.

We assume that you've mastered the mouse—you're completely at ease with clicking, double-clicking, and dragging, and know to watch the mouse pointer for indications of what you can do next. We assume you're comfortable navigating the Web and have mastered the basic skills of Windows. You understand how to

work with files—copy, move, open, close, and delete them—and are at home with the basic Windows interface of menus, buttons, and options. If you're not, we recommend one of two companion books, depending on the version of Windows you're using: *Microsoft Windows ME At a Glance* or *Microsoft Windows XP Plain & Simple*.

A Final Word (or Two)

We had three goals in writing this book:

- Whatever you want to do, we want the book to help you get it done.

- We want the book to help you discover how to do things you *didn't* know you wanted to do.

- And, finally, if we've achieved the first two goals, we'll be well on the way to the third, which is for our book to help you enjoy using Office XP. We think that's the best gift we could give you to thank you for buying our book.

We hope you'll have as much fun using *Microsoft Office XP Plain & Simple* as we've had writing it. The best way to learn is by doing, and that's how we hope you'll use this book.

Jump right in!

2 Jumping Into Microsoft Office

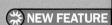

All Microsoft Office programs, by design, have a familiar look, their menus and toolbars are structurally similar, and they take a common approach to many tasks: quitting programs; opening, finding, saving, closing, deleting, and printing files; and getting assistance, whether in the form of a tiny ScreenTip or a full-blown task pane.

This Office–wide consistency makes it possible to offer some efficiency tips—how to work with ever-present toolbars and task panes and our own favorite techniques for working smart. We also show how to take advantage of Office's ability to detect and repair internal problems as well as to recover your files in the event your computer crashes.

Each Office program, however, has its own unique approach that fits hand-in-glove with tasks specific to each program. Microsoft Outlook in particular stands out as unique. Files and folders are all stored and accessed within Outlook, so even though you can perform most of the tasks outlined in this section, in Outlook nearly every task works a bit differently. Note, too, that the steps in this section are general procedures meant to demonstrate how Office programs work in similar ways. A particular Office program might work differently from the others, depending on the options available in that program. Bearing this in mind, turn to the sections on specific programs for guidance in building and producing the e-mail messages, worksheets, presentations, Web pages, and other documents Office makes possible.

Starting an Office Program

Office gives you a half dozen ways to start any of its programs. We've featured two here. One sure-fire method using the Windows Start button works no matter what the configuration of your system; the other, a bit more efficient, uses the Office Shortcut Bar.

The Office Shortcut Bar, with push-button access to every program in Office, can open automatically whenever you start Windows. It's such a nifty gadget and so easy to personalize that you might want to make it home base for your most often-used programs (Office or not), favorite Web links, and even folders you work in routinely.

Open a Program Using the Start Menu

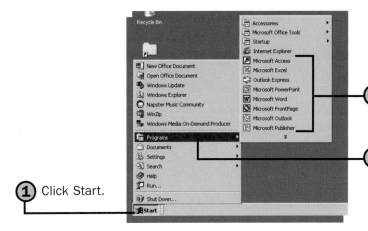

③ Click the Office program you want to open.

② Point to Programs.

① Click Start.

Open a Program Using the Office Shortcut Bar

① On the Office Shortcut Bar, click the button of the Office program you want to open.

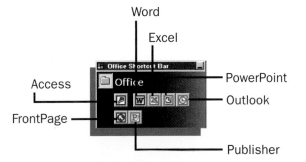

Word

Excel

Access

FrontPage

PowerPoint

Outlook

Publisher

> **TIP:** If you don't see the Office Shortcut Bar when you follow the steps in "Display the Office Shortcut Bar on Windows Startup," it might not have been installed. To install it, insert your Office XP disc into the CD drive, and double-click SETUP.EXE in the dialog box that appears. In the Microsoft Office XP Setup dialog box, click Add Or Remove Features, and then click Next. In the Microsoft Office Tools area, click Microsoft Office Shortcut Bar, click Update, and then follow the directions on your screen. The next time you start Windows, the Office Shortcut Bar will appear.

> **SEE ALSO:** For information about how to move the Office Shortcut Bar just where you want it, see "Working Efficiently Using Toolbars and Task Panes" on page 18.

> **TIP:** If you forget which button opens which program, pause the mouse pointer over the button until a ScreenTip appears with the details.

Display the Office Shortcut Bar on Windows Startup

(1) Click Start.

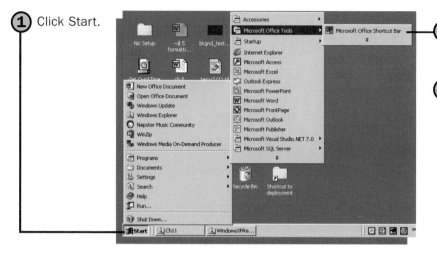

(2) Point to Programs, point to Microsoft Office Tools, and click Microsoft Office Shortcut Bar.

(3) In the Microsoft Office Shortcut Bar dialog box, click Yes to have the Office Shortcut Bar open each time you start Windows.

> ✋ **CAUTION: It can be difficult to restore a shortcut button you've deleted. If you want to remove a program shortcut from the Office Shortcut Bar, hide it by clearing its check box rather than deleting it.**

Personalize the Office Shortcut Bar

(1) Click the Shortcut Bar Control icon, and click Customize.

(2) Click the Buttons tab.

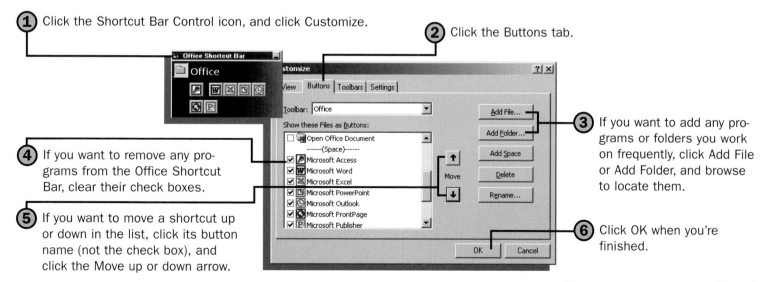

(3) If you want to add any programs or folders you work on frequently, click Add File or Add Folder, and browse to locate them.

(4) If you want to remove any programs from the Office Shortcut Bar, clear their check boxes.

(5) If you want to move a shortcut up or down in the list, click its button name (not the check box), and click the Move up or down arrow.

(6) Click OK when you're finished.

Opening an Existing File

Opening a file is somewhat like a treasure hunt: if you're the one who hid the treasure (or saved the file), then you can go right to it; otherwise, you might have to hunt for it.

Open a File

① Click the Open button. (The button name may differ depending on the program.)

③ Click the Look In down arrow, and browse to locate the file.

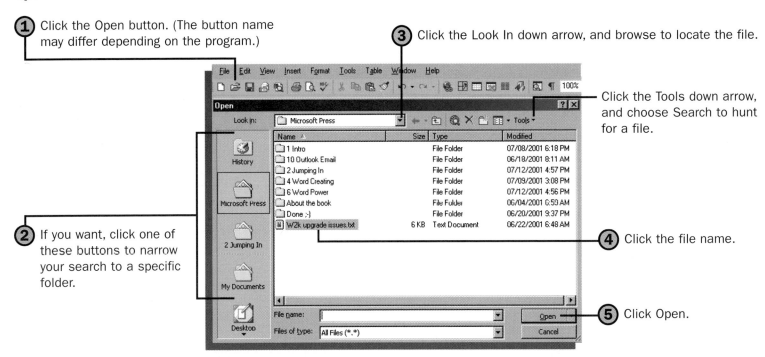

Click the Tools down arrow, and choose Search to hunt for a file.

② If you want, click one of these buttons to narrow your search to a specific folder.

④ Click the file name.

⑤ Click Open.

TIP: There's a shorter way to open the file you worked on most recently. In most programs, choose Task Pane from the View menu, and click the file name in the Open A Document list. If this shortcut appeals to you, you can easily show up to nine files in this list. To do this, choose Options from the Tools menu, and click the General tab. Then enter the number of files you want the program to display at one time in the Recently Used File List box, and click OK.

TRY THIS: You can open a document and its program in one fell swoop. To do so, choose Save As from the File menu, and give your file a name. Click the Desktop icon on the My Places bar, and click Save. The next time you're ready to open the file, simply double-click the file icon on your desktop to open the program and the document.

Finding a File or Text in a File ⊕ NEW FEATURE

You can search for files by name, certainly. And if you remember what you wrote, but not where you stored it, the completely refurbished search feature in Office XP lets you easily look for specific text in files as well. Searching for files or for text is akin to searching on the Web. The more specific your request—an exact file name or a distinctive phrase in a document—the more likely the search engine will speedily retrieve what you want and avoid spinning its wheels finding files you don't want.

> **!** **TIP:** You can narrow your search further to certain types of files—for example, just files from Microsoft Publisher or Microsoft Access. After you complete step 4 in "Search for a File or Text in a File," click the Results Should Be down arrow. Clear the check boxes for the types of files you don't want to search for, and select the ones you do. Return to step 5, and complete the search.

Search for a File or Text in a File

1 Click the task pane down arrow, and click Search. If the task pane isn't open, choose Task Pane from the View menu.

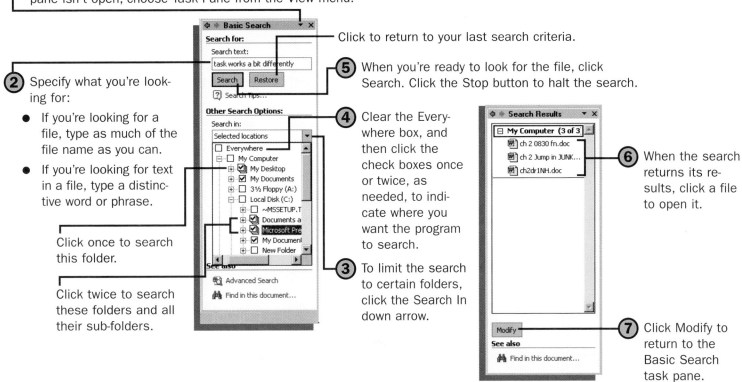

Click to return to your last search criteria.

2 Specify what you're looking for:

- If you're looking for a file, type as much of the file name as you can.
- If you're looking for text in a file, type a distinctive word or phrase.

Click once to search this folder.

Click twice to search these folders and all their sub-folders.

5 When you're ready to look for the file, click Search. Click the Stop button to halt the search.

4 Clear the Everywhere box, and then click the check boxes once or twice, as needed, to indicate where you want the program to search.

3 To limit the search to certain folders, click the Search In down arrow.

6 When the search returns its results, click a file to open it.

7 Click Modify to return to the Basic Search task pane.

Working with Documents in More Than One Program

On occasion you may find it useful to see documents from more than one program at once. Perhaps you want to refer to a Microsoft Excel spreadsheet as you work in Microsoft Word, or you're copying from a Publisher publication into an e-mail message. One way to accomplish this is to *tile* program windows—that is, arrange the windows (and the documents in them) alongside each other like kitchen tiles. Only one tiled window can be active at a time, and a window must be active before you can work in it. However, this is a natural part of working in a file, because clicking in the window when you start to work makes it active.

View Documents from More Than One Program at a Time

① Display each document you want to tile.

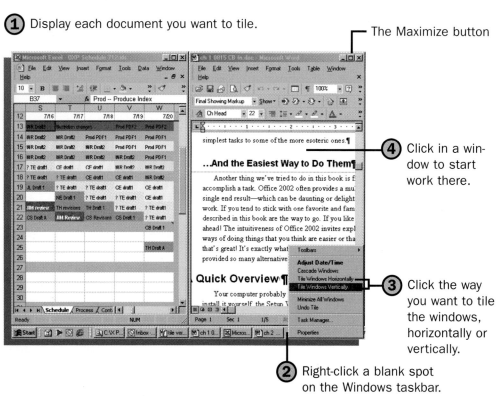

The Maximize button

④ Click in a window to start work there.

③ Click the way you want to tile the windows, horizontally or vertically.

② Right-click a blank spot on the Windows taskbar.

Switch Between Open Programs or Documents

① Hold down the Alt key, and press the Tab key until you select the program or document you want to work with.

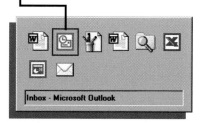

② Release the Alt and Tab keys to display the document or program whose icon is framed in blue—Outlook in our example.

Return to a Single Window

① Click the Maximize button at the upper right corner of the window.

Editing More Than One Document at a Time ⊙ NEW FEATURE

Office XP has sprung a new, highly visual Office Clipboard that makes copying and moving items from place to place a snap. You can use the Clipboard to move or copy anywhere, but because it's so visual, it really shines when you copy or move information within long documents or between programs.

As long as the Clipboard is *active*—that is, open in just one program—anything you copy or cut from any program is placed on the Clipboard, whether it's a paragraph from Word, an image from Publisher, a bulleted list from Microsoft PowerPoint, or a Web address from Microsoft Internet Explorer.

Move or Copy Items to Another File or Program

(1) Open the document you want to copy or move an item from.

(2) Select the text you want to move or copy, and do one of the following:
- Press Ctrl+C to make a copy.
- Press Ctrl+X to cut what you're going to move.

Open the Clipboard

(1) Choose Office Clipboard from the Edit menu.

> ✋ **CAUTION: The Office Clipboard works only when it is open in any Office program—that is, when you see the Clipboard open on the page or the Clipboard icon in the lower right corner of the window on the Windows taskbar.**

Notice that each block of text you copy or cut appears in the Clipboard.

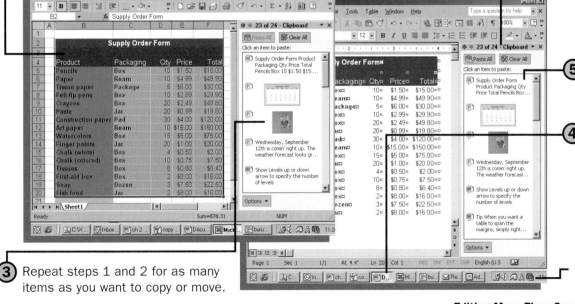

(5) Click the item on the Clipboard you're copying or moving.

(4) Switch to the program or document you're going to copy or move the item to, and click where you're going to insert it. You might have to open the Clipboard in this program as well.

(3) Repeat steps 1 and 2 for as many items as you want to copy or move.

The Clipboard icon indicates that the Clipboard is active.

Saving or Deleting a File

Saving frequently is your first line of defense against power outages and unexpected computer crashes. The first time you save a file, you specify the name of the file and where you want it to be stored. After that, whenever you save a file, the program replaces the old version with the new. But on occasion that won't do.

Perhaps you want to save each draft of your annual budget as it develops or put a PowerPoint slide show on your portable computer. And there will be times when a colleague can't open your report because she uses an earlier version of Word, or another word processing program entirely, such as WordPerfect.

The Office solution to these disparate needs is the Save As feature.

Deleting a file from within an Office program is straightforward—just make sure to close the file before you attempt to delete it because programs cannot delete open files.

Save a File for the First Time

(1) Click the Save button.

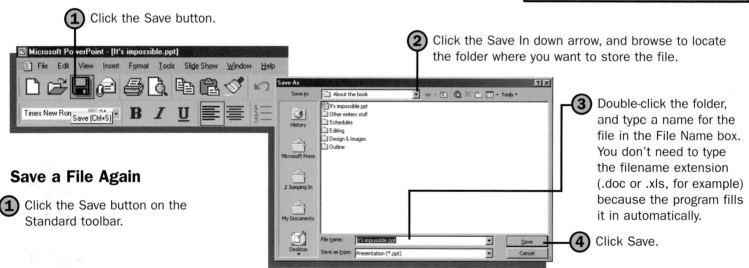

(2) Click the Save In down arrow, and browse to locate the folder where you want to store the file.

Save a File Again

(1) Click the Save button on the Standard toolbar.

(3) Double-click the folder, and type a name for the file in the File Name box. You don't need to type the filename extension (.doc or .xls, for example) because the program fills it in automatically.

(4) Click Save.

> **TIP:** You can direct Office programs to save your work at regular intervals so that you can recover it if there's a power outage or your system crashes. (It's important to note that this is *not* a substitute for saving regularly, as described on this page.) To do this, choose Options from the Tools menu, and click the Save tab. Select the Save AutoRecover Info Every...Minutes check box, and enter the frequency with which you want Office to save your files automatically.

> **TIP:** In Word, you can save all open documents at once: hold down the Shift key while you click the File menu, and then click Save All.

> **TIP:** For information about how to protect your files against loss of data, see the tip in "Recovering Files After a Computer Crashes" on page 23.

Save a File with a Different Name, in a New Folder, or in Another Format

1 Choose Save As from the File menu.

2 If you're saving the file in another folder, click the Save In down arrow, browse to locate the folder where you want to store the file, and double-click it.

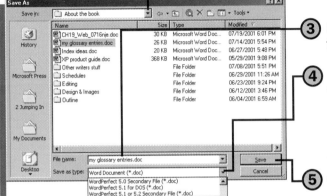

3 If you're changing the name of the file, type a new name for the file.

4 If you're changing the file format, click the Save As Type down arrow, and click the new format.

5 Click Save.

> **! TIP: You cannot delete Access files following these steps.**

MFS
PO Box 43521
Detroit MI 48243-0521

> **! TIP: Ever have that sinking feeling that you deleted something you wish you hadn't? The designers of Windows must have had that experience, because you can reinstate files after deleting them. First, double-click the Recycle Bin on your desktop. Then find the file you deleted, right-click it, and click Restore to return the file to its original folder.**

Delete a File from Within Office

2 Browse to locate the file you want to delete.

1 Make sure the file you want to delete is closed, and then choose Open from the File menu.

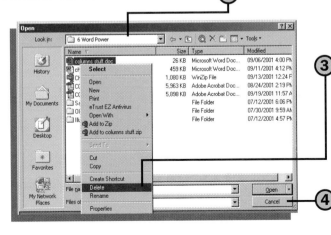

3 Right-click it, and click Delete. When Office asks for confirmation, do one of the following:

- Click Yes to delete the file and send it to the Recycle Bin.
- Click No to cancel deletion and return to the Save As dialog box.

4 Click Cancel to return to your document.

International Affairs
Detroit, Michigan, USA

MFS

Printing in Office

When you print a file, Office presents unique choices depending on the printer you're using and what program you're printing from. We've addressed those differences in the sections on each program. However, certain printing features—how to specify what you want to print, the number of copies and if they should be collated, and so on—cross almost all programs, and we describe those here.

> **SEE ALSO:** For information about how to switch from one printer to another, see "Checking and Printing a Publication" on page 316.

Print a File Quickly

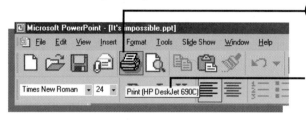

① Click Print.

Pause the mouse pointer over the button to identify the printer you're printing to.

> **TIP:** To stop printing, press the Esc key. If that doesn't work, look for the printer icon, a tiny printer, in the lower right corner of your screen. Double-click it, and in the printer window that appears, right-click the document you want to stop printing, and click Cancel Printing.

Print a File and Specify Your Options

① Choose Print from the File menu.

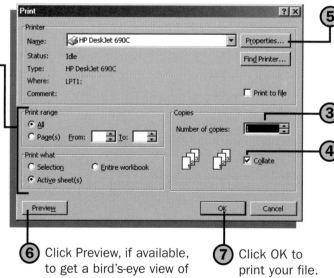

② To specify what you want to print, do one of the following:

- Click All to print the entire file
- Click Pages (or Slides) to print just those you specify.
- Click Selection, if available, to print that portion of the file you selected when you chose to print.
- Click Current Page (or Slide), if available, to print the page the insertion point was on when you chose to print.

⑤ Click Properties to switch between vertical (Portrait) and horizontal (Landscape) orientation of pages or to change the paper size.

③ Enter the number of copies you want to print.

④ Select to print multiple copies in sequential order, or clear to print all of page 1 first, all of page 2 second, and so on.

⑥ Click Preview, if available, to get a bird's-eye view of the file before you send it to the printer.

⑦ Click OK to print your file.

Closing Files and Quitting Office

When you close a file, you close the file that is displayed on your screen; when you quit a program, you choose Exit to close the program and any open files. However, in some programs—Publisher, for example—choosing Exit may close only the file you see on the screen, not all open files. This is because some programs open a fresh instance of the program for each open file. In those programs, follow the steps in "Quit an Office Program" for each open file (and for each instance of the program).

TIP: In Word and Excel, you can close all your open files at once: hold down the Shift key while you click the File menu, and then click Close All.

Close a File

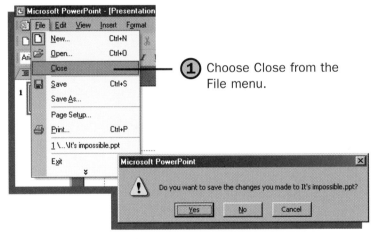

① Choose Close from the File menu.

② If you haven't saved recent changes, Office prompts you to do one of the following:

- Click Yes to save your changes to the file, and then close the file.
- Click No to close the file without saving changes.
- Click Cancel to return to the document without saving changes.

Quit an Office Program

① Choose Exit from the File menu to quit the program, and close all open files. (If there are any files you haven't saved, Office will prompt you to save each one, if you want.)

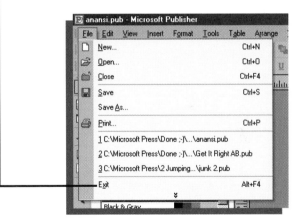

Getting Help

Thorough and thoughtful assistance is more available than ever in Office XP. Tips for practically every object you see on the screen, as well as step-by-step procedures, background information, and even illustrations are often on tap simply by pointing your mouse, but are never more than a couple of clicks away.

The Ask A Question box is your primary key to accessing Help in Office: type a few words in plain English and the program returns with a list of up to nine topics related to your request for information. However, if you don't find the answer you're looking for, the Ask A Question box is backed up by a searchable table of contents, by an index in the form of a keyword search, and by the Answer Wizard, which extends the capabilities of the Ask A Question box.

> **TIP:** To repeat an earlier question, click the Ask A Question down arrow to see the list of topics you've already researched, and click your question in the list.

Ask a Question ⊕ NEW FEATURE

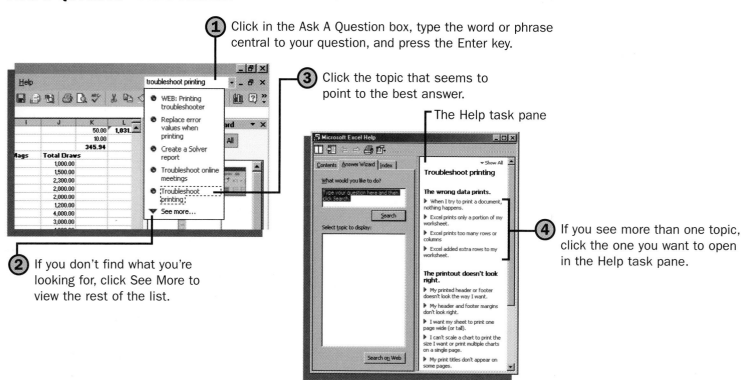

(1) Click in the Ask A Question box, type the word or phrase central to your question, and press the Enter key.

(2) If you don't find what you're looking for, click See More to view the rest of the list.

(3) Click the topic that seems to point to the best answer.

The Help task pane

(4) If you see more than one topic, click the one you want to open in the Help task pane.

Use ScreenTips for a Bit of Information

1 To see the name (and function) of any button, pause your mouse pointer over the button. (The ScreenTip disappears when you move the mouse.)

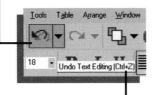

Office includes the keyboard shortcut to undo the last change.

Use ScreenTips for Detailed Information

1 To see a more detailed explanation, pause your mouse pointer over the Office object, and press Shift+F1.

2 When a question mark appears with the mouse pointer, click the object in question—the Word ruler in our example. (The ScreenTip disappears when you click the mouse.)

> **Horizontal ruler** The markers on the horizontal ruler display settings for the paragraph that contains the insertion point. To change the settings for indents, margins, and column widths, drag the markers on the horizontal ruler. To set a tab stop by using the horizontal ruler, click the button at the left end of the horizontal ruler until you see the type of tab you want, and then click the ruler to set a tab stop.

Getting Information About Dialog Box Options

1 In any dialog box, right-click the element you want information about.

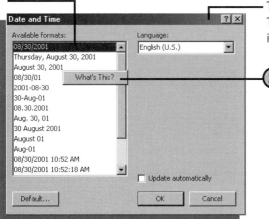

The Date And Time dialog box in Publisher

> **!** TIP: On occasion, you may find an entry in the list that has "WEB" in its title—for instance, "WEB: Printing troubleshooter." Click the title and in most cases you go directly, via the Web, to an appropriate topic. However, if you don't find a suitable topic in the list or via the direct Web link, you can search the Office Web site for information by clicking "None of the above, search for more on the Web." On the other hand, if one of the entries says, "None of the above, search for more on the Web," you will have to track down the information on your own.

2 Click What's This? to display an explanation. (The explanation disappears when you click the mouse.)

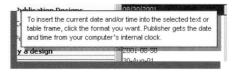

Working Efficiently Using Toolbars and Task Panes

Toolbars and task panes are the Office equivalent of a nip through the back alley to get around a traffic-clogged street. There are other ways to accomplish the tasks set out on every toolbar, but sometimes they are less efficient or accessible. To put a toolbar to work, click one of its buttons and Office springs into appropriate action.

Two toolbars are visible by default: the Standard and Formatting toolbars. Office automatically *docks* these toolbars and others at the margins of the window. Still others, Office assumes you might want close at hand and it *floats* them on the screen—the Picture toolbar, for example. You can add buttons to make sure the tasks you do most often are represented on the toolbar, or remove those you rarely or never use.

Task panes bring otherwise hidden features—and power—to the surface. Some task panes open automatically—for example, when you choose New from the File menu, the task pane for starting new documents opens. Most task panes, however, are available only on demand.

Display or Hide a Toolbar

① Right-click a toolbar.

② Click the name of the toolbar you want to display.

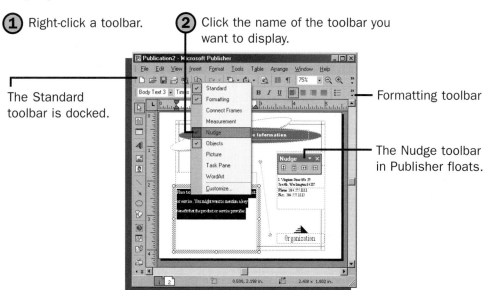

The Standard toolbar is docked.

Formatting toolbar

The Nudge toolbar in Publisher floats.

TIP: Most programs have toolbars tucked into other menus—the Rotate Or Flip toolbar in Publisher, for example, and the Office Shortcut Bar (described earlier in this section), accessible outside Office. You won't be able to follow the instructions in "Display or Hide a Toolbar" to display these toolbars, so prowl the menus for toolbars that may be of use.

SEE ALSO: For information about the keyboard shortcut equivalents to toolbars and menu commands, see "Working Smart" on page 20.

TRY THIS: If you don't see a button on the toolbar for something you do often, you may be able to add it. Click Toolbar Options. (This is the down arrow at the far right of a docked toolbar; on a floating toolbar, the down arrow is to the far right of the toolbar name.) Then point to Add Or Remove Buttons, and point to the toolbar you want to add a button to. Click the button you want to add, and then click outside the toolbar to close it. If the toolbar is docked and shares space with another toolbar, the program might drop a button you haven't used lately if there's not enough room to display the new button.

Put a Toolbar in Its Place

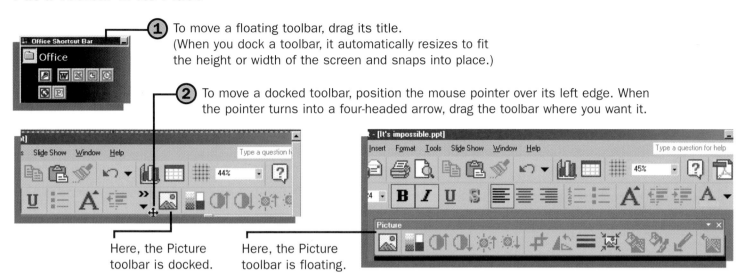

1 To move a floating toolbar, drag its title.
(When you dock a toolbar, it automatically resizes to fit the height or width of the screen and snaps into place.)

2 To move a docked toolbar, position the mouse pointer over its left edge. When the pointer turns into a four-headed arrow, drag the toolbar where you want it.

Here, the Picture toolbar is docked.

Here, the Picture toolbar is floating.

Open Task Panes and Switch Between Them ⊕ NEW FEATURE

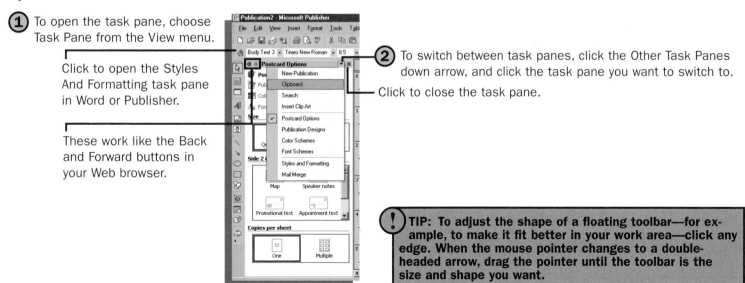

1 To open the task pane, choose Task Pane from the View menu.

Click to open the Styles And Formatting task pane in Word or Publisher.

These work like the Back and Forward buttons in your Web browser.

2 To switch between task panes, click the Other Task Panes down arrow, and click the task pane you want to switch to.

Click to close the task pane.

(!) TIP: To adjust the shape of a floating toolbar—for example, to make it fit better in your work area—click any edge. When the mouse pointer changes to a double-headed arrow, drag the pointer until the toolbar is the size and shape you want.

Working Smart

Everyone who uses Office has favorite tricks for making work easier and more efficient, tactics for uncovering options, and strategies for undoing mistakes. The following are ours.

Undo. Redo. Undo. Redo. Our constant companion, our safety net, there to help us recover from things we didn't mean to do or to restore our original intent when we change our minds. You can undo something as simple as deleting a word or as complex as creating an entire chart. And then change your mind with redo. It's a comfort to know that this feature can undo 100 edits or more.

There are several ways to undo or redo. For the keyboard fans, there's Ctrl+Z to undo an action and Ctrl+Y to redo it. If you're a mouse devotee, refer to the graphic to use the buttons on the Standard toolbar. If your memory is as good as that of Office, you can undo a lot of changes at once: click the Undo down arrow, scroll down the list (backwards in time), and click an earlier "undo" in the list.

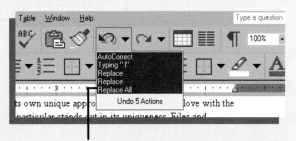

The program will undo this edit and all the edits highlighted above it at once.

> **CAUTION: However omnipotent the Undo command seems, it cannot undo everything, commands from the File menu in particular. As reassurance, however, Office will often warn you before you do something it won't be able to undo.**

Use keyboard shortcuts. For the keyboard enthusiast, Office provides hundreds of shortcuts. Some are well-known—Ctrl+X to cut and Ctrl+P to print, for instance. Others are more obscure, allowing you to control everything from resizing windows and pictures to creating charts or navigating in dialog boxes.

Office distinguishes *accelerators*, which use the Alt key, from other keyboard shortcuts. The menus hold the clues: in each command, an underlined letter indicates the accelerator key. Press the Alt key while you press the underlined letter on your keyboard: *E* for the Edit menu and *C* for the Copy command in our example.

The underlined letters on the menu point out the keyboard accelerators.

Keyboard shortcuts

To uncover the full treasury of Office shortcuts, click in the Ask A Question box in the upper right corner of the window. Type **shortcuts**, and then press the Enter key. Click Keyboard Shortcuts, and browse through the list. Pick a couple that appeal to you, and practice until they become second nature; then add another two or three to your repertoire.

Use toolbars. Toolbars are to the mouse devotee as keyboard shortcuts are to the keyboard enthusiast. Toolbars can sit at the window's edge or sit right next to the action as you work. Click a toolbar's button and Office instantaneously executes your command, whether it's starting an Office program or doing other kinds of work from opening a file and formatting text to jumping to the Web or creating a drawing. You can also customize toolbars, adding buttons for frequent actions and removing buttons for tasks you hardly ever do.

 SEE ALSO: For information about how to display and use toolbars, see "Working Efficiently Using Toolbars and Task Panes" on page 18. For information about accessing and personalizing the Office Shortcut Bar, see "Starting an Office Program" on page 6.

Press the Repeat key. Press the F4 key in Word, Excel, and PowerPoint to repeat virtually any edit you just made—move or delete something, type text, change the format, and so on.

Save often. Without warning, your computer may simply stop responding, or a power outage may cause a system crash. Your best defense against such unpredictability is to press Ctrl+S once in awhile, particularly when you're making many changes.

SEE ALSO: For information about how to save, see "Saving or Deleting a File" on page 12.

Watch for visual cues in Office. Smart tags and lightning bolts, four-headed arrows and tiny hand pointers, ScreenTips, and other tips sometimes pop up when your mouse pointer pauses over something on the screen. Each is an Office clue to helpful information, alternatives for the task you've just completed, or an indication that the program is ready for you

to take a specific action. We call attention to these wherever possible in procedures throughout this book, but you still need to stay alert.

(Note that smart tags give formatting and other options; lightning bolts let you control corrections Office otherwise makes automatically; a four-headed arrow pointer can let you move something you've selected; a tiny hand pointer can indicate that you can jump somewhere else if you click; and ScreenTips give you information about what you're pointing to.)

Right-click and double-click. Stuck? Don't know what to do next? Right-clicking or double-clicking often provide alternatives and give you a way to explore your options. Right-click a slide, a picture, a word, a formula, a toolbar, or a table of contents, and Office generally obliges with a list of a half-dozen things you can do—rename it, edit it in some way, move it, change its look, and more. Double-click an object such as a picture, a WordArt object, clip art, or a chart, and Office often launches a toolbar or window that lets you work with the object in some way.

✪ **NEW FEATURE Talk to Office.** Perhaps you have tendinitis or another condition that makes using the mouse and keyboard difficult, or maybe you just want to tell Office what to do. Whatever the reason, you can now speak commands or have Office convert your spoken words to text.

Help on speech recognition in Office is particularly well-written and thorough, and gives you information about everything from the equipment you'll need (it's minimal) to step-by-step instructions about how to speak to a computer and troubleshooting advice. Click in the Ask A Question box in the upper right corner of the window. Type **speech recognition**, and then press the Enter key. Browse through the list, clicking any topic of interest.

Common Office XP Tasks and Where to Learn About Them

Several sections in this book (including this one) are devoted to tasks that you can do in every Office program: "Enhancing Documents," "Collaborating Using Office," and "Publishing Web Pages in Office." These sections, however, don't tell the whole Office consistency story because there are many other tasks that work in a similar fashion across Office programs. For example, the basics of changing the look of text work exactly the same way in every Office program; they are described, however, in the section on formatting in Word, where our readers are likely to encounter them first.

The following table lists some of these tasks. Note, however, that tasks that work somewhat differently in more than a couple of programs—adding page numbers or using templates, for example—are more likely to be described in the sections on those programs.

Find Out How To Do Common Office XP Tasks

To find out how to do this	Go to this topic
Set character formats: font, font size, and color; bold, italic, and underline	"Changing Font and Size, Italics, Color, and Other Effects" on page 62
Center, justify, left-align, and right-align text	"Aligning and Indenting Text" on page 64
Select text	"Selecting Text" on page 40
Move and copy text, pictures, and other objects within a document	"Moving and Copying Text" on page 41
Move and copy text, pictures, and other objects between programs	"Editing More Than One Document at a Time" on page 11
Search for and replace text	"Finding and Replacing Text" on page 48
Correct typos and spelling	"Correcting Typos and Spelling Automatically" on page 46
Add a border, shaded background, or line around text	"Adding Shading, Borders, and Other Special Effects" on page 70
Insert special characters such as ™ and ¥, different alphabets, nonbreaking spaces, and so on	"Inserting Special Characters and the Date and Time" on page 44
Set and delete tab stops	"Controlling Text Placement with Tabs" on page 67
Insert date and time, both static and updated, each time the document is printed	"Inserting Special Characters and the Date and Time" on page 44
Learn about styles	"What's a Style?" on page 72
Apply styles	"Applying a Style" on page 73
Create and change styles	"Reusing Formats with Styles" on page 74
Search for and replace formatting—bold or font size, for example	"Finding and Replacing Formatting" on page 76
Compose and send e-mail messages	"Composing and Sending an E-Mail Message" on page 154

Recovering Files ● NEW FEATURE

In a perfect world, computers would never fail. But the designers of Office, acknowledging reality, developed a tool that will save any open files just before the computer stops responding. In Word, Excel, and PowerPoint, the program reopens automatically, in most cases displaying two copies of each file that was open when the problem occurred: the original and the file Office created during recovery. (In other Office programs, you can open the file yourself.) Both copies of the file say "repaired," but the recovered file usually contains the most recent changes, while the original file is the one you last saved. (To confirm, compare the times of day each one was saved.)

In most cases, you'll want to save the more recent file (the recovered file) to its original name and overwrite the original to avoid confusion (and clutter on your hard disk). But to be extra safe, keep both until you're confident Office captured all your edits.

> **CAUTION: In spite of the best efforts of Office, there will be occasions when it is unable to recover your files. So, just as you still need to drive carefully even when you're well-insured, there is no substitute for saving your work frequently.**

Recover a File

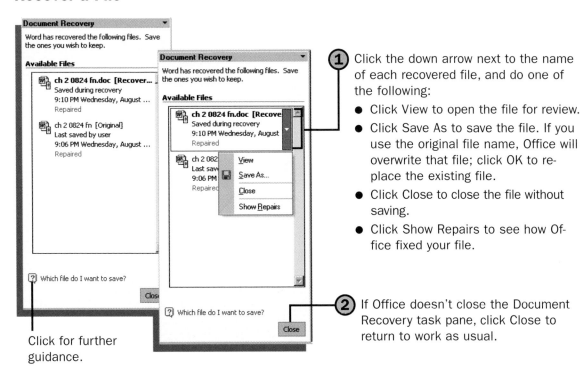

Click for further guidance.

① Click the down arrow next to the name of each recovered file, and do one of the following:

- Click View to open the file for review.
- Click Save As to save the file. If you use the original file name, Office will overwrite that file; click OK to replace the existing file.
- Click Close to close the file without saving.
- Click Show Repairs to see how Office fixed your file.

② If Office doesn't close the Document Recovery task pane, click Close to return to work as usual.

Repairing Office Programs

If you find essential files corrupted—for example, you can't open them—or the program is exhibiting unusual behavior, you can direct Office to locate, diagnose, and repair errors in the program you're working in.

    You have two choices about how Office makes its repairs. First, decide if you want to restore shortcuts on the Windows Start menu. (These shortcuts are instructions that tell what programs and files to open each time you start Windows.) Second, you can direct the repair program to discard potentially corrupt settings and restore the default. Your settings could include ways you've adapted the Office Shortcut Bar, the position of toolbars, the Office Assistant character you chose, and so forth.

> **! TIP:** For a more complete list of the settings you will lose if you choose to discard your settings and restore the defaults, click in the Ask A Question box in the upper right corner of the window. Type automatically repair Office programs, **press the Enter key, and click the topic to open it.**

Repair Problems in an Office Program

> **! TIP:** If you don't see a menu item, double-click the menu. For example, when you're following the steps in "Repair Problems in an Office Program," you might have to double-click the Help menu twice to see Detect And Repair in the list.

① Close all other programs and any open files.

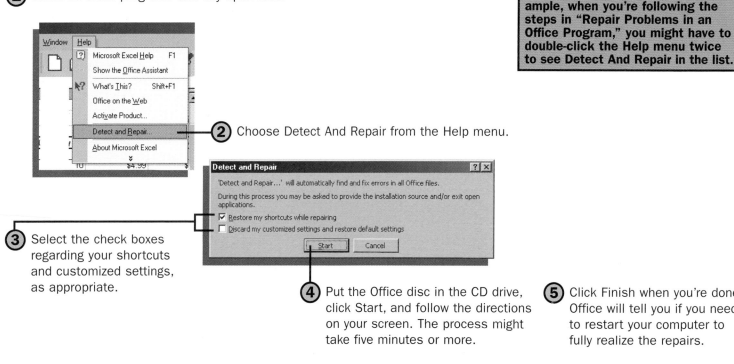

② Choose Detect And Repair from the Help menu.

③ Select the check boxes regarding your shortcuts and customized settings, as appropriate.

④ Put the Office disc in the CD drive, click Start, and follow the directions on your screen. The process might take five minutes or more.

⑤ Click Finish when you're done. Office will tell you if you need to restart your computer to fully realize the repairs.

Enhancing Documents

Is a picture worth a thousand words? Quite often, yes. Including pictures, sounds, and even videos can bring ideas to life, and draw readers to your document. And because Microsoft Office XP makes it easy to add these elements, graphics and other media elements are a common part of many documents. Whether you're including a sound clip in an e-mail message, adding a photograph from the Web to a report, or scanning in the text of a decades-old newspaper article, the tools to help you do these tasks are integrated into each Office XP program.

For starters, the Office XP Media Gallery comes with hundreds of clip art images, animations, and sounds that you can add to your documents. There are also thousands more pieces of media that Office can access online through Microsoft's Design Gallery Live Web site.

Creating and importing your own media elements is also straightforward in Office XP. You can use Office utilities such as Document Imaging, Document Scanning, and Photo Editor to help you make use of content from a variety of different sources.

Adding Pictures to Your Documents

Including pictures in a document can add meaning, depth, and texture to all sorts of presentations and documents. Adding a picture can draw focus to a subject, show information that's difficult to explain with text, or be purely aesthetic. A logo can provide a sense of identity, a photograph can show precise features, and a graph or chart can often be the easiest way to convey complex information. You can use picture files stored on your computer, your local network—even pictures from the Internet—to enhance your documents. You can also use your scanner or digital camera to import your photos into your documents.

Insert a Picture File Stored on Your Computer

1 Point to Picture on the Insert menu, and click From File.

2 Click the Look In down arrow to browse to the location of your graphics file.

3 Click the file you want to insert.

4 Click Insert.

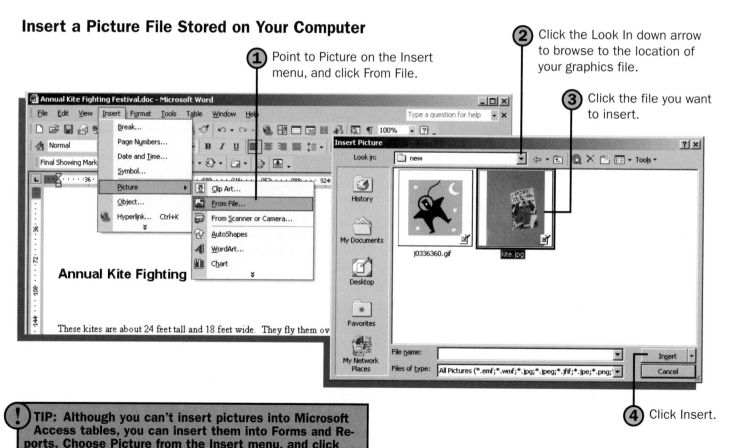

> **! TIP:** Although you can't insert pictures into Microsoft Access tables, you can insert them into Forms and Reports. Choose Picture from the Insert menu, and click the Look In down arrow to browse to the location of your graphics file. Click the file you want to insert, and then click Insert.

Add a Picture from a Scanner or Digital Camera

① Point to Picture on the Insert menu, and click From Scanner Or Camera.

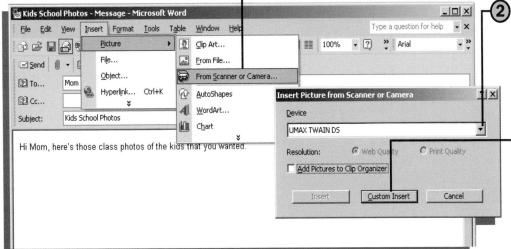

② Click the Device down arrow, and click the scanner or camera that contains the picture you want to add.

③ Do one of the following:

- If your scanner or camera supports Automatic Scan, just click Insert to scan the image into the document.

- If your scanner or camera doesn't support Automatic scan, the Insert button will be dimmed. Click Custom Insert to scan the picture through the scanner or camera's own software.

TRY THIS: If you ever need to use scanned images more than once, adding them to the Clip Organizer—an Office tool that catalogs media files on your computer—can make finding them easy, allowing you to search for scanned pictures in the same way you would look for clip art. Just select the Add Pictures To Clip Organizer check box in the Insert Picture From Scanner Or Camera dialog box. Then search for your scanned images by pointing to Picture on the Insert menu, clicking Clip Art, and clicking Clip Organizer in the Insert Clip Art task pane.

SEE ALSO: For more information about finding pictures using the Clip Organizer, see "Adding Clip Art and Other Types of Media" on page 28.

NEW FEATURE: Scanned pictures and digital images can be extremely large, and they can drastically increase your document's file size. To reduce this size and save space on your hard disk, consider compressing your pictures. To do so, click a picture in your document, and then click the Compress Pictures button on the Picture toolbar. (If you don't see the Picture toolbar after clicking the picture, point to Toolbars on the View menu, and click Picture.)

Adding Clip Art and Other Types of Media

Although photographs and other graphics are great for adding the right touch to a document, they're not the only thing you can add to spruce up your documents. Sound and video files can be included in most Office programs, providing music that sets a mood, sounds that produce warnings, or even an animation to illustrate a technical process. Aside from your own media files, Office includes a large library of clip art, which you can search through to get just the right file for your needs. Also, if you're connected to the Internet, Office searches for clip art in the Design Gallery Live Web site, giving you access to a regularly updated resource of graphics, sounds, photographs, and animations.

Find and Insert Clip Art ⊕ NEW FEATURE

(1) Point to Picture on the Insert menu, and click Clip Art.

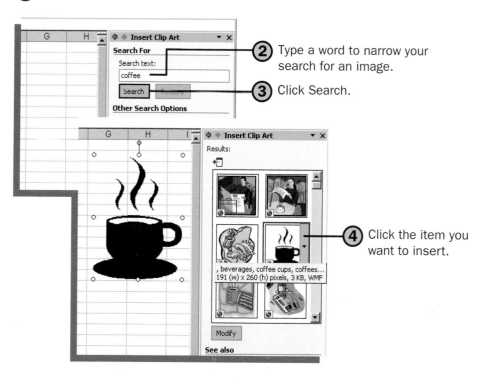

(2) Type a word to narrow your search for an image.

(3) Click Search.

(4) Click the item you want to insert.

TIP: If you're getting a very long list of results, you can further narrow your search by adding words to your search list, specifying where to look for clips, and specifying what type of medium you're looking for. To select where you want Office to search for clips, click the Search In down arrow, and click the collection you want. To narrow your search to a specific type of file, such as an animation or sound file, click the Results Should Be down arrow, and specify which file types you want to search for.

TIP: For information about the image, including how it's categorized (width and height, file size, and type), pause the mouse pointer over any clip art image in the Insert Clip Art task pane. A small icon in the lower left corner of the image gives you more information about the file. For instance, if the icon is a small picture of the Earth, the picture is stored on the Design Gallery Live Web site, so you'll have to stay connected to the Internet to insert it. A CD icon means the picture is stored on the Microsoft Office XP Media Content CD. A star icon indicates the picture is an animation file.

Insert a Sound or Video File

1 Choose Object from the Insert menu.

2 Click the Create From File tab or option, depending on which program you're using.

3 Click Browse.

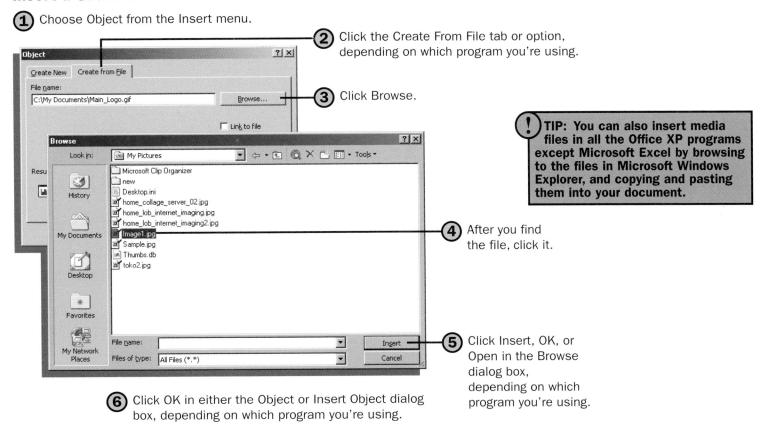

4 After you find the file, click it.

5 Click Insert, OK, or Open in the Browse dialog box, depending on which program you're using.

6 Click OK in either the Object or Insert Object dialog box, depending on which program you're using.

> **TIP:** You can also insert media files in all the Office XP programs except Microsoft Excel by browsing to the files in Microsoft Windows Explorer, and copying and pasting them into your document.

> **TRY THIS:** By default, Office stores a copy of the files you insert within the document, which can make your files quite large. To decrease file size, you can just link to the file, rather than store a copy in your document. To do so, select the Link To File or the Link check box in the Object or Insert Object dialog box (depending on the Office program you're using) when adding an object from a file.

> **TIP:** You can't insert objects directly into Microsoft FrontPage documents using the steps shown here. Instead, you can create hyperlinks to media files in FrontPage by choosing Hyperlink from the Insert menu and browsing to the file in the Insert Hyperlink dialog box.

Changing the Size, Placement, and Content of Pictures

After you've inserted an image, you'll need to make sure it's the right size and in the right place. Also, you might want to *crop* (that is, remove unwanted parts from) your picture. Placement and sizing affect how your pictures are interpreted by readers and create a relationship between the image and the text nearby. Also, cropping extraneous parts of an image can give a report or an article a much cleaner look, which brings focus to the most important parts of the picture. Rearranging and editing your media within Office doesn't take very long and can produce a much more professional-looking document.

Move a Picture

1 Open a document, and click the picture you want to move.

2 Drag the picture where you want it.

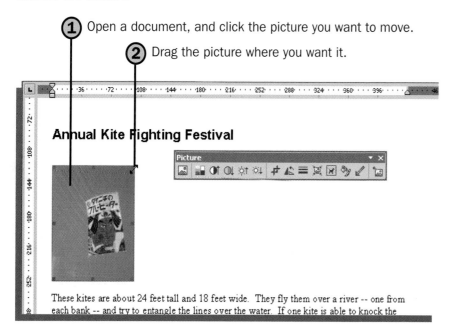

Annual Kite Fighting Festival

These kites are about 24 feet tall and 18 feet wide. They fly them over a river -- one from each bank -- and try to entangle the lines over the water. If one kite is able to knock the

Resize a Picture

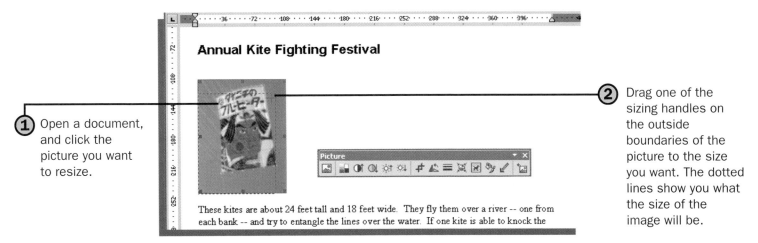

1 Open a document, and click the picture you want to resize.

2 Drag one of the sizing handles on the outside boundaries of the picture to the size you want. The dotted lines show you what the size of the image will be.

Crop a Picture

1 Open a document, and click the picture you want to crop.

2 Click the Crop button on the Picture toolbar. (If you don't see the Picture toolbar, click the picture.)

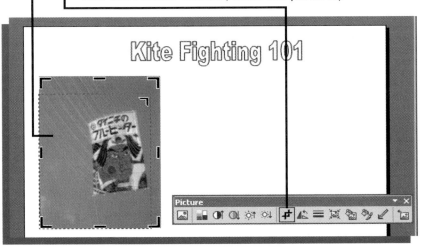

! TIP: Use the Brightness and Contrast buttons on the Picture toolbar to quickly adjust how bright or dark your picture appears, or to sharpen the picture.

! TIP: Cropping a picture doesn't delete the unwanted parts of the image, but simply hides them from view. To show more of the original picture, drag the cropping handles away from the image.

3 Click the cropping handles, and drag the resulting rectangle until it only surrounds the area you want to display, excluding as much of the rest of the image as possible.

Enhancing Pictures with Colors and Borders

Adding a border to a picture and adding background colors can help give your document a more polished, professional look. Like the frame around a picture on a wall, a border can make a photo appear more finished in a brochure or letter, while a solid background can bring a simple diagram into clear focus. For documents containing diagrams or drawings, a simple border or change in background color can help organize space by separating text, images, and different sections of a document.

Add a Border to a Picture

TRY THIS: To manually draw borders and set border settings in Word and Microsoft Outlook, right-click the picture, choose Borders And Shading from the shortcut menu, and then click Show Toolbar. The Tables And Borders toolbar has the tools you need to draw, erase, or modify.

① Right-click the picture you want to add a border to, and choose Borders And Shading from the shortcut menu.

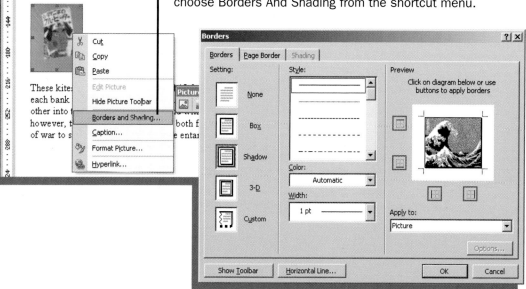

② On the Borders tab, do one or more of the following:

- Click the border you want in the Setting area.
- Click a border style in the Style list.
- Click a border color in the Color list.
- Click a border width in the Width list.

CAUTION: FrontPage, Microsoft PowerPoint, Excel, and Microsoft Publisher don't handle borders in the same way as Word or Outlook. To add a border in FrontPage, click the picture you want, and choose Borders And Shading from the Format menu. Then click the options you want in the Setting and Style areas on the Borders tab.

In PowerPoint, Excel, and Publisher, right-click the picture you want, choose Format Picture from the shortcut menu, and click the Colors And Lines tab. Click the Color down arrow in the Line area, and choose the color you want for the border; then click the Style down arrow, and choose the width of your border.

Change the Background Color of Clip Art

1 Right-click the picture you want to add a background color to, and choose Format Picture from the shortcut menu.

2 Click the Colors And Lines tab.

3 In the Fill area, click the Color down arrow, and click the color you want to use as your background.

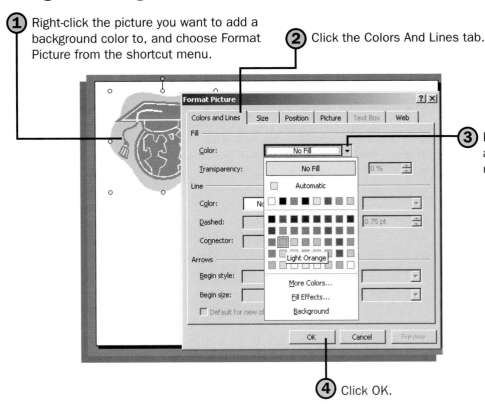

4 Click OK.

> **TIP:** It's easiest to change the background color of a piece of clip art, but you can also edit the backgrounds of other pictures with a few additional steps. With photos and other kinds of graphics, click the Set Transparent Color button on the Picture toolbar, and click the picture's background. Then go through the same steps as you would when changing the background color of clip art.
>
> Note that because the Set Transparent Color tool makes the entire background transparent, this technique only works on images that already contain solid backgrounds, such as schematics, line art, and logos. Photos and other types of graphics without solid backgrounds don't work well with the Set Transparent Color tool.

> **TIP:** FrontPage and Access don't allow you to change background colors of images. However, in FrontPage, you can still use the Set Transparent Color tool to make a picture's background transparent.

Adding and Modifying WordArt

WordArt is a feature within Office programs that makes it painless to include highly stylized, graphical text in your documents. WordArt pictures are handy as titles, or can be used to produce generic watermarks or logos or graphical elements that draw attention to something in a document. WordArt provides high-quality, professional-looking graphics that take little time to create.

> **! TIP:** If you ever need to use your WordArt picture in a non-Office program, such as a graphics program, you can treat WordArt like any other graphic. This allows you to select the WordArt object you want to use, choose Copy from the Edit menu of the Office program, and then choose Paste from the Edit menu of the program that you want to use the WordArt in.

Insert a WordArt Object

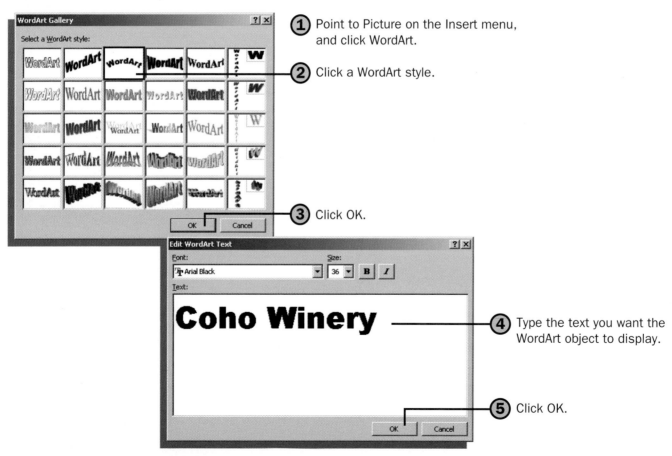

1. Point to Picture on the Insert menu, and click WordArt.

2. Click a WordArt style.

3. Click OK.

4. Type the text you want the WordArt object to display.

5. Click OK.

Change the Style of a WordArt Object

① Click the WordArt object you want to edit. If the WordArt toolbar doesn't appear when you click a WordArt object, point to Toolbars on the View menu, and click WordArt.

② Click the WordArt Gallery button.

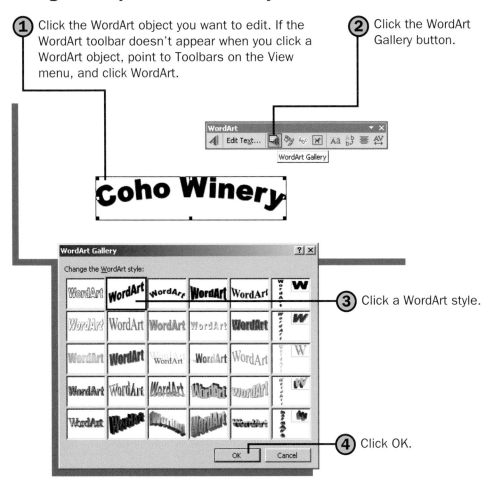

③ Click a WordArt style.

④ Click OK.

Creating, Editing, and Printing a Word Document

Computers work at the speed of light, and Microsoft Word brings that speed to bear on the mundane and repetitive tasks that occupy so much of everyone's writing efforts. So along the way in this section, you'll pick up the efficiencies that Word puts at your disposal—correcting spelling and typos practically without your knowing it, yet putting control at your fingertips to reverse those changes that are not for you; making short work of text you type often; offering a thesaurus that protects you from monotonous language; and providing symbols that make it possible to type such text as "résumé" and "™" accurately.

You'll find out, too, just what view of your document makes the most sense for the kind of work you're doing, and some insider tricks for amplifying the utility of Word's Find and Replace features. We even throw in a few tips on how to address and print envelopes.

With the basics under your belt, on the following pages we'll give you the tools for polishing the look of your document and taking further advantage of Word's power to make light work of your work with words. By the end of this section, you'll have created and edited the words of a basic document, laid them out on the page (adding pages if necessary), and printed them.

Starting a Word Document

There are three paths to getting a Word document up and running: start a new document using a template or a wizard, or start a new document from scratch. Templates and wizards both give you a jump-start by providing formatting and other design elements.

There are some differences between the two. First, as befits a wizard, its icon includes a tiny wand. When you open a wizard, it asks a series of content-related questions and sometimes furnishes a design choice or two. Based on your answers, the wizard designs the document, adding the content you provided. On the other hand, when you open a template, the program furnishes an instant design.

However, it is the similarities between templates and wizards that's most important. In some cases, both offer placeholder text with further instructions for adding content. Ultimately they both give you a leg up on the creation of a document—so use whichever starts the document you want.

> **! TIP:** When you click a wizard or template icon in the Templates dialog box, the preview box might display the message, "Click OK to install additional templates and create a new file." This is because not all the wizards and templates were installed when you set up Office XP. It only takes a minute or two to fix this. Before you click OK, put the Office 2002 disc in the CD-ROM drive. Click OK, and Office takes it from there.

> **TRY THIS:** Word's Fax Wizard will not only design your fax and help you with the content, but it will send it, too, if you have a fax modem. Follow steps 1 and 2 in "Start a Document Using a Wizard." In step 3, click the Letters & Faxes tab, click Fax Wizard, click OK, and then just answer the wizard's questions.

Start a Document from a Template

(1) Choose New from the File menu, and click General Templates.

(2) Click the tab for the type of document you want to create.

(3) Click the icon for the template you want to use, and click OK.

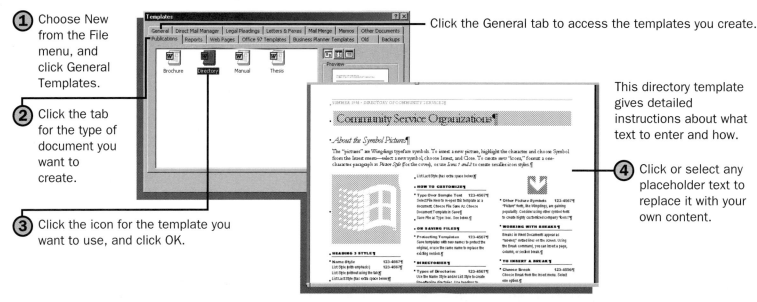

Click the General tab to access the templates you create.

This directory template gives detailed instructions about what text to enter and how.

(4) Click or select any placeholder text to replace it with your own content.

Start a Document Using a Wizard

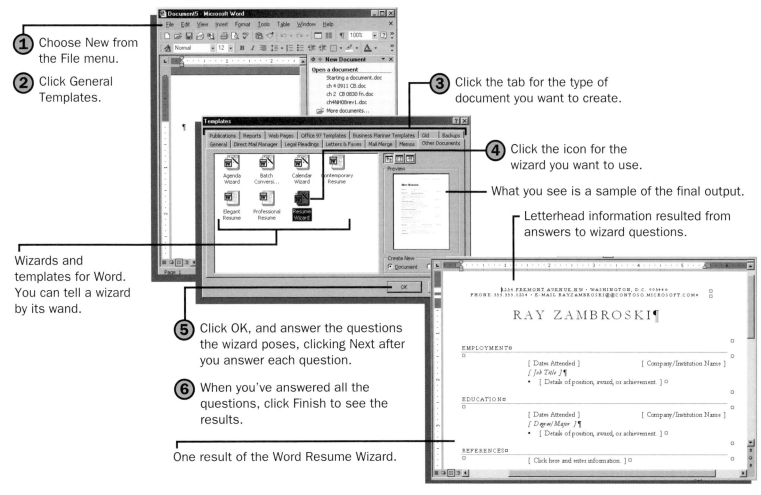

(1) Choose New from the File menu.

(2) Click General Templates.

(3) Click the tab for the type of document you want to create.

(4) Click the icon for the wizard you want to use.

What you see is a sample of the final output.

Letterhead information resulted from answers to wizard questions.

Wizards and templates for Word. You can tell a wizard by its wand.

(5) Click OK, and answer the questions the wizard poses, clicking Next after you answer each question.

(6) When you've answered all the questions, click Finish to see the results.

One result of the Word Resume Wizard.

Start a Blank Document

(1) Choose New from the File menu.

(2) In the New Document task pane at screen right, click Blank Document under New.

Selecting Text

Before you can work with text in Word—change a word, copy a paragraph, boldface or italicize a headline—you must select it. Removing the selection is simplicity itself—simply click anywhere that isn't selected.

You already know how to drag your mouse pointer across the page and select letters, words, phrases, and so on. But to make highlighting faster and easier, we've compiled a few of the handiest shortcuts here. (If you'd like to incorporate these into your routine, consider copying this table and taping the copy to your monitor to follow until these are second nature.)

Shortcuts for Selecting Text

To select:	Do this:
A word and the space that follows it	Double-click the word.
A sentence and the space that follows it	Press the Ctrl key, and then click in the sentence.
A line	Move the mouse pointer to the left of the line you want to select until it changes to an arrow, and then click.
An entire paragraph and its paragraph mark	Triple-click the paragraph.
A column	Press the Alt key as you click in the column.
Any part of a document	Click at the beginning of the text you want to select, and drag through the document to select it.
Noncontiguous words or phrases	Hold down the Ctrl key while you select each word or phrase.
An entire document	Press Ctrl+A.

TIP: Office has a lot of other selection shortcuts, particularly for extending the selection by varying degrees. To check them out, click in the Ask A Question box in the upper right corner of the window. Type shortcuts, and then press the Enter key. Click Keyboard Shortcuts, and then click Editing And Moving Text And Graphics in the list.

TRY THIS: If you find Word helpfully selecting an entire word when you're trying to select just a part of it—for example, selecting *establish* out of *antidisestablishmentarianism*—you can change that behavior. Choose Options from the Tools menu, click the Edit tab, clear the When Selecting, Automatically Select Entire Word check box, and then click OK.

Moving and Copying Text

Word equips you with a half-dozen ways to move and copy text (and pictures or any other object on the page). You might choose a method based on your preference for the mouse, the keyboard, or menus. It turns out, though, that some methods are better suited to moving text shorter distances (that is, from one place on the screen to another), whereas others are more effective for going the distance—across pages, documents, and even programs. (This is the particular province of the brand-new, highly visual Office Clipboard.) We offer two techniques here: using the mouse for copying or moving text over a short distance and the keyboard for locations farther afield.

Move or Copy a Block of Text a Short Distance

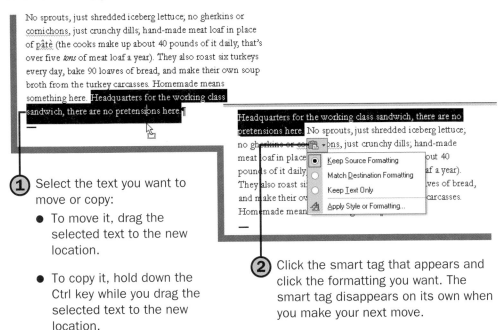

(1) Select the text you want to move or copy:

- To move it, drag the selected text to the new location.

- To copy it, hold down the Ctrl key while you drag the selected text to the new location.

(2) Click the smart tag that appears and click the formatting you want. The smart tag disappears on its own when you make your next move.

Move or Copy a Block of Text to Another Page

(1) Select the text you want to copy or move, and do one of the following:

- Press Ctrl+C to make a copy.

- Press Ctrl+X to cut the text in preparation for moving it.

(2) Go to the new page.

(3) Click in the new location, and press Ctrl+V to paste the text in the new spot.

> **! TIP:** If you're typing along and you suddenly find that Word is "eating" your words, you might have inadvertently pressed the Insert Key and switched into *overtype* mode. Look at the bottom of the Word window: if OVR is black instead of shaded, that's what happened. Press the Insert key again to return to Word's usual mode of inserting text as you type.

> **SEE ALSO:** For information about how to copy text to other documents and programs using the Office Clipboard, see "Editing More Than One Document at a Time" on page 11.

Using Automatic Text

Word's AutoText works a lot like speed dialing on your telephone—you program your telephone to dial a full number when you press a button or two. In Word, you type a block of text you use repeatedly, such as your address or a marketing slogan, and give it a concise name, like "myadd" or "slogan." When you're ready to call up that text in a document, simply type the name, and press the F3 key. Presto! Word deletes the name and replaces it with the text you defined.

You can also draw on a library of AutoText that Word has already prepared for you—for example, the salutation or closing of a letter, or months of the year. You can also create almost anything you can copy as AutoText—a logo or other image, a very long body of text, a symbol, and so forth.

Create Your Own Automatic Text

2 Point to AutoText on the Insert menu, and click New.

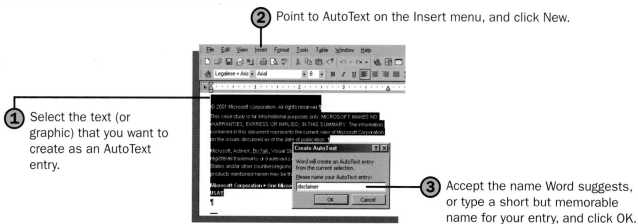

1 Select the text (or graphic) that you want to create as an AutoText entry.

3 Accept the name Word suggests, or type a short but memorable name for your entry, and click OK.

Insert Your Own Automatic Text

1 Click in the document where you want to insert your automatic text (AutoText).

2 Type the name of the AutoText entry, followed by a space or punctuation, and press the F3 key.

Insert AutoText from Word's Library

(2) Point to AutoText on the Insert menu.

(1) Click in the document where you want to insert the text.

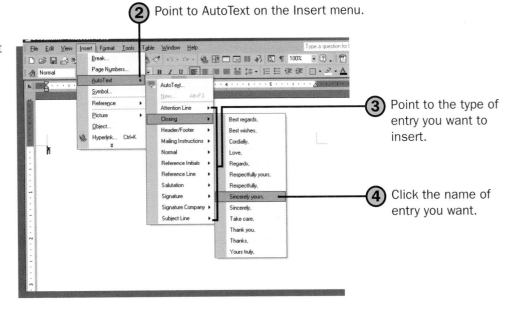

(3) Point to the type of entry you want to insert.

(4) Click the name of entry you want.

TIP: It's easy to change an AutoText entry. To do so, insert it in the document and revise it. Then select your revision, point to AutoText on the Insert menu, and click New. Type the original name, click OK, and when Word asks if you want to redefine the entry, click Yes.

TIP: Perhaps one of the most basic and yet most powerful of Word's editing tools is its Undo feature. Bolstered by a terrific memory that can hold dozens of edits, Undo allows you to press Ctrl+Z to reverse almost any edits you make; if you change your mind again, press Ctrl+Y to redo the change.

Inserting Special Characters and the Date and Time

If you're writing about "cafés" or "Größenwahn," you won't find the characters to express yourself on the standard keyboard. That's where Word's *symbols* come in, putting every conceivable character in Word's thoroughgoing font library on display—from the alphabets of every language from French to Arabic and characters such as a non-breaking space or ©, to entire font sets with nothing but symbols.

It's handy to know that symbols are actually fonts, so they behave like text. You can insert them right into text, make them bigger, or color them—anything you can do with text, you can do with symbols.

You can insert the date and time just as easily as you can symbols—either the current date and time that's immutable or one that changes each time you open or print the document.

TRY THIS: If there's a symbol you use repeatedly—the English pound (£), for example—consider making it faster to enter. Follow steps 1 and 2 in "Add a Special Character or Symbol." In the Symbol dialog box, click the AutoCorrect button, and type a short name for that symbol in the Replace box—pd, for example. Click OK twice. Then, to insert that symbol, type the name (pd), and Word automatically substitutes the symbol (£) for the name.

SEE ALSO: For information about how to format characters, see "Changing Font and Size, Italics, Color, and Other Text Effects" on page 62.

Add a Special Character or Symbol

1 Click in the document where you want to insert the symbol.

2 Choose Symbol from the Insert menu.

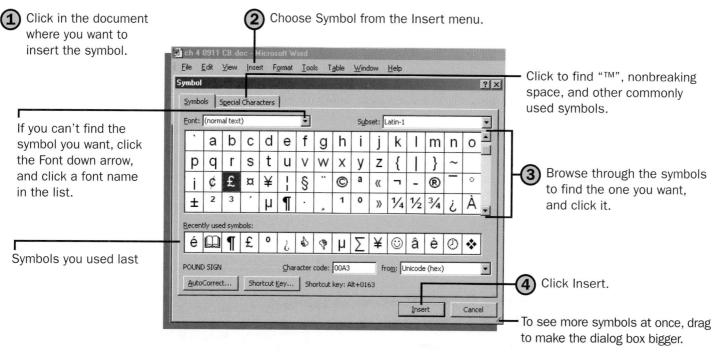

Click to find "™", nonbreaking space, and other commonly used symbols.

If you can't find the symbol you want, click the Font down arrow, and click a font name in the list.

3 Browse through the symbols to find the one you want, and click it.

Symbols you used last

4 Click Insert.

To see more symbols at once, drag to make the dialog box bigger.

TRY THIS: Press the F4 key and Word will repeat exactly what you did last—move or delete something, type text, change the format, and so on. If you don't like the result, reverse it by pressing Ctrl+Z.

TRY THIS: Word is set by default to give your documents a professional shine, right down to quotation marks, which it automatically converts from straight (" or ') to curly (" or '), as typographers prefer. But then how do you use a quotation mark to indicate inches or minutes? As soon as you type a quotation mark, press Ctrl+Z, and Word will straighten it right up.

Add the Date and Time

1 Click in the document where you want the date to appear.

2 Choose Date And Time from the Insert menu.

3 Click the date and time format you want.

4 Specify whether you want the date and time to be constant or changeable:

- Select Update Automatically to update the date and time when you open or print the document.

- Clear Update Automatically to preserve the date and time shown.

5 Click OK.

TRY THIS: You can also insert today's date without lifting your fingers from the keyboard. To do so, type the first four letters of the current month (Augu for August, for example). Then type a space, and Word intervenes with a tip containing the day's date. Press the Enter key to insert the date.

 SEE ALSO: For information about how to format characters, see "Changing Font and Size, Italics, Color, and Other Text Effects" on page 62.

Correcting Typos and Spelling Automatically

Word corrects misspellings, problems with capitalization, and it changes commonly used elements such as 1/2 to ½ or 1st to 1st. (Most corrections are activated by pressing the Spacebar or adding a punctuation mark.) You can add your own problem words to Word's list of automatic corrections. And if you don't want your spelling corrected—say, you've named your company "BRain"—Word supplies an AutoCorrect tag that can reverse its action in one instance or forever.

Using AutoCorrect is easy. Type what you want, and if you make a mistake, Word either corrects it or flags it for you with a wavy red underline.

Adjust Automatic Corrections as You Type

① When you notice that Word has made a correction as you type, move the mouse pointer over the corrected word until you see a thin blue box.

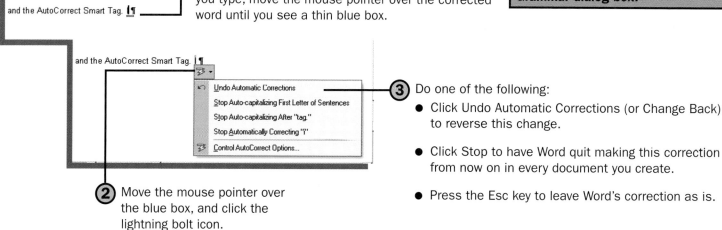

② Move the mouse pointer over the blue box, and click the lightning bolt icon.

③ Do one of the following:
- Click Undo Automatic Corrections (or Change Back) to reverse this change.

- Click Stop to have Word quit making this correction from now on in every document you create.

- Press the Esc key to leave Word's correction as is.

> **TIP:** You can have Word analyze your grammar, too, flagging your document for such problems as capitalization errors, subject and verbs that don't agree, excessive use of the passive voice, and so on. The grammar checker is very thorough and takes time, so it's a tool you'll likely want to use as you're finishing up rather than as you're writing. To do this, choose Spelling And Grammar from the Tools menu. Make sure to select the Check Grammar check box, and follow the instructions in the Spelling And Grammar dialog box.

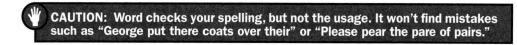

CAUTION: Word checks your spelling, but not the usage. It won't find mistakes such as "George put there coats over their" or "Please pear the pare of pairs."

Add Words to the List of Automatic Corrections

> **TIP: To remove a word or phrase from Word's AutoCorrect list, choose AutoCorrect Options from the Tools menu. Type the first letter or two of the word or phrase you want to delete in the Replace box. Then click it in the list, click the Delete button, and click OK.**

(1) Choose AutoCorrect Options from the Tools menu.

Clear a box to prevent Word from making that correction from now on in every document you create.

(2) In the Replace box, type the incorrect spelling of the word or phrase you consistently spell or type incorrectly.

(3) In the With box, type the correct spelling.

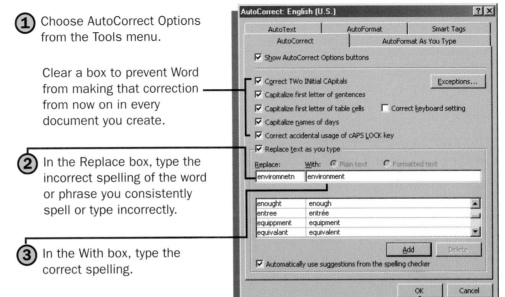

(4) Click OK.

Correct Spelling as You Type

As you type, Word marks mistakes that it does not correct automatically.

(1) Type the correction yourself, or right-click the word in question, and do one of the following:

- Click the correct spelling, if any, to replace the incorrect word with the correct one.

- Click Ignore All to have Word ignore other occurrences of this word in the document.

- Click Add To Dictionary to add a word, such as a name, to your dictionary.

- Click AutoCorrect, if available, to add a word you frequently misspell or mistype to Word's list of automatic corrections.

Finding and Replacing Text

Find and Replace is to writing what the automatic ice-maker is to filling ice-cube trays by hand. Not only can you use Word's Find and Replace features to clean up those double spaces between sentences, but you can use Find and Replace to correct repeated misspellings and to remove those annoying *chevrons* (>>) or paragraph marks in e-mail messages.

It's not limited to these traditional uses either. You can use it to jump to a word in a document. It will also count a given word when you search for it and replace it with the same word—helpful for discovering if you've overused a word.

Find Text

① Choose Find from the Edit menu.

② Type the word or phrase you're looking for.

③ Click More.

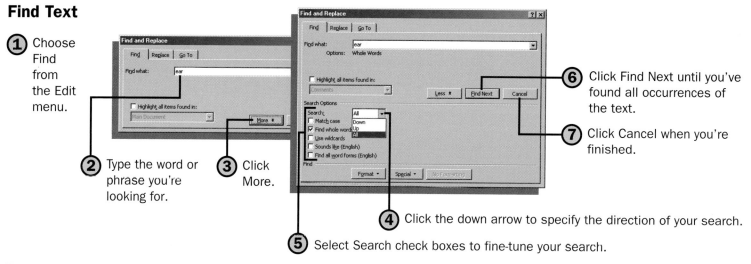

⑥ Click Find Next until you've found all occurrences of the text.

⑦ Click Cancel when you're finished.

④ Click the down arrow to specify the direction of your search.

⑤ Select Search check boxes to fine-tune your search.

Replace Text

① Choose Replace from the Edit menu.

② In the Find What box, type the word or phrase you're looking for.

③ In the Replace With box, type the word or phrase you want to replace it with.

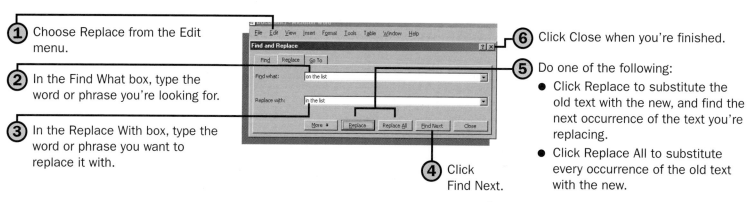

⑥ Click Close when you're finished.

⑤ Do one of the following:
- Click Replace to substitute the old text with the new, and find the next occurrence of the text you're replacing.
- Click Replace All to substitute every occurrence of the old text with the new.

④ Click Find Next.

Undo All the Replacements Just Made

1 Choose Undo from the Edit menu. Word will undo every single replacement.

> **TIP:** To find (or find and replace) text in just one part of a document, select that part before you choose Find (or Replace) from the Edit menu. Word starts its search at the beginning of the selection, giving you the option of continuing in the remainder of the document if you choose.

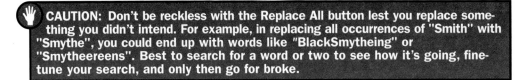

> **CAUTION:** Don't be reckless with the Replace All button lest you replace something you didn't intend. For example, in replacing all occurrences of "Smith" with "Smythe", you could end up with words like "BlackSmytheing" or "Smytheereens". Best to search for a word or two to see how it's going, fine-tune your search, and only then go for broke.

> **TRY THIS:** You know how e-mail messages often have distracting chevrons (>>) or short choppy lines that make you feel as if you're reading in stop-and-go traffic? You can remove them in Microsoft Outlook if Word is your e-mail editor, or you can copy and paste the text into Word and do it there. Search for > and replace it with nothing by deleting everything in the Replace With box. For those hard returns, insert a paragraph mark (which is a special character and Word's name for *hard return*) in the Find What box, and replace it with a space.

Fine-Tuning Your Search

When you choose this in the Find And Replace dialog box:	Word searches like this in your document:
Down or Up	Searches from the insertion point down or up; Word then gives you the option of continuing the search in the rest of the document.
All	Searches the entire document, no matter where you left the insertion point.
Match Case	Matches the exact capitalization of the word you specify, so a search for "cake" does not find "Cake" or "CAKE".
Find Whole Words Only	Finds whole words, so a search for "ear" does not find "ears", "bear", or "rearrange".
Sounds Like	Finds sound-alike words, so a search for "pair" finds "pear" and "pare", but not "repair".
Find All Word Forms	Finds all the forms of a word. A search for "choose" finds "chose", "chosen", and "choosing" and replaces it, with your approval, with the appropriate form of "select". Or a search for "worse" also finds "worst" and replaces it with "better" or "best".
Special	Finds special characters such as a paragraph mark or a manual page break.

Using Word's Thesaurus

In the original Greek, the word "thesaurus" means "treasure" or "storehouse." Word's thesaurus is a treasure for writers—a storehouse of over 100,000 synonyms, antonyms, and related words.

TIP: If you run into problems using Word's thesaurus (or, in fact, any of its proofing tools), click in the Ask A Question box in the upper right corner of the window. Type troubleshoot thesaurus, **and then press the Enter key. Click Troubleshoot Spelling, Grammar, And Other Proofing Tools, and browse through the list.**

Find a Synonym Quickly

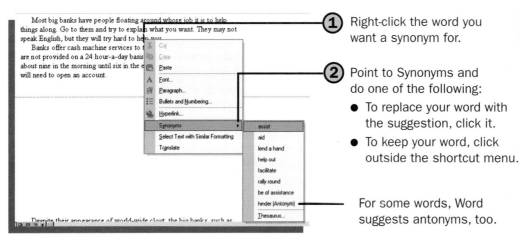

(1) Right-click the word you want a synonym for.

(2) Point to Synonyms and do one of the following:

- To replace your word with the suggestion, click it.
- To keep your word, click outside the shortcut menu.

For some words, Word suggests antonyms, too.

Explore Synonyms

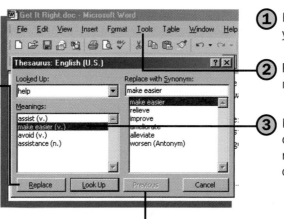

(1) In the document, click the word you want to look up.

(2) Point to Language on the Tools menu, and click Thesaurus.

(3) If there's more than one meaning, click the one that fits the word you're researching most closely, and then click Look Up to explore synonyms.

(4) Repeat step 3 until you find the word you want, and then do one of the following:

- Click Replace to substitute Word's synonym for your word.
- Click Cancel to keep your word and return to the document.

Click to go back to the last version of the list.

Inserting New Pages

Based on margins and page size, Word breaks pages when you fill a page with text or images, and as you add or remove them, the page breaks reflect these changes. There are times, however, when you want to start a new page in a specific spot—for example, before a new heading or to isolate a large illustration or table on its own page. In this case, you force a page break by hand. However, a manual page break (sometimes also referred to as a *hard page break*) functions a bit like a dam—the text won't flow past it, causing the page to break at that spot no matter how little text is on the page. So, before you print, preview your document to make sure pages are breaking as you intended.

Insert a Manual Page Break

3 Click Page Break, and click OK.

2 Choose Break from the Insert menu.

Word's automatic page break

Manual page break

1 Click at the beginning of the line where you want the new page to begin.

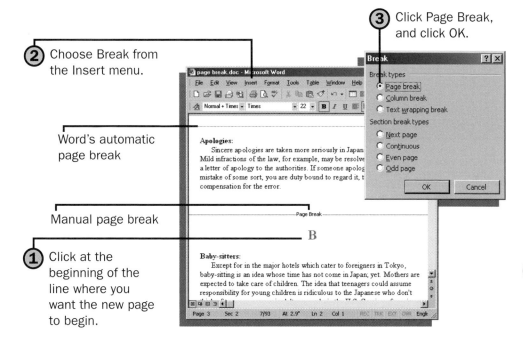

Remove a Manual Page Break

1 Click the manual page break, and press the Delete key. If you don't see the page break mark, choose Normal from the View menu.

Jump to a Page

1 Press the F5 key, type the page number in the Enter Page Number box, and click Go To.

! TIP: You can avoid awkward page breaks in long documents—for example, a page break just after a title. To do so, click the title or other heading, and choose Paragraph from the Format menu. Then click the Line And Page Breaks tab, and select the Keep With Next check box. From now on, at least two lines of that paragraph will stick with the heading.

! TIP: To see how the pages will break when printed, choose Print Layout from the View menu.

Adding and Removing Page Numbers

Everyone recognizes the virtues of page numbers in a document of more than a few pages. Word makes it easy to add, format, and place page numbers in the right spot on every page, and even omit them on the first page of documents, such as a letters.

You can see the page numbers when you are in Print Layout view, Print Preview, or on the printed page. Their pale gray color is Word's cue that the numbers appear on every page. If you want something more elaborate—chapter titles or the date—use headers and footers instead.

> **SEE ALSO:** For information about how to add headers and footers to a document, see "Repeating Text and Pictures on Every Page" on page 88.

Number Every Page

1 Choose Page Numbers from the Insert menu.

2 Click the Position down arrow, and click where you want to put the page numbers.

3 Click the Alignment down arrow, and click the horizontal alignment you want.

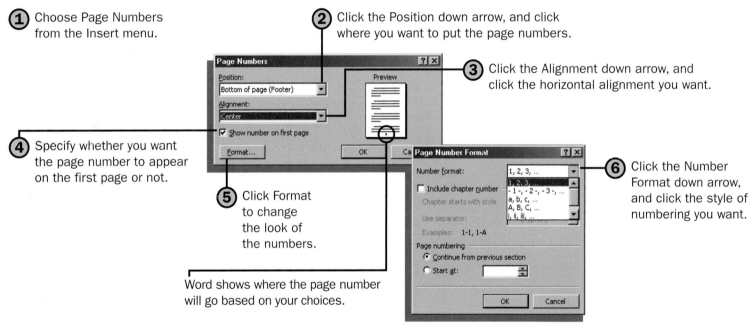

4 Specify whether you want the page number to appear on the first page or not.

5 Click Format to change the look of the numbers.

6 Click the Number Format down arrow, and click the style of numbering you want.

Word shows where the page number will go based on your choices.

7 Click OK twice. If you don't see the page numbers, choose Print Layout from the View menu, and scroll to see them.

Remove Page Numbers

③ Right-click, and click Cut. Word removes the page numbers from every page in the document.

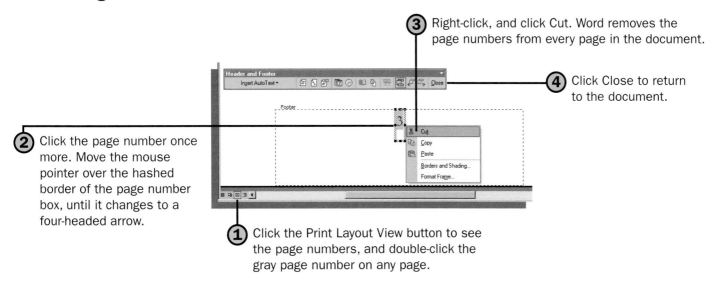

④ Click Close to return to the document.

② Click the page number once more. Move the mouse pointer over the hashed border of the page number box, until it changes to a four-headed arrow.

① Click the Print Layout View button to see the page numbers, and double-click the gray page number on any page.

TIP: If page numbers are clipped on the printed page, they might not have enough space. To give them room, choose Page Setup from the File menu. Then click the Layout tab, and adjust the space in tiny increments in the From Edge boxes. Use the up arrows to adjust the measurements in the Header box (if the numbers are at the top of the page) or in the Footer box (if they're at the bottom). Click OK. You might have to do this more than once to get it just right.

TIP: If you have any problems with page numbers, click in the Ask A Question box in the upper right corner of the window. Type troubleshoot numbers, and then press the Enter key. Click Troubleshoot Page Numbers And Line Numbers, and click the problem that applies.

Setting Up Pages

When you set up pages in Word, your considerations include page margins (Word's defaults are set at 1.25" on the left and right and 1" at the top and bottom), the orientation (horizontal or vertical), and the size of the paper you'll print on. Word stores information on various paper sizes—letter and A4 (the standard paper size used outside the U.S.), various envelopes, index cards, and the like. These settings apply to the entire document unless you create a special section in a document and specify otherwise.

All these specifications serve as cues for the printer—how much white space to leave around the edges of the paper and whether to print a document vertically (portrait) or horizontally (landscape, as for a wide table or spreadsheet).

SEE ALSO: For information about creating special sections and setting margins and page orientation within a section, see "Creating a Document with More Than One Section" on page 86.

Adjust Margins

1 Choose Ruler from the View menu.

2 Click the Print Layout View button, and click in the document.

3 Point to the gray boundary on the horizontal or vertical ruler until the pointer changes to a double-headed arrow.

Use the horizontal ruler to set left and right margins.

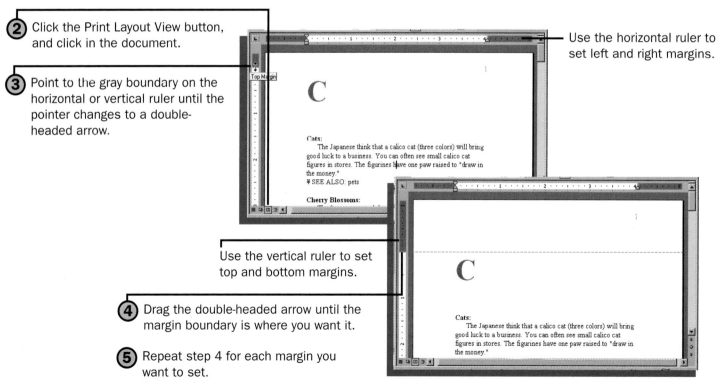

Use the vertical ruler to set top and bottom margins.

4 Drag the double-headed arrow until the margin boundary is where you want it.

5 Repeat step 4 for each margin you want to set.

Set Page Orientation

1 Choose Page Setup from the File menu.

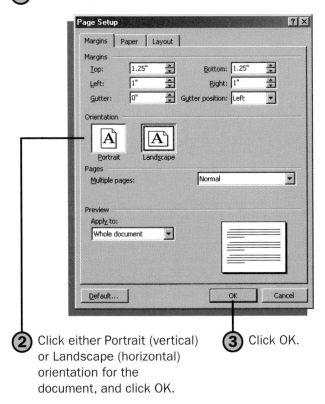

2 Click either Portrait (vertical) or Landscape (horizontal) orientation for the document, and click OK.

3 Click OK.

> **! TIP:** You can use portrait and landscape orientation in the same document—for example, to include a wide table in an otherwise vertical document. To do this, select the page(s) whose orientation you want to change. Follow the steps in "Set Page Orientation," and then click Selected Text in the Apply To list. Click OK. Word automatically inserts the pages with different orientations as new sections.

Set Paper Size

1 Choose Page Setup from the File menu.

2 Click the Paper tab.

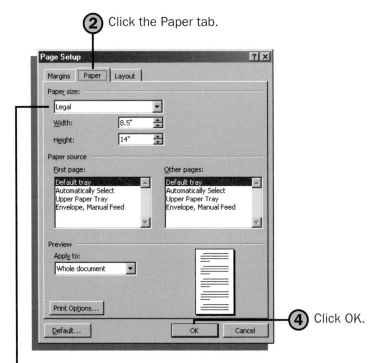

4 Click OK.

3 Click the Paper Size down arrow, and click the type of paper you'll be printing on. If you're printing on a special size of paper, choose Custom Size at the bottom of the list, and enter the dimensions in the Width and Height boxes.

> **! TIP:** If your printer has more than one tray, you can use the lists in the Paper Source area to direct Word to print the first page on different paper—letterhead, for example—than subsequent pages.

Addressing and Printing Envelopes and Label Sheets

You can address envelopes in several ways: have Word take the address from an open document, type the address, or track it down in your Outlook Contacts list. You can choose to print the envelope as you address it, or save it and print it at a later date.

When you get ready to feed the envelope into the printer, remember that the envelope must pass over a curved paper path in many printers and can be wrinkled in the process. So help the printer out. Press the envelope as flat as you can with your hands.

Address and Print a Single Envelope

And avoid bulky envelopes or ones with metal or string-tied clasps that might also damage the printer.

We all know that addresses go on envelopes. But labels have a larger life than just displaying return addresses—you can create sheets of labels as bookplates or as labels for disks or your collection of videos. And don't limit yourself to the brand-name labels Word suggests—there are many brand-x labels that mimic them perfectly, and even have the product number of their brand-name counterpart on the packaging.

1 If you have a letter you want to print an envelope for, open it.

2 Point to Letters And Mailings on the Tools menu, and click Envelopes And Labels.

3 Type or edit the delivery address.

Click the Insert Address button to find the address in your Outlook Contacts list.

4 Accept the return address (if Word supplies one), type one, or select Omit to leave off the return address if you're printing on letterhead.

5 To print the envelope now, put an envelope in the tray in the feed direction indicated, and click Print.

6 To print the envelope later, click Add To Document, and then save and close the document.

Click to choose an envelope other than a standard business envelope (No. 10), to change the address font, and so on.

Feed the envelope into the printer this way, or click to change it.

> ✋ **CAUTION: If you use an inkjet printer, which uses heat to fix ink on the page, buy only those labels marked specifically for use with such printers or you could end up with a gooey mess inside your printer or worse, with the need for a new printer. For the same reason, don't print on envelopes that have peel-off strips.**

Print a Sheet of Labels with Identical Text

(1) Point to Letters And Mailings on the Tools menu, and click Envelopes And Labels.

(2) Click the Labels tab.

(3) Type the text you want to appear on every label. It doesn't have to be an address. If you're making a return address label, you can select the Use Return Address check box.

(4) Click Options.

Word shows the kind of label you've chosen in the Label Options dialog box.

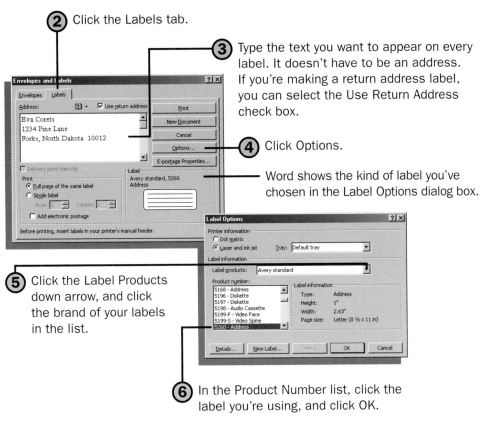

(5) Click the Label Products down arrow, and click the brand of your labels in the list.

(6) In the Product Number list, click the label you're using, and click OK.

(7) Put label paper in the tray, and click Print. You might want to test this on plain paper first, to save the expense of label paper.

Print an Envelope You've Already Addressed

(1) When you're ready to print the envelope, open the document you created in "Address and Print a Single Envelope."

(2) Put the envelope in the printer tray, and choose Print from the File menu.

(3) In the Page Range area, type 0 (zero) in the Pages box, and click OK. To print the letter first, and then the envelope, type 1,0 in the Pages box.

> ✋ **CAUTION: Printing envelopes can be tricky. The printer and the computer come to a document from different vantage points, so the transfer of information between the two is not always as straightforward as we might imagine. For example, Word and the printer might miscommunicate about the layout of the address on the envelope or the orientation of the envelope in the printer tray, so you'll need to experiment with the Feed options in Word and how to put the envelope into the printer.**

Viewing a Document

We'll spotlight three ways to look at your Word document here—Normal view, Print Layout view, and Print Preview. Normal view is designed to show as much of the working document as possible so you can focus on content, dispensing with such niceties as page numbers and margins. (Note, however, that the line lengths in this view are controlled by margin settings.)

Print Layout view shows you how the printed document will look while you work on it. Print Preview, on the other hand, is designed more to help you catch problems than to fix them. It gives you a bird's eye view of your document, so you can see a page or more at a glance. Akin to that last check in the mirror before you leave home, Print Preview helps ensure there are no unsightly page breaks, the page numbers are visible, and so on.

Work in Normal View

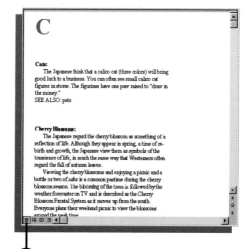

(1) Click the Normal View button to switch to Normal view.

Work in Print Layout View

(1) Click the Print Layout View button to switch to Print Layout view.

Preview a Document for Printing

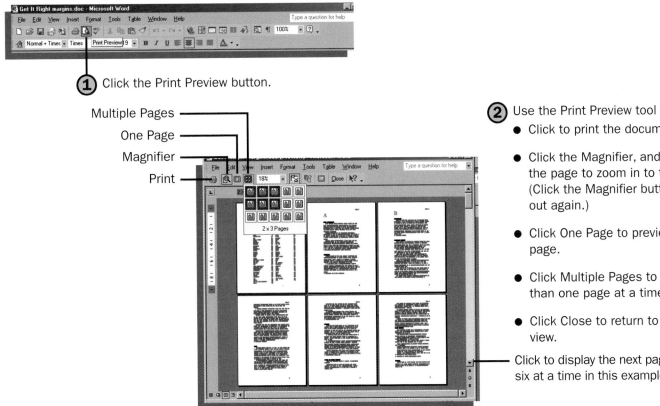

① Click the Print Preview button.

Multiple Pages

One Page

Magnifier

Print

② Use the Print Preview tool as follows:
- Click to print the document instantly.
- Click the Magnifier, and then click the page to zoom in to the details. (Click the Magnifier button to zoom out again.)
- Click One Page to preview a single page.
- Click Multiple Pages to preview more than one page at a time.
- Click Close to return to your working view.

Click to display the next pages—six at a time in this example.

> **TIP:** If you have problems viewing documents, click in the Ask A Question box in the upper right corner of the window. Type viewing documents, and then press the Enter key. Click Troubleshoot Document Views And Screen Displays, and browse through the list.

Printing from Word

Word's printing choices transform even the humblest printer into a printer-copier combo. Of course you can direct the printer to print all or part of a document and as many copies as you want. But like a copier, you can also have your printer collate pages and print on both sides of the paper (even though duplex printing is not one of your printer's features). Word can instruct your printer to scale a document to fit a certain size of paper—enlarge a document designed for smaller paper or reduce the size of a document to fit on smaller paper—for example, print a legal-size page onto letter-size paper.

Print a Word Document

TIP: Convert a printer that prints on only one side of the paper to a machine that prints duplex. To do this, you'll use the steps in "Print a Word Document" as a guideline. Start with paper that's heavy enough to keep the words from showing through on the reverse side. Then print the odd pages first, choosing Odd Pages in step 2.

Now, to print the even pages, flip or rotate (depending on your printer) the stack of paper. (If you're not sure which way to feed the paper into the printer, test it with a couple of pages.) Then follow step 1 again, and choose Even Pages in step 2. Click the Options button, select the Reverse Print Order check box, and click OK twice. When you're done, go back and clear the Reverse Print Order check box.

Select a portion of the document before you choose to print, and when you click Selection Word will print just that.

(1) Choose Print from the File menu.

(2) Specify what you want to print.

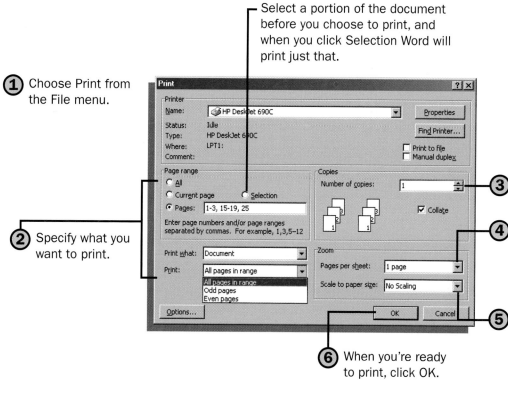

(3) Enter the number of copies you want.

(4) Click the Pages Per Sheet down arrow, and click the number of pages you want to print on one sheet of paper.

(5) Click the Scale To Paper Size down arrow, and click the size of paper you want to print your document on.

(6) When you're ready to print, click OK.

Formatting a Word Document

After you've created a basic Microsoft Word document, it's time to turn your attention to how it looks. But before you plunge into italicizing and coloring text, adding borders, and mastering styles, it's important to understand the Word—and Microsoft Office XP—approach to formatting.

In Office, formatting can apply to three distinct elements: characters, paragraphs, and documents:

- Character (or font) formats—font and size, boldface, italics, color, and so on—are devoted to letters, numbers, and spaces. To apply character formats, you must highlight every character you want to change.

- Paragraph formats apply to, well, paragraphs. A paragraph can be as short as a headline, a bullet point (like this one), or a paragraph as we commonly think of them. To format one paragraph, you need only click in the paragraph; to format more than one just make sure the selection touches every paragraph.

- Document formats concern themselves with the layout of pages. This not only includes margins, page orientation (vertical and horizontal), and page size but also includes the position of page numbers, headers, and footers. To format a document, you need only have it open.

You can apply any of these formats before you type a word in a new document, while you're typing, as well as after you've finished.

Changing Font and Size, Italics, Color, and Other Effects

The Bold, Italic, and Underline buttons work just like switches. You click one of these buttons to turn on the style for selected text, and then click it again to turn the style off. For your choice of font, font size, and color, you choose from a list—or in the case of color, from a palette of colors. You can combine as many of these effects as you want—in fact, many, such as color, are enhanced by boldface.

You can also ~~strikethrough~~ text, ^{superscript} or _{subscript}, condense or e x p a n d it. You can even make it blink or sparkle. To explore your font options, select any text, and choose Font from the Format menu. Then experiment with other effects on the Character Spacing and Text Effects tabs.

Set Character Formats

① Select the text you want to format.

② Click the Font down arrow, and click the font you want.

③ Click the Font Size down arrow, and click the point size you want.

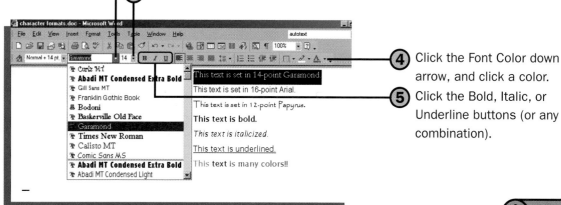

④ Click the Font Color down arrow, and click a color.

⑤ Click the Bold, Italic, or Underline buttons (or any combination).

Setting the Space Between Lines and Paragraphs ⊕ NEW FEATURE

Setting the space between lines in a paragraph, and between paragraphs in a document, can lend readability to your documents. For example, adding space between lines can provide extra room for hand-written corrections and comments; extra spacing between paragraphs can help organize a document visually. Word gives you greater control over the space between paragraphs than simply adding extra carriage returns, as you would with a typewriter (remember those?).

When you've set the spacing of the paragraph the way you want, Word applies the changes to the next paragraph after you press the Enter key at paragraph's end.

> **TIP: To avoid more space than you bargained for when you set line spacing, add space either before or after a paragraph, but not both.**

Set Line Spacing

① Select the paragraph(s) you want to change.

② Click the Line Spacing down arrow, and click the line spacing you want.

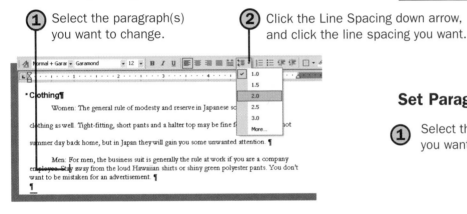

Set Paragraph Spacing

① Select the paragraph(s) you want to change.

② Choose Paragraph from the Format menu.

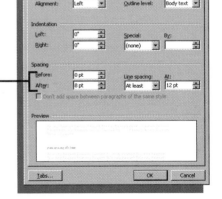

③ On the Indents And Spacing tab, type the amount of extra space (in points) you want to add before or after the paragraph, and click OK.

> **TIP: You can change line spacing right from the keyboard. Select the paragraphs you want to change, and then press Ctrl+2 for double-spacing; press Ctrl+5 for 1¹/₂ spacing; and press Ctrl+1 for single spacing. (Use the numbers at the top of the keyboard, *not* the numbers on the keypad.)**

Aligning and Indenting Text

Text alignment refers to the horizontal placement of lines within paragraphs—*left-aligned* (even on the left edge of a paragraph and the most common alignment); *justified* (aligned on the right and left edges, like a newspaper column); centered; and *right-aligned* (even on the right edge). Indenting text controls the extent to which a paragraph or its first line is indented from the margins—for example, the first line of each paragraph or a long quotation indented from both margins.

Without ever touching the Spacebar, Word lets you perfectly align and indent text using buttons on the toolbar or by moving markers on the ruler.

TIP: Both alignments and indents are paragraph formats stored in the mark at the end of each paragraph. Delete that mark and you delete the formats.

SEE ALSO: For information about how to close up those white holes that can plague justified text, see the Try This on page 69.

Center, Justify, Left-align, and Right-align Text

1 Select the paragraph(s) you want to align.

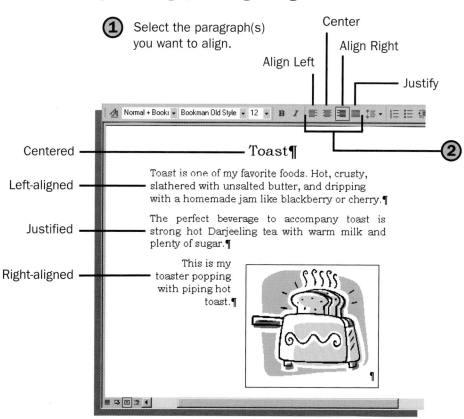

2 Click the alignment you want:

- Click the Center button to center text.
- Click the Align Left button to align text to the left.
- Click the Justify button to justify text.
- Click the Align Right button to align text to the right.

Indent Text

(1) If the ruler is not already visible, choose Ruler from the View menu.

Left Indent

First Line Indent

Right Indent

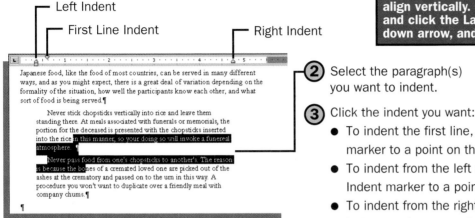

Japanese food, like the food of most countries, can be served in many different ways, and as you might expect, there is a great deal of variation depending on the formality of the situation, how well the participants know each other, and what sort of food is being served.¶

Never stick chopsticks vertically into rice and leave them standing there. At meals associated with funerals or memorials, the portion for the deceased is presented with the chopsticks inserted into the rice in this manner, so your doing so will invoke a funereal atmosphere. ¶

Never pass food from one's chopsticks to another's. The reason is because the bones of a cremated loved one are picked out of the ashes at the crematory and passed on to the urn in this way. A procedure you won't want to duplicate over a friendly meal with company chums.¶

(2) Select the paragraph(s) you want to indent.

(3) Click the indent you want:

- To indent the first line, drag the First Line Indent marker to a point on the ruler.
- To indent from the left margin, drag the Left Indent marker to a point on the ruler.
- To indent from the right margin, drag the Right Indent marker to a point on the ruler.

Create Different Levels in a List

(1) Select the paragraph(s) you want to indent.

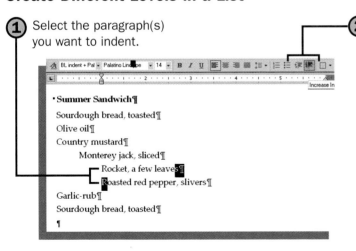

Increase In

• **Summer Sandwich**¶

Sourdough bread, toasted¶
Olive oil¶
Country mustard¶
Monterey jack, sliced¶
Rocket, a few leaves¶
Roasted red pepper, slivers¶
Garlic-rub¶
Sourdough bread, toasted¶
¶

(2) Click the indent option you want:

- Click the Increase Indent button to move the paragraph(s) to the right .5 inch.
- Click the Decrease Indent button to move the paragraph(s) to the left .5 inch.

Creating Bulleted and Numbered Lists

The buttons for bulleted and number lists worked like switches—click a button to turn on numbers and click it again to stop numbering. This makes it simple to create bulleted and numbered lists, because you just type your list by pressing the Enter key after each item. Then you select the list and turn on the bullets or numbers. Word indents each paragraph properly, adding the bullet or number, and (for numbers) automatically numbering each paragraph in order. Each new item you add to the list by pressing Enter adopts the bullet or number format.

Make a Numbered List

1 Select the paragraph(s) you want to number.

2 Click the Numbering button.

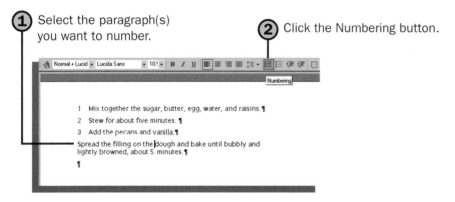

Make a Bulleted List

1 Select the paragraph(s) you want to bullet.

2 Click the Bullets button.

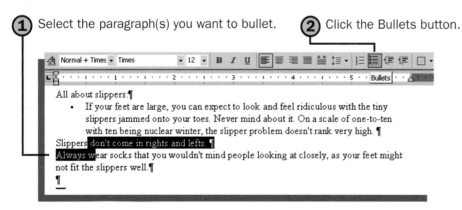

TIP: Word makes it easy to re-order a numbered list. For example, in the procedure "Make a Numbered List," if you wanted step 3 in the illustration to come first—add the pecans and vanilla before stewing—you'd select the text in step 3 and drag it before step 2. Word would instantly renumber the steps.

TIP: To discontinue bullets or numbering as you type, select the paragraph (or even an entire list) where you want to remove the bullets or numbers. Then click the Numbering or Bullets button.

TIP: You can start a numbered list simply by typing "1." and then typing the first item. When you press the Enter key at the end of the line, Word numbers the following paragraphs as part of the list automatically. Press the Enter key twice after the last item to discontinue the numbered list.

NEW FEATURE: If your numbered list begins with the wrong number, right-click the first item in the list and choose Restart Numbering from the shortcut menu.

Controlling Text Placement with Tabs

Tabs are great for very basic tables, but if you need more than a quick alignment of a word or two per column, using tables instead may be your best approach.

A bit of advice as you plunge into using tabs: don't use the Spacebar to line up columns. Most of the fonts you're using are *proportionally spaced*. That is, each letter takes up a different amount of space—for example, the *m* is fatter than an *i* or *l*. This means the extra spaces that worked in one line may go awry in the next. Instead, select the unruly lines and tweak the tab stop.

Position Text using Tabs

(1) If the ruler is not already visible, choose Ruler from the View menu.

(2) Press the Tab key, and type the first item on your list.

(3) Click the Tab button until you get the type of tab stop you want—left, right, centered, decimal, or bar.

(4) Click the ruler where you want to insert the tab stop.

Show/Hide ¶ button

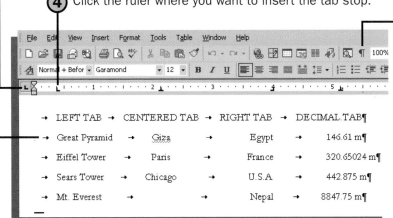

(5) Repeat steps 2 through 4 to add more than one tab stop.

SEE ALSO: For information about how to build tables, see "Creating a Table" on page 78.

TIP: To see the tab marks—not a bad idea when you're first learning to use tabs—click the Show/Hide ¶ button on the Standard toolbar. (The tab marks show up as arrows, as in the figure.)

Delete a Tab Stop

(1) Select the paragraphs containing the tab stop you want to remove.

(2) Drag the tab stop off the ruler.

TIP: To move a tab stop, select the text containing the tab stop you want to adjust. Then drag the tab marker on the ruler to reposition the tab stop.

Arranging Text in Newspaper-style Columns

Word makes it easy to create columns for newsletters and other documents in which the text flows without interruption from the bottom of one column and continues at the top of the next. When you insert text in the middle of one of these columns, it pushes the text in front of it forward. If you want text to stay in place, as with a schedule, it's better to use tables. In tables, when you put text into a cell, it stays there, unaffected, while you type text into other cells or columns.

Word gives you quite a bit of control over columns, making it easy to create a *banner heading* (the heading unfurls across more than one column of text) or columns of uneven widths, and to break columns just where you want. But remember: you can only see and work with columns in Print Layout View; other views show only one column at a time.

Lay Out Text in Columns ⊗ NEW FEATURE

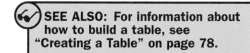

SEE ALSO: For information about how to build a table, see "Creating a Table" on page 78.

TIP: If you run into problems arranging text in columns, Word may have some suggestions. Type newspaper columns **in the Ask A Question box in the upper-right corner of your screen. Click** troubleshoot newsletter-style columns, **and press the Enter key.**

(2) Select the text you want to arrange in columns, or press Ctrl+A to select the entire document.

(1) Click the Print Layout button.

(3) Click the Columns button, and click the number of columns you want.

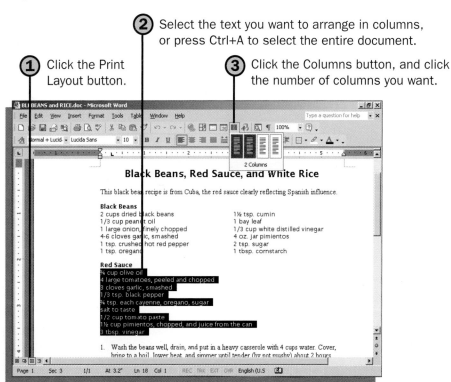

TIP: If you're creating a document destined for the Web, don't bother to arrange the text in newspaper-style columns because Web browsers won't display more than one column.

Create a Banner Heading ⊕ NEW FEATURE

1 Select the paragraph you want to make into a heading.

2 Click the Columns buttons, and click the single-column layout.

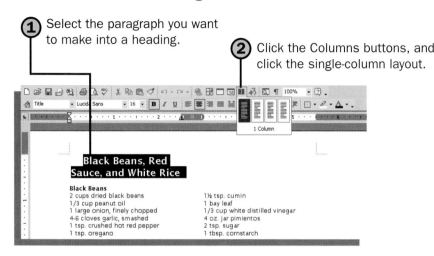

Create Uneven Columns

1 Choose Ruler from the View menu.

2 Click the column you want to adjust.

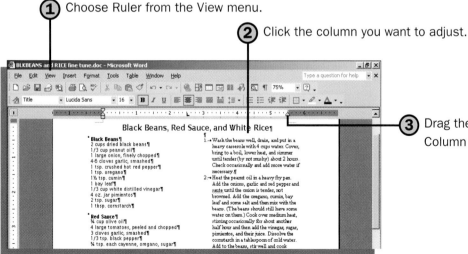

3 Drag the appropriate Move Column marker on the ruler.

Force a Column Break

1 Click in the paragraph where you want the new column to start.

2 Choose Break from the Insert menu.

3 Click Column Break, and then click OK.

> **TRY THIS: If the text in columns is punctuated with little chunky white spaces or a very ragged right edge, hyphenating might help. Choose Language from the Tools menu, and then click Hyphenation. Click Automatically Hyphenate Document, and click OK.**

> **TIP: To remove columns, select the text you want to return to one column. Click the Columns button, and click the single-column layout.**

> **TIP: You can fine-tune columns further—for example, adjust the space or add a vertical line between columns. Choose Columns from the Format menu, and make the adjustments you want.**

Adding Shading, Borders, and Other Special Effects

It's easy to add all kinds of special effects to text in Word—so easy, in fact, that the key to a handsome document is a sense of restraint more than anything. Here are a few effects to play with that can add emphasis and style to any document. A *drop cap* (or dropped capital letter) is a large first letter that can give an opening line some panache. Shading the background helps a paragraph stand out from a crowd.

Add a Drop Cap

1 Click the Print Layout button.

2 Click the paragraph where you want the drop cap.

3 Choose Drop Cap from the Format menu.

Remove a Drop Cap

1 Choose Drop Cap from the Format menu.

2 Click None, and click OK.

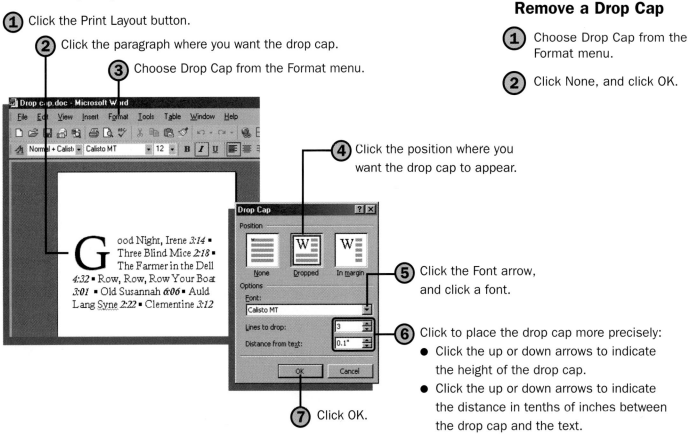

4 Click the position where you want the drop cap to appear.

5 Click the Font arrow, and click a font.

6 Click to place the drop cap more precisely:
- Click the up or down arrows to indicate the height of the drop cap.
- Click the up or down arrows to indicate the distance in tenths of inches between the drop cap and the text.

7 Click OK.

Add a Border, Shaded Background, or Line to a Paragraph

TIP: To remove a border or shading, select the paragraph(s) and choose Borders And Shading from the Format menu. On either the Borders or the Page Border tab, click None. On the Shading tab, click No Fill.

(2) Choose Toolbars from the View menu, and click Tables And Borders.

(3) Click the Line Style down arrow, and click a style.

(4) Click the Line Weight down arrow, and click the line or border thickness.

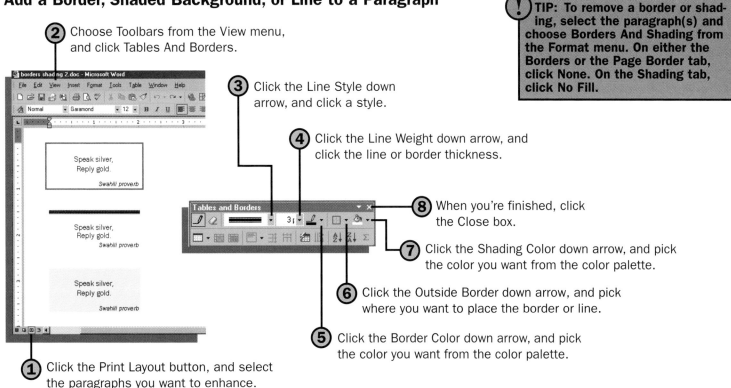

(8) When you're finished, click the Close box.

(7) Click the Shading Color down arrow, and pick the color you want from the color palette.

(6) Click the Outside Border down arrow, and pick where you want to place the border or line.

(5) Click the Border Color down arrow, and pick the color you want from the color palette.

(1) Click the Print Layout button, and select the paragraphs you want to enhance.

TIP: To repeat a format, no matter how complex, press the F4 key—the "repeat the last action" key—at the top of your keyboard *immediately after* you've completed the formatting.

TIP: Don't let the Tables And Borders toolbar get in your way—to move it, drag it by the grey bar at the top of the box. If you drag it on top of the toolbars at the top of the screen, it will pop right in.

What's a Style?

A *style* is a collection of formatting rules with a name. For example, a heading (as shown in "Discover What's in a Style" below) gathers together character formats (font and size, bold and italic) and paragraph formats (alignment, indentation, and spacing). It's somewhat akin to the way a diner offers breakfast: No. 1 (eggs, hash browns, and toast), No. 2 (eggs, bacon, hash browns, and toast), and so on. You order your breakfast by number and the kitchen knows what to fix. In the same way, when you apply a style by name, you order up the entire collection of formats as you do so.

Discover What's in a Style

① Select the text you're curious about.

② Choose Reveal Formatting from the Format menu to see the formatting details.

The powers of styles are many. They make formatting changes a snap—change a style and you instantly change every instance of text formatted with that style. Styles establish consistency, whether within a document (for example, ensuring that every headline has the same format) or among documents—for example, making sure that each chapter heading in a book looks the same, no matter who wrote it.

Every Word document uses a collection of styles called a *template*. In fact, the basic underpinning of every document is the Normal template. It puts dozens of styles at your disposal—choose from half a dozen bulleted list styles, nine different headings, and so on.

You can create your own style collections, or templates. When you modify or create styles, you can save the settings as part of a template which you can easily apply to any document. We've focused on the basics of styles here, but the principals and uses of styles apply to every Office program.

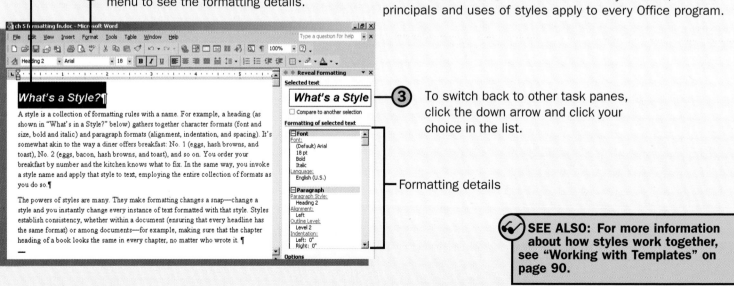

③ To switch back to other task panes, click the down arrow and click your choice in the list.

Formatting details

> SEE ALSO: For more information about how styles work together, see "Working with Templates" on page 90.

Applying a Style

Word has a half dozen ways to make formatting simple. We'll show you a couple of ways to apply formats—one for the spontaneous (using the Format Painter as you go) and the other for the more methodical (using a named, pre-defined style). The Format Painter lets you literally paint a collection of both character and paragraph formats onto text. An existing style works the same way, only you apply it by name.

TRY THIS: To copy selected formatting to more than one spot when you're copying an existing style, double-click the Format Painter button (instead of just clicking) as you do step 2. When you've painted all the text you want, press the Esc key.

Apply Formats as You Go

(1) Click in the paragraph containing the formatting you want to copy.

(2) Click the Format Painter button.

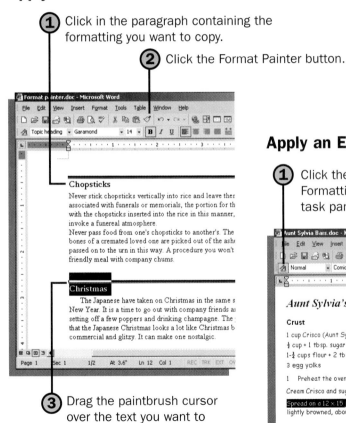

(3) Drag the paintbrush cursor over the text you want to apply the new format.

Apply an Existing Style ⊕ NEW FEATURE

(1) Click the Styles And Formatting button if the task pane isn't open.

(2) Select the text to which you want to apply a pre-defined style.

(3) In the Styles And Formatting task pane, click the style you want to apply.

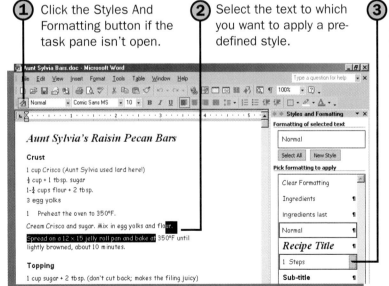

Reusing Formats with Styles

Creating a new style can be as simple as naming a format you've already created—for example, QUOTE, an indented italicized style in a small font size for quotations. When you change a style, however, you cash in on the power of styles: edit the style in one place and the change ripples throughout the entire document.

For example, if we wanted to change the black text to white in the "See Also" references in this book, we'd change the style just once, and instantly the text would change throughout the book.

> **TRY THIS: You can change any style (except the Normal paragraph style) by copying a format. For example, format your heading just so. Click the paragraph you've just changed and point to the *original* style name in the Styles And Formatting task pane. Click the down arrow, and click Update To Match Selection.**

Create a New Style

1 Click in the paragraph containing the text with the format you want.

2 Click in the style box.

3 Type a short, memorable name for the new style.

4 Press the Enter key.

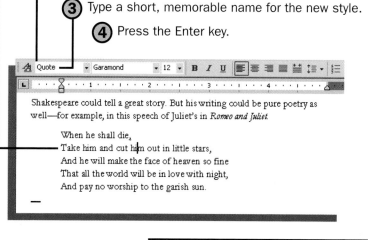

Delete a Style ⊕ NEW FEATURE

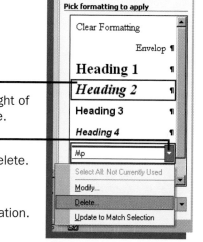

1 In the Styles And Formatting task pane on the right of your screen, point to the style you want to delete.

2 Click the down arrow, and click Delete.

3 Click Yes when Word asks for confirmation.

Change a Style

(1) Click a paragraph containing the style you want to change.

(2) Click the Styles And Formatting button.

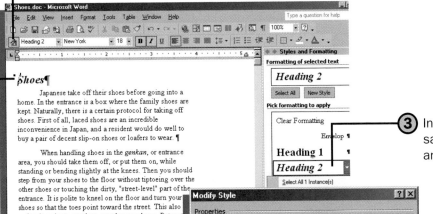

(3) In the task pane, point to the same style name, click the arrow, and then click Modify Style.

(4) Click to choose the character formatting you want.

(5) Click to choose the alignment, line and paragraph spacing, and indents you want.

(7) Click OK.

(6) To fine-tune the style further, click the Format button, and experiment with choices there.

Finding and Replacing Formatting

You're no doubt familiar with Word's powerful tool for finding words (among other things) and replacing them with other words. But did you know that you can use that same tool to search for one kind of formatting and replace it with another. Now you can wait until the last moment to switch all the bold text in your document to italics or change all instances of your company name from boring black to bright orange.

Find and Replace Formatting

(1) Choose Replace from the Edit menu, and then click the More button.

(2) Click the Format button, and click the format you want to find.

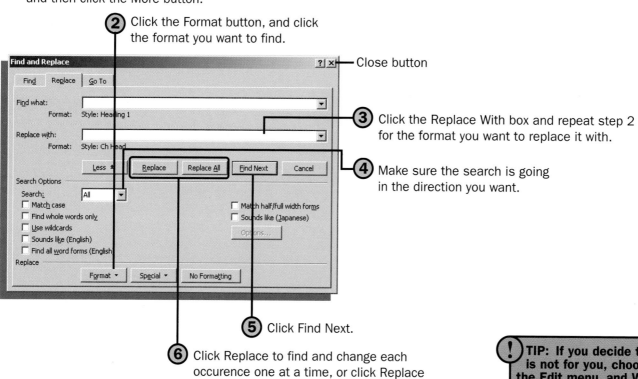

Close button

(3) Click the Replace With box and repeat step 2 for the format you want to replace it with.

(4) Make sure the search is going in the direction you want.

(5) Click Find Next.

(6) Click Replace to find and change each occurence one at a time, or click Replace All to replace all instances at once.

> **! TIP:** You can replace something with nothing. Let's say you want to return all instances of italicized text to normal formatting. In the Find What box, choose Italics for Font. In the Replace With box, press the Delete key. Click Replace All and presto! The italics are gone.

> **! TIP:** If you decide the new format is not for you, choose Undo from the Edit menu, and Word will undo every single replacement you just made.

Building Complex Documents Using Word

6

Now that you've mastered the basics of creating and formatting a document, you may be ready to turn your attention to some of the features that make Microsoft Word a powerhouse when it comes to organizing information, taming lengthy documents, automating repetitive work, and even translating words into other languages.

In this section we'll exercise Word's organizational ability with tables, starting from building a table, adding text to it, stretching or shrinking it to accommodate your additions, and making it both handsome and readable. We'll touch on Word's features for handling long documents—how to create a separate section within a document (basically a document within a document), add text that's repeated on every page to orient your readers, and call on Word to build a table of contents for you.

We'll also illustrate Word's ability to lighten the burden of boring work, show you how to reuse the format of documents you've created, and spotlight Word's superb Mail Merge Wizard, which makes the process of merging and printing your mailing list on a package of labels as simple as it can get.

Creating a Table

It takes just the click of a button to create a table that fits between the margins of a document. Don't fuss over getting just the right number of columns and rows because they're easy to add later—content is, too. You can type text or even insert a picture, and the cells expand in height to accommodate whatever you put there. Navigating within a table requires a couple of tricks, but nothing taxing. And if you've already built a table using tab stops that isn't working the way you would like, Word can rescue your efforts by converting the text to a table.

Trying to decide whether to use newspaper-style columns or a table? When you want text to flow from column to column as you add or delete text (as in a newspaper article), use columns. If you want to expose the structure of your information—as in a schedule or a résumé—use tables.

Start a Table

(1) Click in the document where you want to put the table.

(2) Click the Insert Table button.

(3) Drag the mouse pointer diagonally to specify the number of columns and rows you want, and release the mouse button.

5 x 2 Table

Word inserts a table with five rows and two columns.

SEE ALSO: For information about how to create newspaper-style columns, see "Arranging Text in Newspaper-style Columns" on page 68.

TRY THIS: Word's table conversion ability is a two-way street: you can also remove the table structure, leaving the text behind. This is useful when you want to make table content into a narrative—for example, to turn a script with columns for action and dialog into a story. To do this, select the table you want to convert, point to Convert on the Table menu, and click Table To Text. Decide how you want to separate the text—with paragraph marks, tabs, commas, or hyphens—and click OK.

TIP: To see how your table looks on the page, choose Print Layout from the View menu.

Convert Text with Items Separated by Tab Stops to a Table

(1) Select the entire block of text with each item destined for a column separated by tab stops. For best results, make sure that each line (paragraph) has the same number of tab stops, and there are no extraneous paragraph marks.

(2) Point to Convert on the Table menu, and click Text To Table.

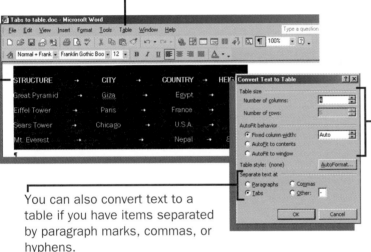

You can also convert text to a table if you have items separated by paragraph marks, commas, or hyphens.

TRY THIS: Before you convert text to a table, you'll have better control over the results if you can actually see the tab stops and paragraph marks. To show them, click the Show/Hide ¶ button on the Standard toolbar at the top of the window.

(3) Click the number of columns and rows and any other options you want, and click OK.

(4) You might need to tweak the table a bit.

STRUCTURE¤	CITY¤	COUNTRY¤	HEIGHT¤	¤
Great Pyramid¤	Giza¤	Egypt¤	146.61·m¤	¤
Eiffel·Tower¤	Paris¤	France¤	320.6502·4 m¤	¤
Sears Tower¤	Chicago¤	U.S.A.¤	442.875·m¤	¤
Mt.·Everest¤	¤	Nepal¤	8847.75·m¤	¤

Navigate and Work in a Table

To do this:	Press the:
Move to the next column	Tab key
Move to the previous column	Shift+Tab keys
Move up or down in a table (from row to row)	Up Arrow or Down Arrow key
Start a new paragraph *within* a cell	Enter key
Add a new row	Tab key in the last cell of the table

Delete a Table

(1) Click the table.

(2) Point to Delete on the Table menu, and click Table.

Adding, Deleting, and Moving Table Rows and Columns

In general, the boundaries of a table are limited by the margins of the page. You can add columns with abandon until the table fits between the margins; after that, Word reduces the width of existing columns. Moving rows and columns isn't hard: the existing rows move up or down around the newly moved rows, the existing columns shift right or left. When you delete a row, column, or table, say goodbye to all the contents as well.

TIP: When you've got a table set up just so—exactly the right look, column widths, and number of rows—you can reuse it, by clearing all or part of its contents, but keeping the table framework. Just select what you want to delete, and press the Delete key.

Insert Blank Rows or Columns

1 Select the same number of rows or columns you want to add next to existing rows or columns—for example, to add two columns, select two columns.

2 Point to Insert on the Table menu.

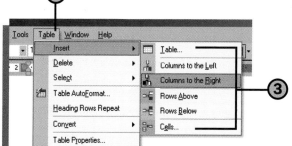

3 Click what you want to insert—columns or rows—and where.

In this example, Word inserted two new columns to the right of the selected columns.

Numero de train	17	19		
Paris-Gare-de-Lyon	07.54	10.54		
Chambery-Chalet-les-Eaux	11.01	14.02		
Modane	15.08	14.02		
Bardonecchia-Stazione	12.25	15.25		

TIP: To add a row at the end of a table as you type, press the Tab key in the last cell of the table.

Delete Rows and Columns

① Select as many rows or columns as you want to delete.

② Right-click the selected rows or columns, and click Delete Rows or Delete Columns.

! TIP: How do you insert a paragraph mark before a table at the very top of a document? Easy. Click in the first cell of the table, and press Ctrl+Shift+Enter. This works to split a table in two as well: click in any cell in the leftmost column, and Word will add a paragraph mark before it.

Move Rows and Columns

① Select the row or column you want to move.

② Drag it to the new location.

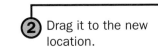

Selecting a Table or Its Parts

To select:	Do this:
Cell(s)	Click in a cell, and drag the mouse pointer to select one or more cells.
Row(s)	Move the mouse pointer to the left of the row until it changes to a right-pointing arrow, and then click. To select more than one row, drag the mouse pointer up or down.
Column(s)	Move the mouse pointer above the column until it changes to a down arrow, and then click. To select more than one column, drag the mouse pointer to the right or left.
A table	Click in the table, point to Select on the Table menu, and then click Table.

Adjusting Table Cells, Rows, and Columns

When you want a title to span several columns (or even an entire table), you can run cells together to make a single wide cell. Or, if you want to divide a column or row to display information with more precision, you can accomplish this by splitting cells.

As you make columns wider or narrower, Word generally keeps the width of the table the same (although there are ways around this). When you expand a column by dragging it, Word shrinks the columns to right of the column you're widening. However, if you drag the outermost column boundaries on the left or right, the sky's the limit—you can even go so far as to make the table spill into a place where it disappears.

Display the Tables And Borders Toolbar

 Point to Toolbars on the View menu, and click Tables And Borders.

Split Cells

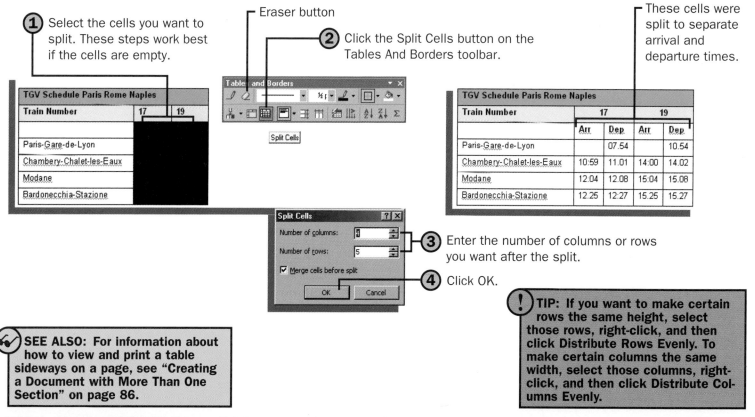

① Select the cells you want to split. These steps work best if the cells are empty.

Eraser button

② Click the Split Cells button on the Tables And Borders toolbar.

These cells were split to separate arrival and departure times.

Split Cells

TGV Schedule Paris Rome Naples		17		19	
Train Number		Arr	Dep	Arr	Dep
Paris-Gare-de-Lyon			07.54		10.54
Chambery-Chalet-les-Eaux		10:59	11.01	14:00	14.02
Modane		12.04	12.08	15:04	15.08
Bardonecchia-Stazione		12.25	12:27	15.25	15.27

Split Cells

Number of columns: 4

Number of rows: 5

☑ Merge cells before split

OK   Cancel

③ Enter the number of columns or rows you want after the split.

④ Click OK.

> ⚬ **SEE ALSO:** For information about how to view and print a table sideways on a page, see "Creating a Document with More Than One Section" on page 86.

> ❗ **TIP:** If you want to make certain rows the same height, select those rows, right-click, and then click Distribute Rows Evenly. To make certain columns the same width, select those columns, right-click, and then click Distribute Columns Evenly.

Merge Cells

1 Select the cells you want to merge.

2 Click the Merge Cells button on the Tables And Borders toolbar.

In this example, three cells were merged to accommodate the title of the table.

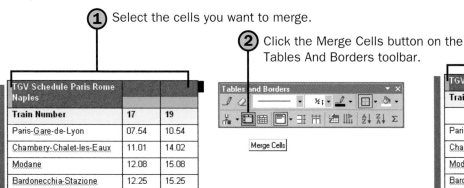

Adjust the Width of a Column

1 Point to the right column boundary of the column you want to adjust.

2 When the mouse pointer changes to a double-headed arrow, do one of the following:

- Drag the vertical gridline to the width you want, and shrink or expand the column just to the right, keeping the table width constant.
- Hold down the Ctrl key while you drag to shrink or expand the columns to the right proportionally, keeping the table width constant.
- Hold down the Shift key while you drag to keep the columns to the right constant, expanding or shrinking the table width in the process.

Numero de train¤	17¤	19¤
Paris-Gare-de-Lyon¤	07.54¤	10.54¤
Chambery-Chalet-les-Eaux¤	11.01¤	14.02¤
Modane¤	15.08¤	14.02¤
Bardonecchia-Stazione¤	12.25¤	15.25¤

This column was adjusted simply by dragging.

Numero de train	17	19
Paris-Gare-de-Lyon	07.54	10.54
Chambery-Chalet-les-Eaux	11.01	14.02
Modane	15.08	14.02
Bardonecchia-Stazione	12.25	15.25

TRY THIS: You can literally erase the lines between cells you want to merge. Simply click the Eraser button on the top row of the Tables And Borders toolbar and then use it just as you would a real eraser. Press the Escape key to restore the standard mouse pointer.

Formatting and Positioning Tables

For instant good looks and readability, Word offers almost four dozen different table styles. (You can also tweak the position of text in cells and relocate the table on the page.) Varying the colors or shading of rows and columns is particularly useful for large and very wide tables. It makes the structure of a table easier to grasp, and simplifies the task for your reader's eye as it traverses a wide row or tall column.

Change the Look of a Table Using Built-In Formats

1 Click the table you want to format.

2 Click Table AutoFormat on the Tables And Borders toolbar. If you don't see the toolbar, point to Toolbars on the View menu, and click Tables And Borders.

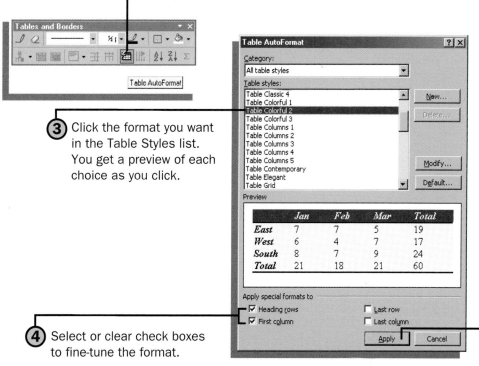

3 Click the format you want in the Table Styles list. You get a preview of each choice as you click.

4 Select or clear check boxes to fine-tune the format.

5 Click Apply when you're satisfied with the look of your table.

> **TIP:** When you want a table to fit between the margins, simply right-click the table, point to AutoFit on the shortcut menu, and then click AutoFit To Window. Word will expand or shrink the table to fit within the margins you've set. You might need to adjust individual column widths when Word is done.

> **TRY THIS:** If you have a table that continues beyond one page, you can make reading it easier by repeating table headings on every page. To do this, select the heading row or rows. (The selection must include the first row of the table.) Choose Heading Rows Repeat from the Table menu. You will see the repeated headings when you print or switch to Print Layout view. One note: Word repeats headings only when tables break as a result of automatic page breaks and not when you insert a manual page break.

Align Text Within Cells

(1) Select the cells, rows, or columns whose horizontal or vertical alignment you want to change.

(2) Click the cell alignment down arrow on the Tables And Borders toolbar, and click the alignment you want. If you don't see the toolbar, point to Toolbars on the View menu, and click Tables And Borders.

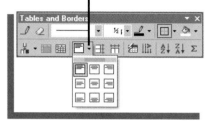

Move or Resize a Table

(1) Choose Print Layout from the View menu.

Move Handle

Numero de train	17	19
Paris-Gare-de-Lyon	07.54	10.54
Chambery-Chalet-les-Eaux	11.01	14.02
Modane	15.08	14.02
Bardonecchia-Stazione	12.25	15.25

Resize Handle

(2) Pause the mouse pointer over the table until you see the Move and Resize handles. Then do one of the following:

● To move the table, point to the Move handle; when it changes to a crosshair pointer, drag the table to a new location.

● To change the size of the entire table, point to the Resize handle; when it changes to a double-headed arrow, drag the table until it's the size you want.

TRY THIS: When you want to indent a table within a body of text—say, for emphasis—click the table, and choose Table Properties from the Table menu. On the Table tab, click Left in the Alignment area. In the Indent From Left box, enter the amount you want the table to be indented, and then click OK.

TRY THIS: To keep a table (or any portion of it) on one page, select the entire table or that part you want to keep together. Choose Paragraph from the Format menu. Then click the Line And Page Breaks tab, select Keep Lines Together, and click OK.

SEE ALSO: For information about how to add a border to a table, see "Adding Shading, Borders, and Other Special Effects" on page 70.

Creating a Document with More Than One Section

There will be occasions when the layout of your document just won't work for every page—a wide table might need to be viewed sideways, you might want a table of contents in two columns, and so on. Word accommodates this requirement by creating a new section. A *section* is rather like a document within a document in which you can control such attributes as margins, page orientation, and the number of columns, to name a few.

TIP: You can add a border to a section—for example, a title page—by following the instructions in "Enhancing Pictures with Colors and Borders" on page 32. In step 2, click the Page Border tab and follow the instructions as shown.

Create a New Section in a Document

(1) Click in the paragraph where you want the new section to begin.

(2) Choose Break from the Insert menu.

The table of contents section will be two columns wide.

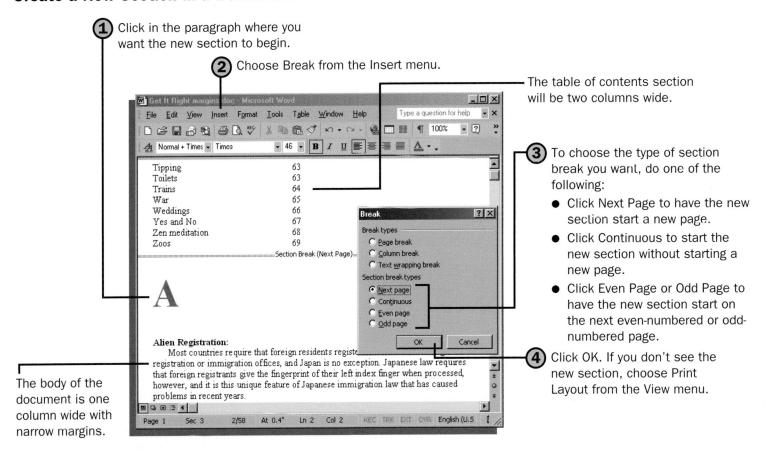

(3) To choose the type of section break you want, do one of the following:
- Click Next Page to have the new section start a new page.
- Click Continuous to start the new section without starting a new page.
- Click Even Page or Odd Page to have the new section start on the next even-numbered or odd-numbered page.

(4) Click OK. If you don't see the new section, choose Print Layout from the View menu.

The body of the document is one column wide with narrow margins.

Remove a Section Break

(1) Click the section break, and press the Delete key. If you don't see the section break, choose Normal from the View menu.

Set Margins and Page Orientation for a Section

(1) Click the section where you want to set margins or change page orientation.

TRY THIS: For information about how to add page numbers, see "Adding and Removing Page Numbers" on page 52. You can make the page numbers different in a section—for example, it's customary to have the table of contents numbered with lowercase Roman numerals. Follow the steps as outlined, changing the numbering style in the Page Number Format box. Then specify whether you want the page numbers to Continue From Previous Section or Start At a number you specify, and click OK.

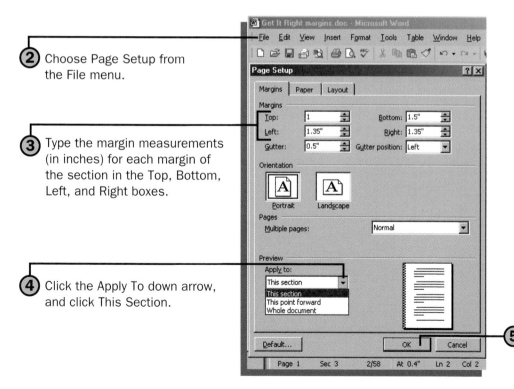

(2) Choose Page Setup from the File menu.

(3) Type the margin measurements (in inches) for each margin of the section in the Top, Bottom, Left, and Right boxes.

(4) Click the Apply To down arrow, and click This Section.

(5) Click OK. To see the new section layout, choose Print Layout from the View menu.

Repeating Text and Pictures on Every Page

Text (including page numbers) or pictures (such as a company logo) that are repeated on every page are aptly known as *headers* if they appear at the top, as *footers* if they're repeated at the bottom. As an example, the headers in this book reiterate the section title and the footers include the name of the task at hand and page numbers.

When you turn to editing headers and footers, you can do so from any page because they are repeated throughout the document. And take note: to see a header or footer, your document must be in Print Layout view.

Add a Header or Footer

1 Choose Header And Footer from the View menu.

2 Do one of the following:
- To start a header, enter text or graphics in the header area.
- To start a footer, click the Switch Between Header And Footer button, and enter text or graphics in the footer area.

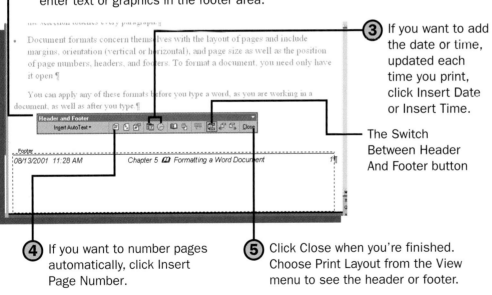

3 If you want to add the date or time, updated each time you print, click Insert Date or Insert Time.

The Switch Between Header And Footer button

4 If you want to number pages automatically, click Insert Page Number.

5 Click Close when you're finished. Choose Print Layout from the View menu to see the header or footer.

CAUTION: If you've inserted page numbers following the directions in "Adding and Removing Page Numbers" on page 52, don't insert them again in a header or footer. It's best not to mix these two features, but rather choose your approach—for simple page numbers, go the route of inserting them; for something more elaborate, add a header or footer.

SEE ALSO: For information about how to format headers and footers, see "Formatting a Word Document" on page 61.

SEE ALSO: For information about how to give clipped headers or footers more space, see "Adding and Removing Page Numbers" on page 52.

Remove a Header or Footer

1 Choose Print Layout from the View menu to see the header or footer.

2 Double-click the header or footer, and then triple-click the header or footer to select all of it.

3 Press the Delete key, and click Close. Word removes the header or footer from every page in the document.

Working on Two Parts of the Same Document

When you're working in a long document, it can be useful to see different parts at the same time—for example, to ensure you're making consistent references throughout or to compare something you've written earlier. *Splitting* a Word document is akin to a split screen on television—you edit and navigate in each part of the document independently of the other, but both are views into the same document.

SEE ALSO: For information about viewing more than one document at once, even from different programs, see "Working with Documents in More Than One Program" on page 10.

View Two Parts of One Document Simultaneously

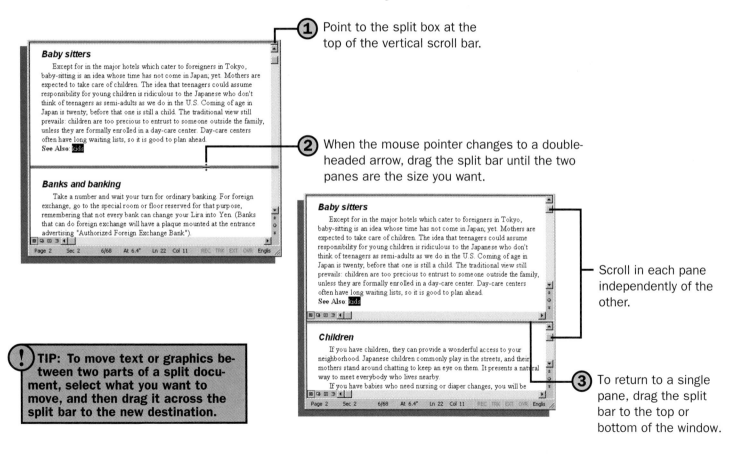

1 Point to the split box at the top of the vertical scroll bar.

2 When the mouse pointer changes to a double-headed arrow, drag the split bar until the two panes are the size you want.

Scroll in each pane independently of the other.

TIP: To move text or graphics between two parts of a split document, select what you want to move, and then drag it across the split bar to the new destination.

3 To return to a single pane, drag the split bar to the top or bottom of the window.

Working with Templates

All documents are built on templates starting with Word's default, the Normal template. A *template* is a collection of styles, page setup information, AutoText entries, placeholder text, and so on. Word's Normal template has no content, but includes three different heading styles, body text set in 12-point Times New Roman, and all the default AutoText entries.

You can save any document as a template—for example, a letter you've perfected for your company letterhead—using it as the foundation of future documents or attaching it after the fact. The letterhead template could include the salutation and preferred closing, margin settings, and even the logo. Creating templates capitalizes on your formatting efforts by recycling formats; using templates is helpful in establishing a consistent look when there is more than one person writing to a style.

 SEE ALSO: For background information about styles in Word, see "What's a Style?" on page 72.

Save a Document as a Template

1 Open the document that will serve as the basis for the template.

2 Choose Save As from the File menu.

4 Type a name for the new template, and click Save. Word saves the template in the Template folder with the filename extension, dot.

5 Add and format any text or graphics you want to appear in all new documents based on this template, and delete any items you don't want to appear.

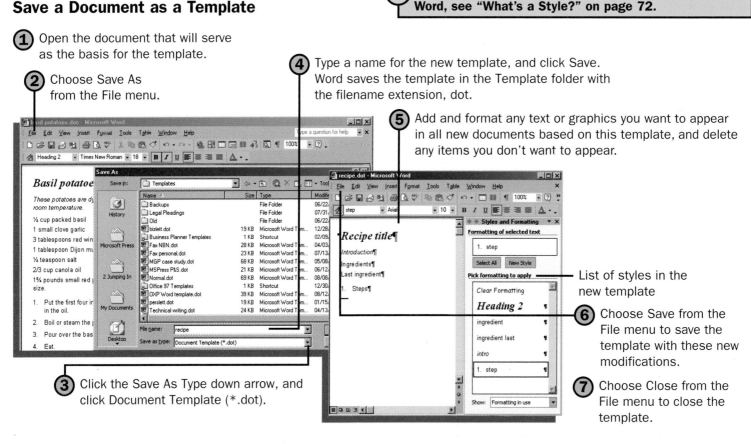

List of styles in the new template

6 Choose Save from the File menu to save the template with these new modifications.

3 Click the Save As Type down arrow, and click Document Template (*.dot).

7 Choose Close from the File menu to close the template.

Switch Templates in a Document

① Open the document you want to apply the new template to, and choose Templates And Add-Ins from the Tools menu.

Aunt Billy's Jerusalem Artichoke Relish

This could be either a *picalilly* or a *chow chow*—the kind of relish you'd see on a Southern Sunday dinner table along with the celery, carrot sticks, and those black olives you can impale on your fingers.

Vegetables

4 quarts Jerusalem artichokes, peeled
3 large white onions (or 2 cups)
4 red peppers
4 green peppers
1/2 large bunch celery
1 small white cabbage
 Cut up these ingredients into small dice. Let soak overnight in water to cover mixed with 1 cup salt.
 Drain well.

CAUTION: In order to apply the new styles, the style names must be the same in both documents. If they're not the same, the text will keep its original formatting.

② Click Attach. In the Attach Template dialog box, click the template you want, and click Open.

Templates and Add-ins

Document template
C:\Documents and Settings\Carol Brown\App
☑ Automatically update document styles
☐ Attach to all new e-mail messages

Global templates and add-ins
Checked items are currently loaded.
☐ printed guide.dot

Full path: C:\...\Templates\printed guide.dot

Attach... | Linked CSS... | Add... | Remove
Organizer... | OK | Cancel

③ Select the Automatically Update Document Styles check box.

④ Click OK.

New look with new styles

Aunt Billy's Jerusalem Artichoke Relish

This could be either a picalilly or a chow chow—the kind of relish you'd see on a Southern Sunday dinner table along with the celery, carrot sticks, and those black olives you can impale on your fingers.

Vegetables

4 quarts Jerusalem artichokes, peeled
3 large white onions (or 2 cups)
4 red peppers
4 green peppers
1/2 large bunch celery
1 small white cabbage

1. Cut up these ingredients into small dice. Let soak overnight in water to cover mixed with 1 cup salt.
2. Drain well.

TIP: For information about how to start a document using a template you created, see "Starting a Word Document" on page 38. Follow the steps in "Start a Document from a Template"—you'll find your template on the General Templates tab.

TIP: If you have any difficulty using templates, click in the Ask A Question box in the upper right corner of the window. Type troubleshoot templates, and then press the Enter key. Click Troubleshoot Templates And Letters in the list.

Inserting a Table of Contents

Like Word's automatic page numbers and dates, a table of contents is dynamic. When you generate a table of contents, Word tracks down every heading level you indicated and notes which page it's on. Each time you print or when you specifically request to update the table of contents, Word goes through this process again—updating page references and altering any table of contents entries to reflect changes in document headings.

Although Word makes it possible to generate a table of contents with up to nine levels, our advice is to limit it to three. Bear in mind that a table of contents is a tool to help people grasp the big picture and build their own concept of your document. Wading through one that's too detailed defeats that purpose.

Generate a Table of Contents

1 Click the point in the document where you want the table of contents to start (generally at the top). Make sure all the headings you want to include in the table of contents are formatted with heading styles, levels 1 through 9.

2 Point to Reference on the Insert menu, and click Index And Tables.

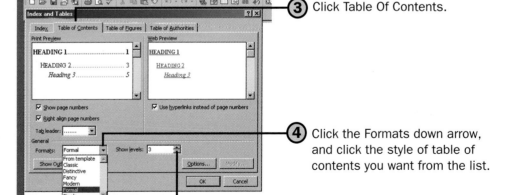

3 Click Table Of Contents.

4 Click the Formats down arrow, and click the style of table of contents you want from the list.

5 Click the Show Levels arrows to specify the number of levels you want to appear in your table of contents, and click OK. (You don't have to show all the heading levels in the document.)

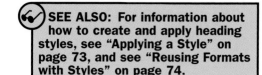

SEE ALSO: For information about how to create and apply heading styles, see "Applying a Style" on page 73, and see "Reusing Formats with Styles" on page 74.

TIP: You can use a table of contents as a navigational tool—that is, jump to a page—by pressing the Ctrl key as you click the table of contents entry.

TIP: To edit a table of contents, change the headings in your document and the follow the steps in "Update the Table of Contents." To delete a table of contents, drag the mouse pointer over the first letter or two to select the entire table of contents, and then press the Delete key.

Update the Table of Contents

1 Right-click the table of contents, and click Update Field.

2 If the Update Table Of Contents dialog box appears, click either Update Page Numbers Only or Update Entire Table.

Automating Mailings

There may be occasions when you want to send a mailing to a list—for instance, to promote the services of your business or announce a sale. You don't have time to craft a special letter to each person and address each envelope by hand, but you want something more personal than "Resident."

Word offers the services of its meticulous and thorough Mail Merge Wizard to make it as easy as possible to create labels for a mass mailing (which we feature here), print customized form letters and accompany them with addresses printed directly onto envelopes, or send e-mail or faxes to a wide audience. The wizard will even help you create a directory or catalog from a database.

So how does *mail merge* work? (Technically, it's not always a "mail" merge, but because that is the most widely used application of this feature, we'll explain it from that perspective.) Basically the wizard fills in a form (known as the *main document*), by drawing from a list of names and addresses to create individual documents—labels (a very tiny document!), letters, e-mail messages, and so on—customized for each recipient.

The Mail Merge Wizard prompts you to create the following elements essential to any mail merge:

Identify your list of recipients. Your mailing list options include using your Contacts list from Microsoft Outlook (or other electronic address book), a database from Microsoft Excel, Microsoft Access, or another program, or creating another list on the spot. After you specify which list you'll use, you then tell the wizard how to sort it—postal code order for a bulk mailing, for example—and select who will receive the mailing (if not the entire list).

Set up the form (or main document). This works just like a blank form (First Name, Last Name, Middle Initial, and so on), but it also contains instructions that tell the Mail Merge Wizard how to fill in the form with data from your list. For example, you'll see one such merge instruction in the mailing labels—"<<Address Block>>", a meta-instruction that includes the name and address. A merge letter would be more complex, including a salutation ("Dear <<First Name>>,") and a body that could also differ by recipient.

Run the merge to produce the result. The wizard uses the instructions to merge the list with the form (main document) to create customized documents—letters, faxes, labels, and so on. Although the merge is meant to be printed as it's completed, in most cases it can be saved for later or repeated use.

> **! TIP:** Word's assistance for its merge feature is so thorough that we enthusiastically recommend you use it as a companion to our instructions when you go through your first mail merge. Click in the Ask A Question box in the upper right corner of the window. **Type** mail merge, **and then press the Enter key. Click the topic in the list for the type of merge you're running. Consider printing the topic so you have it handy as you work.**

> **! TIP:** Look for this same mail merge functionality in Microsoft Publisher.

Creating and Printing Labels for a Mass Mailing ⊕ NEW FEATURE

Be prepared. Good advice not only for life, but for running a mail merge as well. Start with research at the postal service to find out if your mailing is large enough to qualify for bulk mailing rates; if so, you'll need to sort the list in postal code order. The mail merge process will also go more smoothly if your mailing list is in good order, and if you know the exact path to its location. Make sure, too, you have the right kind of labels on hand that work for your printer.

One last note before you plunge in: there isn't room in this book to describe every detail of a mail merge. We've tried, however, to provide reassurance that you're on the right track and point you in the direction of assistance when you might need it.

> **SEE ALSO: For more information about choosing the right kind of labels, particularly if you're using an inkjet printer, see "Addressing and Printing Envelopes and Label Sheets" on page 56. Or refer to the manual that came with your printer for further advice.**

Generate Mailing Labels

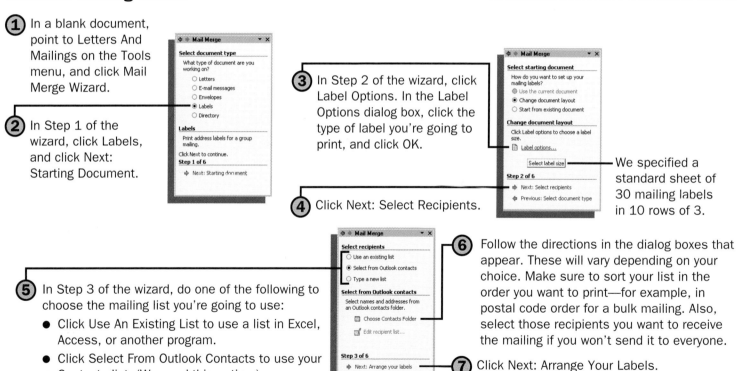

(1) In a blank document, point to Letters And Mailings on the Tools menu, and click Mail Merge Wizard.

(2) In Step 1 of the wizard, click Labels, and click Next: Starting Document.

(3) In Step 2 of the wizard, click Label Options. In the Label Options dialog box, click the type of label you're going to print, and click OK.

(4) Click Next: Select Recipients.

We specified a standard sheet of 30 mailing labels in 10 rows of 3.

(5) In Step 3 of the wizard, do one of the following to choose the mailing list you're going to use:

- Click Use An Existing List to use a list in Excel, Access, or another program.
- Click Select From Outlook Contacts to use your Contacts list. (We used this option.)
- Click Type A New List to create a mailing list on the spot.

(6) Follow the directions in the dialog boxes that appear. These will vary depending on your choice. Make sure to sort your list in the order you want to print—for example, in postal code order for a bulk mailing. Also, select those recipients you want to receive the mailing if you won't send it to everyone.

(7) Click Next: Arrange Your Labels.

!TIP: To save the labels for later use—perhaps you want to reprint these exact labels at another time—follow these instructions in "Generate Mailing Labels" through step 12. In step 13, after you click Next, click Edit Individual Labels. In the Merge To New Document dialog box, indicate which labels to save, and then click OK. Word opens a single document that contains all the labels you just requested. You can then save the document for later use, just as you would any other Word document. When you're ready to print or edit them, you simply open the document you saved.

!TIP: If you have any problem at all with the merge—either while you are using the Mail Merge Wizard or afterward—get help. Click in the Ask A Question box in the upper right corner of the window. Type mail merge, and then press the Enter key. Click Troubleshoot Mail Merge in the list, and click the problem that applies.

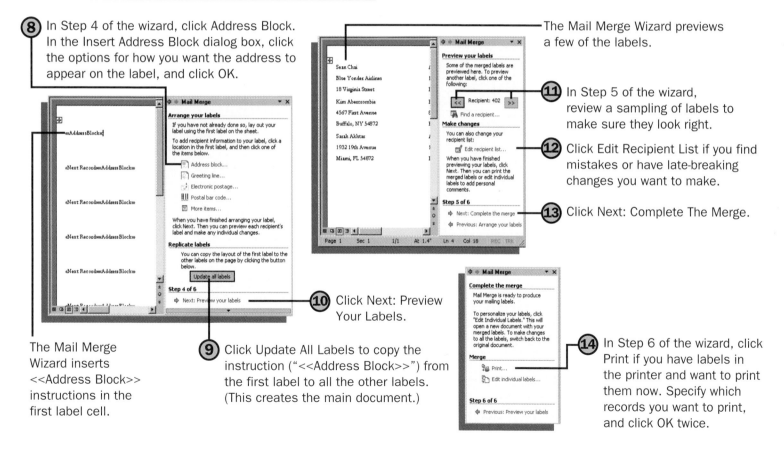

8 In Step 4 of the wizard, click Address Block. In the Insert Address Block dialog box, click the options for how you want the address to appear on the label, and click OK.

The Mail Merge Wizard inserts <<Address Block>> instructions in the first label cell.

9 Click Update All Labels to copy the instruction ("<<Address Block>>") from the first label to all the other labels. (This creates the main document.)

10 Click Next: Preview Your Labels.

The Mail Merge Wizard previews a few of the labels.

11 In Step 5 of the wizard, review a sampling of labels to make sure they look right.

12 Click Edit Recipient List if you find mistakes or have late-breaking changes you want to make.

13 Click Next: Complete The Merge.

14 In Step 6 of the wizard, click Print if you have labels in the printer and want to print them now. Specify which records you want to print, and click OK twice.

Translating Text ⊕ NEW FEATURE

E-mail and the Web make worldwide communication a reality for everyone with an Internet connection. Chances are you'll receive a document in a language that you don't speak. In our multilingual world, being able to translate your documents from one language to another can greatly expand your readership and make communication possible with people who speak other languages.

Translate a Word

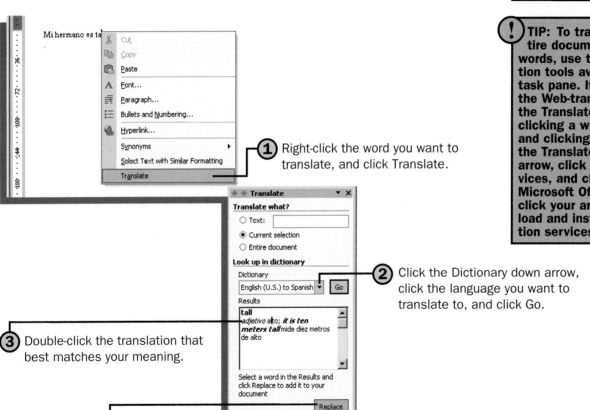

① Right-click the word you want to translate, and click Translate.

② Click the Dictionary down arrow, click the language you want to translate to, and click Go.

③ Double-click the translation that best matches your meaning.

④ Click Replace.

If the language you're looking for isn't in the list, you can find additional translators here.

CAUTION: Translation software is useful, but not infallible. When writing sensitive documents such as contracts, technical references, or other works that must be accurate or can be easily confused, make sure you have someone fluent in the language you're writing proofread the document.

TIP: To translate phrases or entire documents, rather than single words, use the Web-based translation tools available in the Translate task pane. If you don't have one of the Web-translation add-ins, open the Translate task pane by right-clicking a word in your document and clicking Translate. Then click the Translate Via The Web down arrow, click More Translation Services, and click Go. When the Microsoft Office Update site loads, click your area of origin, and download and install one of the translation services.

7 Creating an Excel Worksheet

Microsoft Excel gives you the tools to work with numbers efficiently and accurately. An Excel *workbook*—which is simply an Excel file—stores your information, just as a green ledger pad used to, and works with it, as a calculator does. Think of an Excel workbook as the twenty-first century version of your trusty three-ring binder, full of information that you can move around, dive into, and work with as you please.

As you work with Excel, you'll become familiar with the way it helps you organize your data.

Cells, which are organized by columns and rows, are the building blocks of Excel. A cell can contain words, numbers, or a formula. Almost all of your work will involve entering and manipulating information in cells. By formatting the cells with borders, colors, or special fonts, you can create readable tables that help you and your audience understand your data.

Worksheets, which are made up of cells, are like individual sheets of paper within a notebook, but they can hold much more information than a real piece of paper. Use worksheets as the main organizers of your data—each month or each salesperson might get its own worksheet, perhaps.

Workbooks, which contain a set of related information located on one or more worksheets, take the place of your old three-ring binder. Use a workbook for each set of data that you want to work with—for example, all the data for a single year or for a certain event.

Getting Started with Excel

Whether you're working with numbers, words, or both, all you need to do to work in Excel is open a workbook, and then type in new information or edit your previous work. When you type a number in a cell, Excel treats it as a *value*—something that could be part of a calculation, such as addition or multiplication. Each cell can hold only one value.

You'll use *text*—words, or words combined with numbers in a single cell—to describe columns or rows, provide a title, or footnote your sources. Text cells can contain many words. If you enter text next to a row or column of numbers, Excel will treat the text as a *label* for that data. Labels are useful for organizing and explaining your data and for creating charts.

> **! TIP:** If you open Excel without choosing an existing file, you'll see a new, blank workbook.

Open a New or Existing Workbook

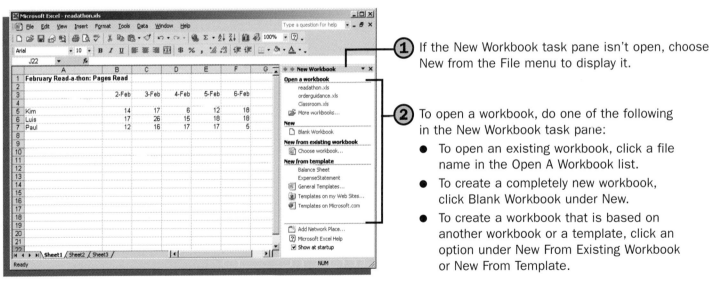

(1) If the New Workbook task pane isn't open, choose New from the File menu to display it.

(2) To open a workbook, do one of the following in the New Workbook task pane:

- To open an existing workbook, click a file name in the Open A Workbook list.
- To create a completely new workbook, click Blank Workbook under New.
- To create a workbook that is based on another workbook or a template, click an option under New From Existing Workbook or New From Template.

> **NEW FEATURE:** The Open A Workbook area in the New Workbook task pane displays the Excel files you've used most recently. If the file you want doesn't appear in the list, click More Workbooks.

> 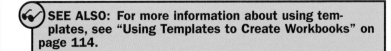 **SEE ALSO:** For more information about using templates, see "Using Templates to Create Workbooks" on page 114.

Enter a Value or Text

(1) Click the cell where you want the information to appear.

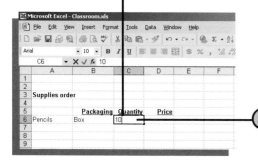

(2) Type the number or characters, and press the Enter key.

Edit a Cell

(1) Double-click the cell. **(2)** Use the left and right arrow keys to place the insertion point at the character(s) you want to change.

(3) Type to insert new characters, or press the Delete key to delete characters.

(4) Press the Enter key.

The Formula Bar shows the contents of the cell as you edit it.

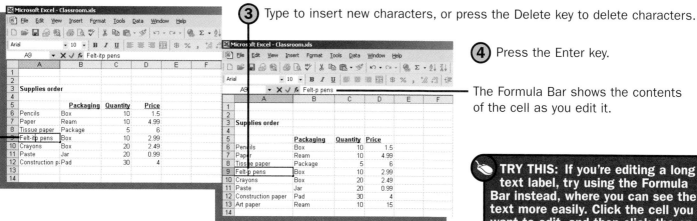

Working with Cells and Ranges

An Excel worksheet is made up of millions of cells. As you're working, you tell Excel which of the millions to modify by selecting either a single cell or a group of cells. Select a single cell when you need to enter data or text, or set up formatting for just that cell. Select *ranges*, which are blocks of cells, when you want to work with a larger area of your worksheet. Select *nonadjacent* areas—cells, ranges, rows, or columns that aren't next to each other—to work with several parts of your worksheet at once (for example, to put text in italic). A selected cell or area is called *active*, meaning that it's ready for modification.

After you've learned shortcuts for selecting cells or ranges, you'll move through your worksheet more quickly and make changes more efficiently.

Select a Cell

1 Click the cell. The active cell appears with a thick border.

Moving Between Cells

Key Strokes	Direction
Right arrow, Tab key	Move right
Down arrow, Enter key	Move down
Left arrow, Up arrow	Move left, move up
Home	First cell in current row
Ctrl Home	Top left corner of worksheet (cell A1)
Ctrl End	Bottom right corner of data area

Select a Range

1 Point to the cell at the top left corner of the area you want to select.

2 Hold down the mouse button, and drag to the last cell.

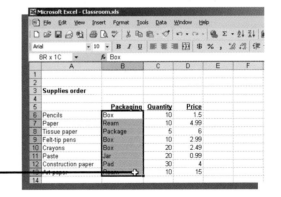

> **TRY THIS:** Instead of using the mouse to select a range, hold down the Shift key, and press an arrow key. Watch how your range area shrinks and expands with the use of the arrow keys.

Select Entire Rows or Columns

(1) Click the row heading (which contains the row number) or the column heading (which contains the column letter).

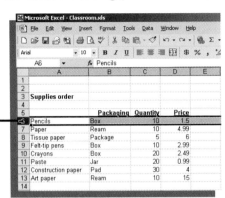

(2) To select more than one row or column, drag the mouse pointer to include the additional rows or columns.

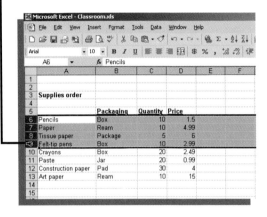

Select Nonadjacent Worksheet Areas

(1) Select the first cell, range, column, or row, and release the mouse button.

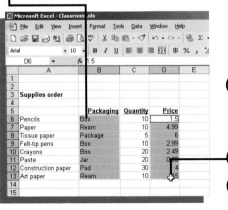

(2) Hold down the Ctrl key.

(3) Select another cell, range, column, or row by dragging the mouse pointer.

(4) Repeat steps 2 and 3 for each additional area.

Inserting, Deleting, and Moving Areas of a Worksheet

As you work with a worksheet you've created, you'll probably discover that you need to rearrange your data. You can add or delete one or more columns, rows, or cells with a minimum of fuss—and, most importantly, without messing up the work you've already done. If you want to rearrange your data, you can move cells to a different part of your worksheet or to a different worksheet altogether.

When you move, add or delete cells or ranges, Excel tries to adjust formulas or charts that use your data so that they still reflect the right data. But if you've deleted the data that formulas or charts depend on, Excel won't be able to adjust the formulas or charts, and you'll need to correct them yourself.

Insert or Delete a Column or Row

1 Right-click a column or row heading, and do one of the following:

- Click Insert to place a new column to the left of the selected column, or to place a new row above the selected row.
- Click Delete to remove the selected column or row.

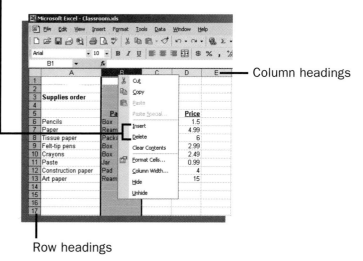

Column headings

Row headings

Delete a Cell or Range

1 Select the cell or range.

2 Right-click the cell or range, and click Delete.

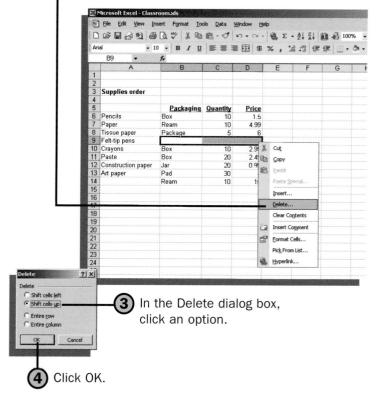

3 In the Delete dialog box, click an option.

4 Click OK.

> ✎ **TRY THIS:** To erase the contents of a cell or range without deleting the cells themselves, select the area you want to erase, and press the Delete key.

Insert a Cell or Range

① Select the cell or range where you want to add the new cells. To add a block of cells, select a range.

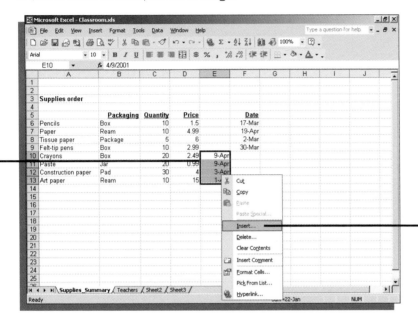

CAUTION: If you click one of the Shift Cells options when you insert or delete a cell or range, check your worksheet carefully to make sure that the changed area of your worksheet still matches your requirements. When you shift cells—rather than inserting entire columns or rows—column and row labels might not end up aligned with the data that was moved.

② Right-click the cell or range, and click Insert.

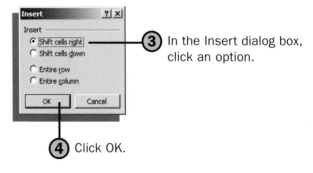

③ In the Insert dialog box, click an option.

④ Click OK.

TIP: When you insert a cell or range adjacent to formatted cells, the inserted cells will be assigned the same format as the neighboring cells. If you don't want that formatting, you can remove it: click the Insert Options smart tag (the paintbrush that appears where you inserted the cells), and click Clear Formatting.

Move a Cell or Range

① Select the cell or range you want to move.

② Right-click the cell or range, and click Cut.

③ Right-click the cell where you want to place the data, and click Paste.

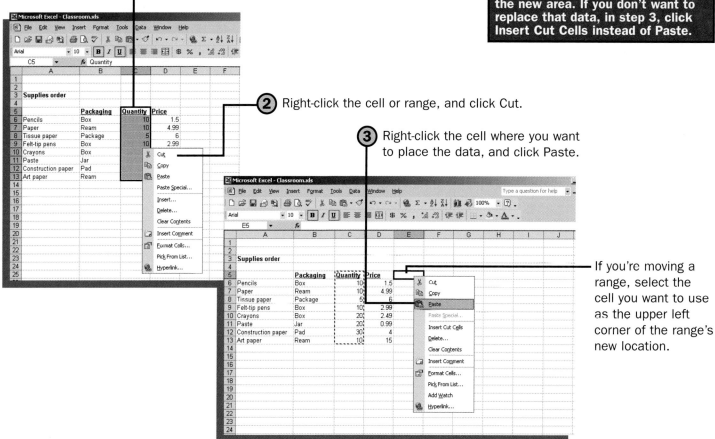

If you're moving a range, select the cell you want to use as the upper left corner of the range's new location.

TIP: You can hide columns or rows that contain data you need to keep, but don't want to see. To do so, click the column or row heading, right-click, and click Hide.

TIP: To move an entire column, right-click its column heading, and click Cut. Right-click the heading of the column to the right of where you want to place the cut column, and click Insert Cut Cells. Excel inserts a new column that contains the cut data.

Formatting Text and Numbers

Think of a page in a newspaper, and consider what makes it easy to read—text arranged in neat blocks and headlines in eye-pleasing fonts and sizes. You can apply these same design techniques to give structure to your worksheet—for example, to make the proverbial bottom line stand out or to illuminate important findings in a budget analysis. With Excel's formatting tools—many of which are similar to those you'll find in other Microsoft Office XP programs—you can make the data visually appealing to any kind of audience.

Change Font or Font Appearance

1 Select the cell or range, and click one or more of the following buttons on the Formatting toolbar:

- Click the Font down arrow, and click a font.
- Click the Font Size down arrow, and click a font size.
- Click the Bold, Italic, or Underline button to change the font style.

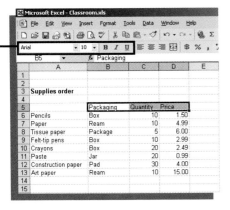

Add Comma, Percentage, Currency, or Decimal Formatting to Numbers

1 Select the cell or range, and click one or more of the following buttons on the Formatting toolbar:

- To add a currency symbol, click the Currency Style button.
- To add a percent sign, click the Percent Style button.
- To add commas, click the Comma Style button.
- To add more decimal places, click the Increase Decimal button.
- To remove decimal places, click the Decrease Decimal button.

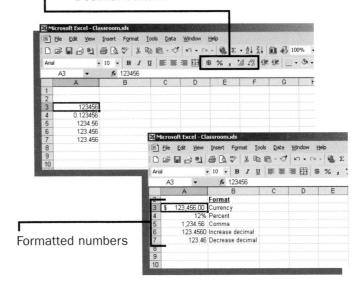

Formatted numbers

> **! TIP:** Click the Bold, Italic, or Underline button a second time to undo these formats.

Apply Numeric Formats

(1) Select the cell or range.

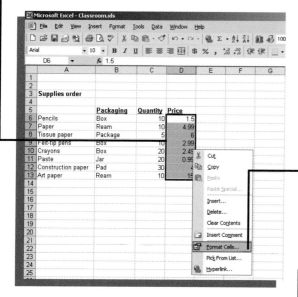

TIP: If you're entering calendar dates as data labels or for some other purpose, take advantage of the wide range of formats available for dates. Select the cell or range, right-click it, and click Format Cells. Click Date in the Category list on the Number tab, and specify a date format.

TRY THIS: Use the Special format category to customize the display of certain kinds of numbers, such as ZIP codes or telephone numbers.

(2) Right-click the cell or range, and click Format Cells.

(3) Click the Number tab.

(4) In the Category list, click a type of formatting.

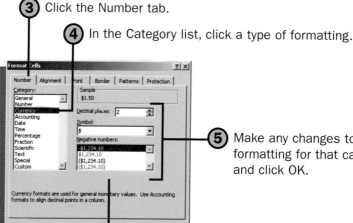

(5) Make any changes to the formatting for that category, and click OK.

Options for formatting will be different, depending on the category you choose.

TIP: Use the Number tab in the Format Cells dialog box to change a format you've set with the Comma Style, Currency Style, or Percent Style button.

Adjusting the Way Text Is Displayed

Even though the most important part of your worksheet is likely to be the numbers, don't neglect your text! Clear, easy-to-read labels and titles will enhance your data and help your audience understand what the data says. To help you make your text look its best, Excel lets you control how text appears in cells—*aligned* with the right, left, or center of a column; *shrunk* to fit a specific cell's size, or *wrapped* within a cell, so that the text fits within the width of the cell (like a newspaper column) and the cell height stretches to display the entire text.

Align Text

(1) Select the cell or range containing the text.

(2) Click the Align Left, Center, or Align Right button on the Formatting toolbar.

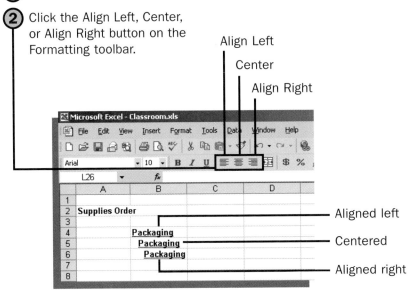

Align Left

Center

Align Right

Aligned left

Centered

Aligned right

> ! **TIP:** You can also control how text is positioned between the top and bottom of a row, or take advantage of additional options for positioning text within the column. Right-click the cell, and click Format Cells. Click the Horizontal or Vertical down arrow on the Alignment tab, and make your choices.

> **TRY THIS:** If you'd rather not make all the formatting decisions yourself, use the AutoFormat tool. AutoFormat provides over a dozen built-in designs for text and tables. To use AutoFormat, select the range you want to format. Choose AutoFormat from the Format menu, and scroll through the choices. Click the format you want, and then click OK.

Customize Text Placement Within a Cell

(1) Select the cell or range containing the text.

(2) Right-click the cell or range, and click Format Cells.

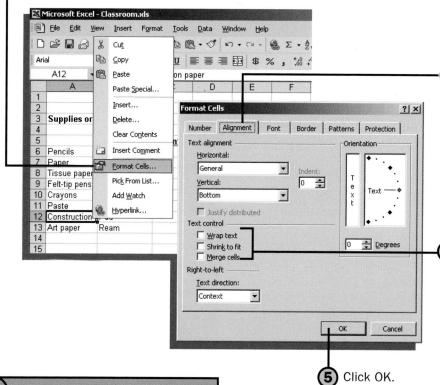

(3) Click the Alignment tab.

TIP: If you set a row to have a specific height, you may not be able to see all of your wrapped text. To display all the wrapped text, double-click the lower boundary of the row heading.

(4) Select one or more of the check boxes in the Text Control area:

- To display the text in a block within the cell, select the Wrap Text check box. The cell's row height will expand to fit the wrapped text.

- To shrink the text font size so that the text fits within the current size of the cell, select the Shrink To Fit check box.

- To combine two or more cells so that your text can be displayed in the combined area, select the Merge Cells check box. (If you haven't selected the cells you want to merge, click OK, select the range, and start with step 1.)

(5) Click OK.

TIP: If you know that columns, rows, or ranges will contain a lot of text, set their alignment before you begin typing in the text. That way, it will be easier for you to review your work and notice any typing errors.

Adjust Column Width or Row Height

① Point to the right boundary of a column heading or the lower boundary of a row heading.

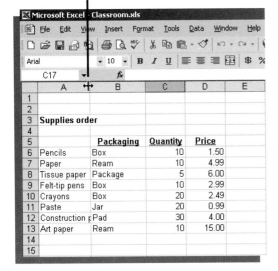

② When the mouse pointer changes to a double-headed arrow, drag the heading to its new size.

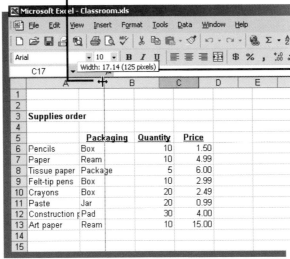

As you drag the column heading, the ScreenTip displays the new width.

! **TIP: By double-clicking the right boundary of a column heading, you can match the column width to the longest entry.**

! **TIP: You can change the width of several columns at once. To select several columns, click the first column's heading, and then drag the mouse pointer to select the other columns. To change their width, point to the right boundary of one of the columns, and then drag the mouse pointer.**

Adding Colors and Patterns to Cells

Colors and patterns highlight important cells or ranges, and help set one area of a worksheet apart from another. When you're working with a cell or range, you can change the color of its contents, its background color, or both. Patterns provide another way to make certain parts of your spreadsheet stand out. You can even combine colors and patterns.

Try to limit the number of patterns and colors you use so that the worksheet doesn't appear too busy. And remember that, depending on your printer, the colors you see on your screen may be somewhat different from those you see on paper. It's a good idea to review colors both on the screen and in a printed draft before printing out a finished version.

Add Color to a Cell or Range

1 Select the cell or range.

2 To add a background color to the cell, click the Fill Color down arrow on the Formatting toolbar, and click a color on the palette.

3 To change the color of the font, click the Font Color down arrow on the Formatting toolbar, and click a color on the palette.

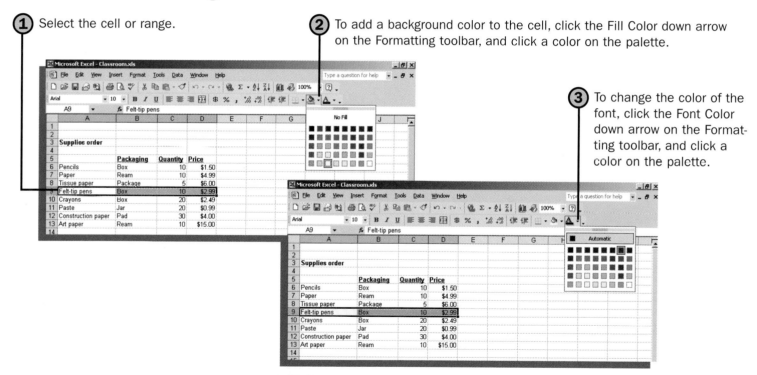

TRY THIS: To add color to an entire worksheet, right-click the box in the far upper left corner of the worksheet (above the row headings and to the left of the column headings), and then follow steps 1 and 2.

Add a Pattern to a Cell or Range

(1) Select the cell or range.

(2) Right-click the cell or range, and click Format Cells.

✋ **CAUTION: Patterns can make it hard to read the cell, so use them carefully.**

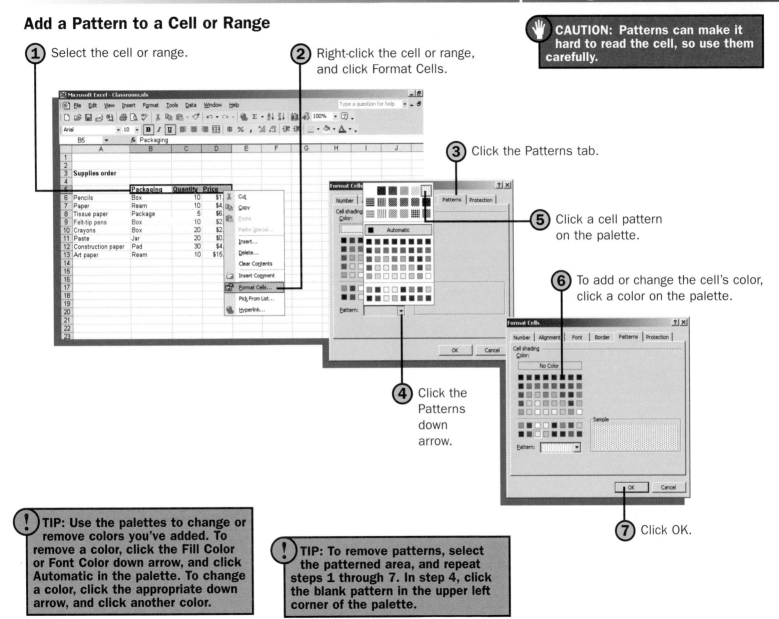

(3) Click the Patterns tab.

(5) Click a cell pattern on the palette.

(6) To add or change the cell's color, click a color on the palette.

(4) Click the Patterns down arrow.

(7) Click OK.

❗ **TIP: Use the palettes to change or remove colors you've added. To remove a color, click the Fill Color or Font Color down arrow, and click Automatic in the palette. To change a color, click the appropriate down arrow, and click another color.**

❗ **TIP: To remove patterns, select the patterned area, and repeat steps 1 through 7. In step 4, click the blank pattern in the upper left corner of the palette.**

Adding Borders to Cells

Use *borders*—outlines that appear around the outside of cells or ranges—as a way to help organize a worksheet's appearance. Borders appear in both the on-screen and printed versions of your worksheet.

Excel lets you quickly apply borders to a selected area in a worksheet. You can also customize the appearance of borders by changing their color, pattern, and thickness.

Add a Custom Border to Part of a Worksheet

(1) Select the cell or range of cells you want to surround with a border.

(2) Right-click the cell or range, and click Format Cells.

> **TIP:** To apply standard borders quickly, use the Borders button on the Formatting toolbar. Select a range, click the Borders down arrow, and click a border style on the palette. You can also use this button to remove all borders—just click the No Border style in the upper left corner of the palette.

> **TRY THIS:** To change the style or color of a border you've added, click the new style or border, and then click the border in the Preview area.

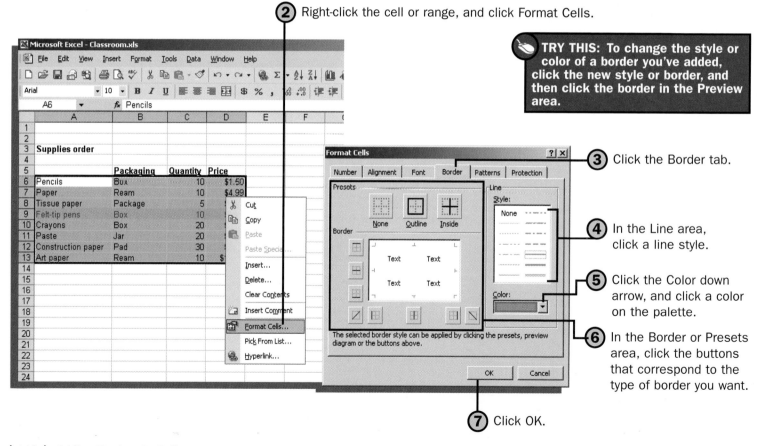

(3) Click the Border tab.

(4) In the Line area, click a line style.

(5) Click the Color down arrow, and click a color on the palette.

(6) In the Border or Presets area, click the buttons that correspond to the type of border you want.

(7) Click OK.

Copying a Table from the Web to Excel

Depending on the kind of work you're doing, you may well find that the Web is chock-full of helpful data. First, of course, you'll need to verify that data you've found on the Web is available for copying and that you've satisfied all requirements related to copying or using the information. After you have permission to use the data, you can copy and paste the data into an Excel worksheet with a minimum of fussing to make the data look right once you get it.

CAUTION: Be prepared to edit the worksheet containing the copied Web table. The process of copying a Web table will capture all of the data in the table and might fill up your worksheet with more data than you need.

Copy and Paste a Table from the Web into a Worksheet

1 Open the Excel worksheet where you'll place the copied data.

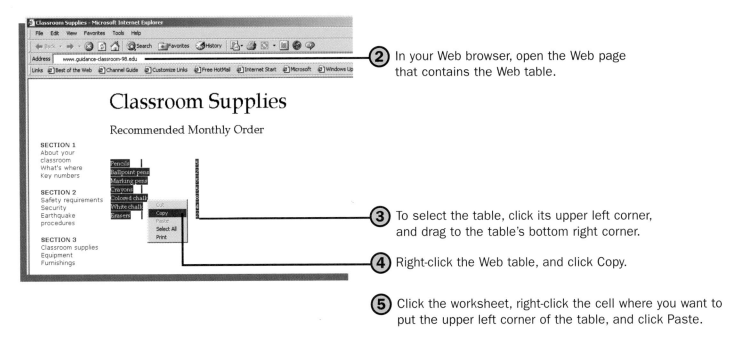

2 In your Web browser, open the Web page that contains the Web table.

3 To select the table, click its upper left corner, and drag to the table's bottom right corner.

4 Right-click the Web table, and click Copy.

5 Click the worksheet, right-click the cell where you want to put the upper left corner of the table, and click Paste.

TIP: To learn more about using Web data in Excel worksheets, click in the Ask A Question box in the upper right corner of the window. Type about getting data from a Web page, and then press the Enter key.

Using Templates to Create Workbooks

No matter how much you love your work, doing the same thing over and over again gets a little old. If you often create worksheets that have a similar purpose, but use different data—for example, invoices for clients or monthly sales summaries—you'll save time and reduce boredom by using templates. A *template* contains the formatting, data, and formulas that you want to reuse. When you need to create a workbook, just open the template, add your new information, and save your workbook as a new file.

You can use Excel's templates or save your own workbook as a template. When you save a workbook as a template, all the worksheets in that workbook will appear each time you open the template. If you don't need all those worksheets, streamline your files by deleting the extras before you save the template.

> **!** **TIP:** Some cells in Excel's built-in templates, such as the labels and the formulas, are *protected*—meaning that you can't change them. If you want to customize those cells, you'll have to unprotect the worksheet: point to Protection on the Tools menu, and click Unprotect Worksheet.

Start a Document from an Excel Template

① Choose New from the File menu, and click General Templates in the New Document task pane.

② Click the tab for the type of workbook you want to create.

③ Click the template you want to use.

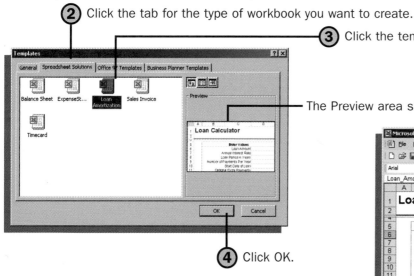

The Preview area shows you part of the template.

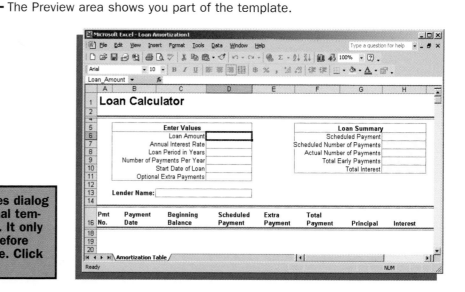

④ Click OK.

> **!** **TIP:** When you click a template in the Templates dialog box, you might see "Click OK to install additional templates and create a new file" in the Preview area. It only takes a minute or two to install the templates. Before you click OK, put the Office XP CD in the CD drive. Click OK, and Office takes it from there.

Create a Template from an Existing Workbook

1 Open the workbook you want to use as a template.

2 Choose Save As from the File menu.

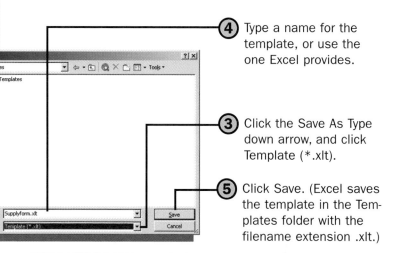

4 Type a name for the template, or use the one Excel provides.

3 Click the Save As Type down arrow, and click Template (*.xlt).

5 Click Save. (Excel saves the template in the Templates folder with the filename extension .xlt.)

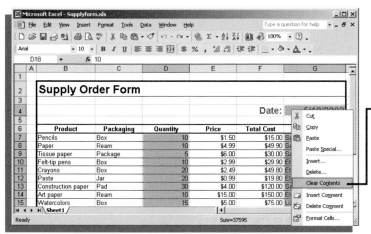

TIP: To use a template you've created, choose New from the File menu, and click General Templates in the New Workbook task pane. In the Templates dialog box, click the General tab, and then click your template.

6 To remove data you don't want to appear in the documents based on this template, select the range or ranges, right-click, and click Clear Contents.

7 To save the template with these modifications, choose Save from the File menu.

8 To close the template, choose Close from the File menu.

Naming, Adding, and Moving Worksheets

Worksheets help you structure your information so that you can locate key elements quickly. You can name worksheets, creating the equivalent of the little plastic tabs on manila dividers, and arrange and rearrange them according to your requirements. Excel inserts three worksheets into each new workbook. You can insert more worksheets or remove ones you don't need.

Before you plunge into entering data, take a couple of moments to think about how you want to organize your numbers, and then start arranging and naming your worksheets to match. Plan to put related data on a single worksheet. And whatever you decide, remember that you can move things around later very easily!

> ❗ **TIP: Worksheet names can includes spaces and capital or lowercase letters, but they can't include these symbols: : \ / ? * [ ]**

> ❗ **TIP: To switch to a different worksheet, click its sheet tab.**

Rename a Worksheet

① Double-click the sheet tab.

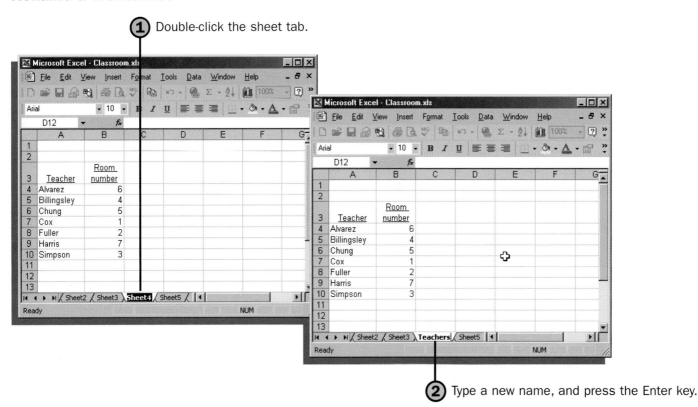

② Type a new name, and press the Enter key.

Insert a New Worksheet

(1) Right-click the sheet tab, and click Insert.

(2) Click Worksheet on the General tab, and click OK.

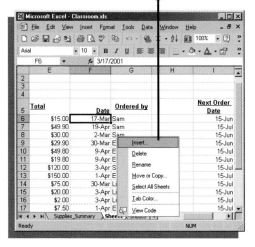

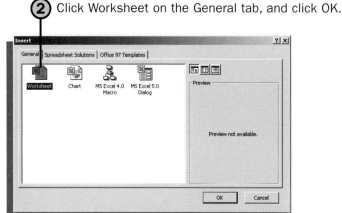

Move a Worksheet

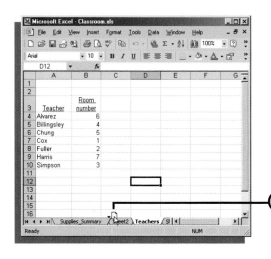

(1) Click the sheet tab, and drag the sheet tab along the bottom of the window to the new location.

> **!** TIP: When you insert a worksheet, it will be inserted *before* (to the left of) the sheet tab you clicked.

> **!** TIP: To delete an entire worksheet, right-click its sheet tab, and click Delete. But be careful—once you delete a worksheet, it's gone! The Undo button can't be used to reverse a worksheet deletion.

Printing from Excel

Printing your worksheet can be the first step toward sharing your work with others. Before printing, take a minute to determine how much of your worksheet (or how many of the worksheets in your workbook) you need to print. Depending on what you decide, you can print small areas, large projects, and a patchwork of ranges in between. After you've decided what to print, preview what it will look like on the page, and make tweaks based on what you see. If your audience needs to see your work as it appears on the screen—complete with gridlines, column headings, and row headings—Excel can deliver this, too.

Set a Print Area

1 Select the range you want to print.

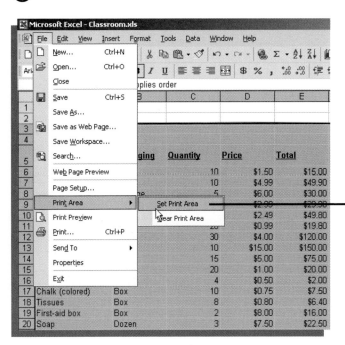

> **TIP:** To stop using the print area you selected, point to Print Area on the File menu, and click Clear Print Area.

> **TIP:** If you want to print a chart that is part of a worksheet, but don't want to print the rest of the worksheet, select the worksheet cells *behind* the chart as the print area. (If your chart appears over cells with data or text, drag the chart to an empty area of the worksheet and then select the blank cells behind it.)

2 Point to Print Area on the File menu, and click Set Print Area.

> **TRY THIS:** If you just want to add cells to a print area, you don't have to clear the print area and then reset it. Instead, choose Page Break Preview from the View menu. Select the cells you want to add, right-click, and then click Add To Print Area.

> **TIP:** To learn more about printing in Excel, click in the Ask A Question box in the upper right corner of the window. Type about printing, and then press the Enter key.

Format a Print Area

(1) Choose Page Setup from the File menu.

The other tabs in the Page Setup dialog box provide additional formatting options for your printed worksheet.

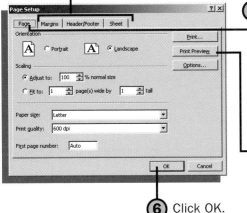

(2) Click the Page tab, and do one or more of the following:

- To select a page orientation, click the Portrait or Landscape option. Portrait is better for tables that are taller than they are wide; landscape is better for wide tables.
- To reduce or enlarge the worksheet's appearance on the page, click Adjust To, and click a percentage.
- To resize the worksheet to fit on a specific number of pages, click Fit To, and click the arrows to choose a number of pages.

(3) Click Print Preview to see how your document will appear on the page.

(4) On the Preview screen, click Setup to return to the Page Setup dialog box.

(6) Click OK.

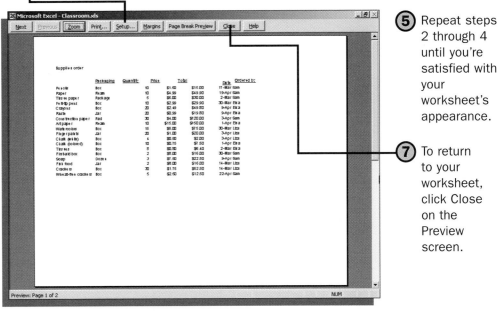

(5) Repeat steps 2 through 4 until you're satisfied with your worksheet's appearance.

(7) To return to your worksheet, click Close on the Preview screen.

> **!** **TIP:** Gridlines can make a table easier to read. To print gridlines, choose Page Setup from the File menu, and click the Sheet tab. In the Print area, select the Gridlines check box, and then click OK.

> **!** **TIP:** The Preview screen may not show all cell details (such as borders) clearly. To get a better sense of how they'll look, click the Zoom button on the Preview screen to get a magnified view of the print area.

Print a Worksheet

1 Choose Print from the File menu.

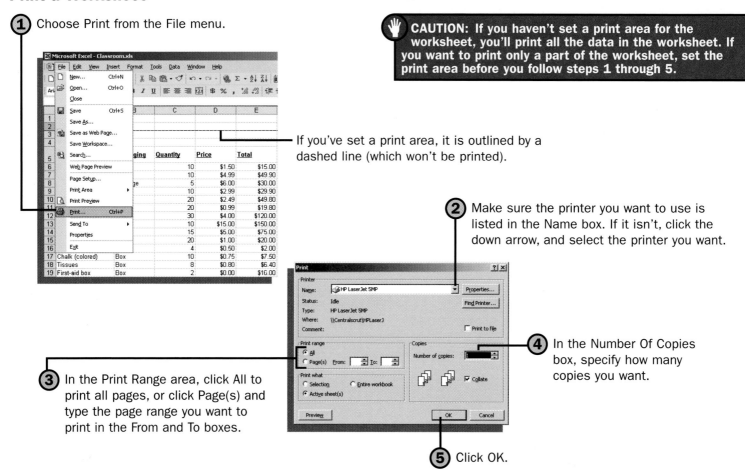

CAUTION: If you haven't set a print area for the worksheet, you'll print all the data in the worksheet. If you want to print only a part of the worksheet, set the print area before you follow steps 1 through 5.

If you've set a print area, it is outlined by a dashed line (which won't be printed).

2 Make sure the printer you want to use is listed in the Name box. If it isn't, click the down arrow, and select the printer you want.

4 In the Number Of Copies box, specify how many copies you want.

3 In the Print Range area, click All to print all pages, or click Page(s) and type the page range you want to print in the From and To boxes.

5 Click OK.

TIP: To instantly print the active worksheet, click the Print button on the Standard toolbar. This works best for small worksheets that will fit on a single page.

Previewing and Moving Page Breaks Before Printing

It isn't always apparent from looking at your screen how your worksheet will look when it's printed. Before printing, it's a good idea to get a bird's-eye view of your entire worksheet, page by page. Excel lets you preview your *page breaks*—where Excel will stop printing one page and start printing the next—and adjust them so you can organize the printed version the way you want it

Preview and Move a Page Break

(1) Choose Page Break Preview from the View menu.

(2) To move a page break, move your mouse pointer to the page break line. When the pointer changes to a double-headed arrow, drag the page break to its new location.

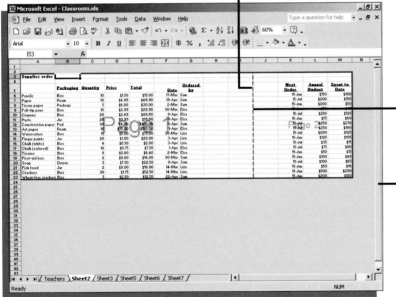

! TIP: If your worksheet is more than one page wide and one page long, Excel assumes you want to print *down* the worksheet, so that each set of columns is printed completely before the next set of columns is printed. To override that, choose Page Setup from the File menu, and click the Sheet tab. In the Page Order area, click Over, Then Down.

Page breaks appear as thick, dashed blue lines.

Click on the scroll bars to review page breaks for the entire worksheet.

! TIP: To display your worksheet on the screen without page breaks, choose Normal from the View menu.

8

Working Efficiently with Data and Calculations

Using Microsoft Excel to work with your data means saying goodbye to punching equations into calculators over and over again. You'll streamline any workbook, large or small, with Excel's efficiency tools, which fall into three main groups:

- **Tools that simplify calculations.** After you've entered your numbers, you can use them again in different calculations without retyping them, using *formulas* (calculations you create) or *functions* (formulas that Excel sets up for you, using data you specify).

- **Tools that help you reuse information.** You'll save even more time by reusing information you've already entered. Create a formula once, and then copy it and apply it to many different numbers. When you're working with data that comes in a series (for example, all the months in the year, or the even numbers from 2 to 1000), you can enter just the first few numbers, and AutoFill will complete the series for you.

- **Tools that speed up data review and error correction.** Excel helps you check your work thoroughly and efficiently. Use special display options and shortcuts to move easily through your data. Then, when you find the inevitable mistake, fix it faster with visual auditing tools and one-click error corrections.

Using Formulas to Work with Your Data

Formulas are calculations—simple or complex—that use the data entered in your worksheet. Excel does the computational heavy lifting; you just tell Excel where the numbers are and what to do with them.

To create a formula, you'll tell Excel where the numbers are by using *cell references*—combinations of column number and row letter, such as B3 or AA19, that identify specific worksheet cells. You'll tell Excel what to do with these numbers by using *operators* (symbols such as "+" or "–"). For example, to add the numbers in the fourth row of columns B, C, and D, type the formula =**B4+C4+D4** in the cell where you want the total to appear. The actual result of the calculation appears in the cell—but the formula is still there, and you can see it in the Formula Bar.

TIP: A formula can use references to cells in different worksheets. In step 3 of "Create a Formula," click the sheet tab for the cell, and then click the cell.

Arithmetic Operators

Operator	Example	Operation
^	=10^4	Raises 10 to the fourth power
/	=8/2.5	Divides 8 by 2.5
*	=12*20	Multiplies 12 by 20
- (hyphen)	=1001-259	Subtracts 259 from 1001
+	=257+341	Adds 341 to 257

TIP: To learn more about operators and the order of precedence, click in the Ask A Question box in the upper right corner of the window. **Type** about calculation operators, **and then press the Enter key.**

CAUTION: To avoid getting the wrong result from a formula, the operators in a formula must be in the *order of precedence*, or the order in which a series of mathematical operations is completed. In Excel, the order is the following: exponentiation; division or multiplication; and addition or subtraction.

If you use parentheses to organize your formula, Excel performs calculations inside parentheses first and then uses the order of precedence to do the rest of the calculation. For example, Excel calculates the formula "=2*3+5" as 11, performing multiplication first (2*3=6) and then addition (6+5=11). The formula "=2*(3+5)" returns 16, because Excel does the calculations inside the parentheses (3+5=8) and then computes the rest of the formula.

Create a Formula

1 Select the cell where you want the result to appear.

2 Type **=** to begin the formula.

Formula Bar

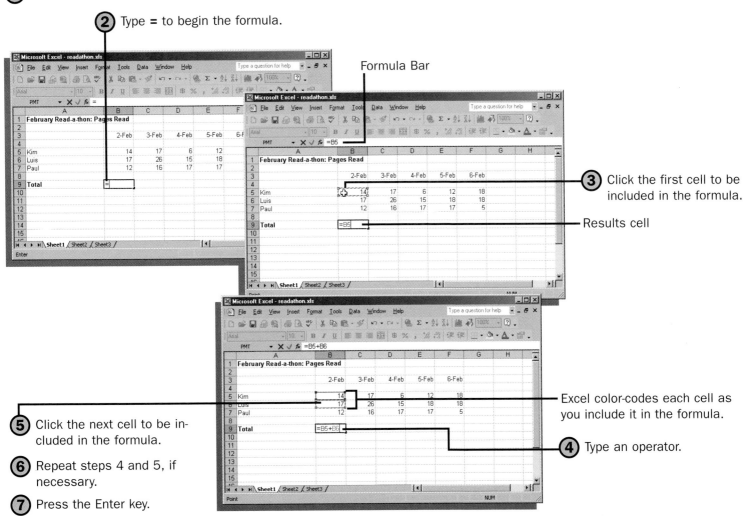

3 Click the first cell to be included in the formula.

Results cell

5 Click the next cell to be included in the formula.

6 Repeat steps 4 and 5, if necessary.

7 Press the Enter key.

Excel color-codes each cell as you include it in the formula.

4 Type an operator.

Simplifying Calculations Using Functions

You'll probably use some calculations more often than others—getting the total of a list of numbers, for example, or finding their average. Excel makes these routine operations convenient, and more likely to be free of errors, by providing *functions*, which are built-in formulas that you apply to a range of numbers. You just select the cells you want included in the calculation and choose a function. The rest of the work is done for you—quickly, automatically, and accurately.

Excel gives you quick access to the most common functions. If your needs are more complex, you can search through dozens of sophisticated functions that provide calculations for statistical, financial, engineering, and other kinds of analysis.

Use Common Functions in a Worksheet ⊛ NEW FEATURE

(1) Select the cell where you want the result to appear.

Formula Bar

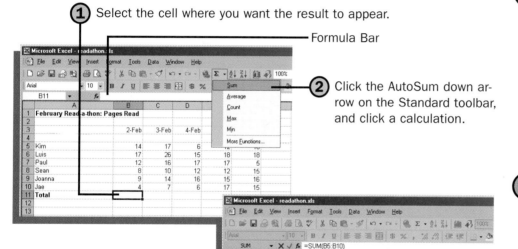

(2) Click the AutoSum down arrow on the Standard toolbar, and click a calculation.

(3) Select the range to use in your formula. If the function is near other data, Excel will choose a range (shown by a colored outline). To change it, select the range you want to use.

(4) Press the Enter key.

! TIP: You can include more than one range in your function. To do so, click the AutoSum down arrow, click a function, and select the first range or cell (or keep the range that Excel has selected for you). On your keyboard, hold down the Ctrl key while you select the next range or cell. When you've finished selecting data, release the Ctrl key, and then press the Enter key.

! TIP: Use the Formula Bar to edit functions you've entered. (To display it, choose Formula Bar from the View menu.) To work with a function, click the worksheet cell where the formula's result appears. The function will appear in the Formula Bar. To edit it, click in the Formula Bar, and make your changes.

✋ CAUTION: If you delete or move cells that you've used in a formula, the formula may no longer be accurate.

Use Specialized Functions to Analyze Data ⊕ NEW FEATURE

① Select the cell where you want the result to appear.

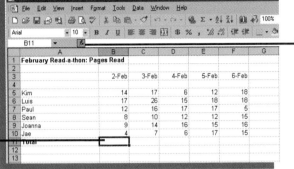

② Click the Insert Function button on the Formula Bar.

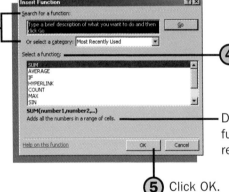

③ Search for the function you want in one of the following ways:

- To search by what you want to do, type a few words in the Search For A Function box, and click Go.

- To browse by category (such as financial or statistical functions), click the Or Select A Category down arrow, and click a category.

④ Click a function in the Select A Function list.

Description of the highlighted function's purpose and data requirements

⑤ Click OK.

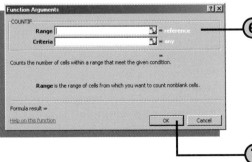

⑥ Review the Function Arguments dialog box, and select the data to use in the function. The Function Arguments dialog box is customized to each function's data requirements.

⑦ Click OK.

Copying Formulas

After you've created a formula, you can apply it to as many numbers as you like. If you've already set up a formula to add up monthly sales for one year, for example, copy it and use it to add up sales for other years, too.

Reuse a Formula by Copying It

(1) Click the cell where the result of your formula appears.

CAUTION: You should always double-check the copied version of a formula to make sure it uses the cells you intended. If it doesn't, you may need to change part of the formula from *relative* cell references to *absolute* cell references. To confirm that the copied formulas are using the cells you want, select the cell with a copied formula, and then look in the Formula Bar to see the cells the formula uses. For more information about cell references and how to use them, see "Using Relative and Absolute Cell References" on page 129.

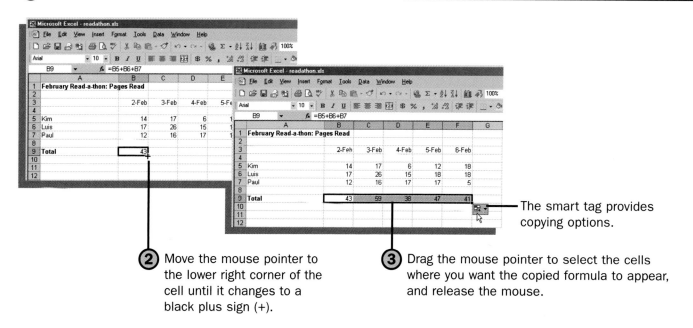

The smart tag provides copying options.

(2) Move the mouse pointer to the lower right corner of the cell until it changes to a black plus sign (+).

(3) Drag the mouse pointer to select the cells where you want the copied formula to appear, and release the mouse.

TIP: To copy a formula to an area that isn't right next to the original formula, right-click the cell containing the original formula, and click Copy. Then select the cell or range where you want the copied formula to appear, right-click, and click Paste.

NEW FEATURE: If your original formula contains formatting that you don't want to use in the copies, click the smart tag, and then click Fill Without Formatting.

Using Relative and Absolute Cell References

When you copy a formula or function, you're really copying a set of instructions that tell Excel where to find the data it needs for your calculation. Those instructions—the cell references—come in two flavors, *relative* and *absolute*, and understanding their differences will make your formulas more effective and more accurate.

Relative Cell References

Excel's formulas are based on *relative cell references*. This means that when you copy a formula, the results of the formula change because the copied versions use different data. (The copied versions look for cells based on the cells' location *relative* to the cell where you've entered the formula.)

In this example, cell B& calculates the square footage of the "Living Room" in "House A" by multiplying the numbers in the two cells above it (B6 and B7). When the formula is copied to other cells, the copied versions use the values in the two cells above the copied formula. For the "Kids' Room" in "House B," the formula is in E14, so it uses cells E12 and E13.

Absolute Cell References

Sometimes, though, you'll want a copied formula to use some of the information that the original formula uses—for example, to calculate the total cost of carpeting a room, you'd multiply each room's square footage by the same price per square foot of carpet. Copies of a formula will use the same cells as the original when you use *absolute cell references*. Absolute cell references appear in the Formula Bar with dollar signs ($) before the column letter and row number. Many formulas include both absolute and relative references.

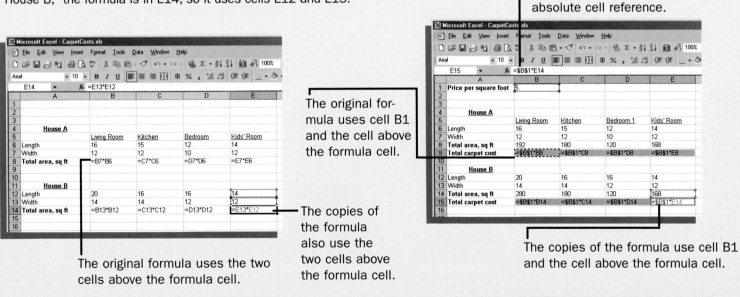

Dollar signs indicate an absolute cell reference.

The original formula uses cell B1 and the cell above the formula cell.

The copies of the formula also use the two cells above the formula cell.

The copies of the formula use cell B1 and the cell above the formula cell.

The original formula uses the two cells above the formula cell.

Switching Between Relative and Absolute References

Any time you enter a cell reference in a formula, Excel assumes it is a relative reference. To override that, edit the original formula in the Formula Bar.

Change a Relative Reference to an Absolute Reference

(1) Select the cell with the original formula.

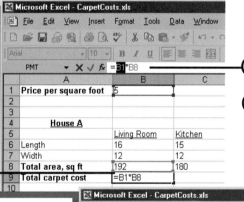

(2) Click in the Formula Bar, and select the cell reference.

(3) Press the F4 key. To change the reference back to a relative reference, press the F4 key repeatedly until all dollar signs are removed from the reference.

The selected reference becomes an absolute reference, and the rest of the formula remains unchanged.

TIP: You can also create *mixed references*, which make either the cell or the row of a reference absolute, but leave the rest of the reference relative. To create a mixed reference, select the reference in the Formula Bar, and press the F4 key until a dollar sign appears before the letter (if you want the column to remain fixed) or the number (if you want the row to remain fixed).

TIP: To learn more about cell references, click in the Ask A Question box in the upper right corner of the window. Type about cell references, **and then press the Enter key.**

TRY THIS: Use absolute references any time you need to use a certain number in many formulas. If, for example, you need to calculate a markup on your prices, put the markup percentage in a cell and refer to it in your formulas. That way, if the markup percentage changes, you can just change the cell instead of changing all the formulas.

Using Data from Different Workbooks

Big projects usually mean lots of data, which in turn often means that the information you'll use in one workbook has already been collected in another. No need to copy that information—instead, use formulas to link your workbook to the data you need. By linking, you ensure that any updates made to the original information will be reflected in your work, too.

Keep in mind, though, that if the structure of the other workbook changes—if rows or columns are deleted, for example—your formulas may no longer be correct. Try to link to workbooks that you control, so that you'll know when changes are made that could affect your work.

Link a Cell to a Different Workbook

 SEE ALSO: For more information about entering formulas, see "Create a Formula" on page 125.

1 Open both workbooks.

- To make it easier to move between your workbooks, arrange them side by side. Choose Arrange from the Window menu, and click Vertical in the Arrange Window dialog box.

2 In the cell that you want to contain a reference to the other worksheet, type the formula, beginning with an equal sign (=).

3 To include the reference to the cell in the other workbook, click the other workbook, and select the cell.

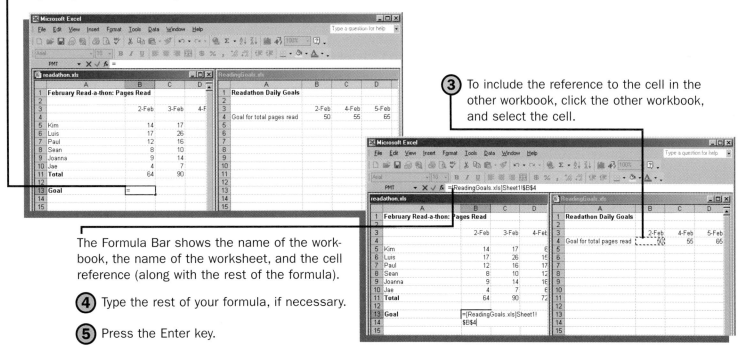

The Formula Bar shows the name of the workbook, the name of the worksheet, and the cell reference (along with the rest of the formula).

4 Type the rest of your formula, if necessary.

5 Press the Enter key.

Entering Data Automatically

Some of your data—especially the information you use to label your rows or columns—might fall in a logical sequence. For example, in a list ranking your 100 favorite movies, you'd want to put the numbers from 1 to 100 next to the movie titles. Or, in a worksheet showing daily ice cream sales, you'd probably label each row (or column) with the day of the month.

Instead of typing every one of those numbers or days, use AutoFill to streamline the effort. After you type the first entry or two, Excel can fill in the rest of the data. Whether you're creating a set of date or time labels, copying a formula, or setting up a list of numbers, using AutoFill will speed up your work and reduce typing errors.

Fill In Repeated or Sequential Data ⊛ NEW FEATURE

1 Select the cell that you want to use as the starting point of your data.

2 Move the mouse pointer to the lower right corner of the cell until it changes to a *fill handle* (a black plus sign [+]).

3 Drag the fill handle to the last cell you want to fill with data, and release the mouse.

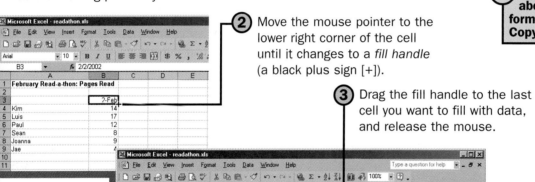

4 Click the down arrow of the AutoFill smart tag.

5 Click an option in the list that specifies how you want the range to be filled.

> **TIP:** To fill in a range with data that follows a certain pattern, you'll need to enter enough data for Excel to figure out what the pattern is. For example, to create a list of the numbers from 1 to 10, type 1 in the first cell and 2 in the second cell. (This tells Excel that you want the list to increase by one.) Then select both cells, and drag the fill handle to select the range you want filled.

> **SEE ALSO:** For more information about using this method to copy formulas, see "Reuse a Formula by Copying It" on page 128.

Naming Cells and Ranges

As you work with your data, you may find yourself using the same ranges time and again. For example, if you've calculated a set of monthly totals, you might display them in a graph, use them in a formula for an annual total, and highlight them in a summary worksheet. Or you might put an interest rate in a cell, and use that cell in several formulas that calculate loan payments.

To make it easier to put a cell or range to these different uses, you can name it, and then use the name to refer to the data in the formula or chart. By using the name, you skip the tedious—and sometimes error-prone—process of navigating to a range and selecting it.

Assign a Name to a Cell or Range

1 Select the cell or range.

2 Type a name for the cell or range in the Name Box.

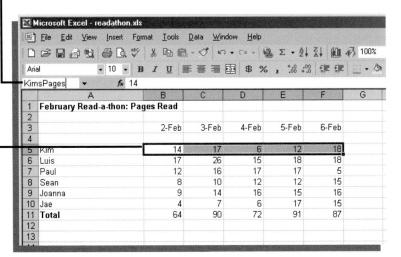

3 Press the Enter key.

CAUTION: Range names must follow a few rules. Start the name with a letter, and don't use spaces. To make your names clearer, use capital letters or the underscore (_). For example, you could name a range "Feb02Reading" or "Feb02_Reading," but not "Feb02 Reading" or "02FebReading."

TRY THIS: Use a range name in a formula to help anyone looking at the formula understand its purpose. For example, if the cells that show July's sales figures of each sales representative are in a range named "July," then a formula for total sales would be "=sum(July)" or a formula for average sales per salesperson would be "=average(July)".

TIP: To go to a cell or range you've named, click the Name Box down arrow, and click a name in the list. Excel will select the named area and display it on the screen.

Tracking and Correcting Errors in a Worksheet

Almost all worksheets will contain an error somewhere. A formula might use a cell that's been deleted, divide a number by an empty cell, or add up June's data instead of July's.

When Excel finds a cell with a possible calculation error, it inserts a green triangle in the cell. If the error is so severe that Excel can't complete the calculation, the cell also displays an *error message*, such as "#DIV/0!". Use Excel's error assistance tools to figure out what caused the error and how to fix it.

Excel won't be able to alert you to all errors, though—for example, Excel won't know that you meant to use July, not June, numbers in a formula. To find these subtle errors, you'll need to go through your worksheet carefully, a process simplified by Excel's auditing tools.

> **! TIP: Keep in mind that a green triangle means it's possible, but not certain, that a formula contains an error. That's why the Error smart tag menu includes the "Ignore Error" command. Choose this if you believe the formula is correct.**

Review and Correct Errors Identified by Excel ⊕ NEW FEATURE

(1) Select a cell that contains a green triangle in the upper left corner.

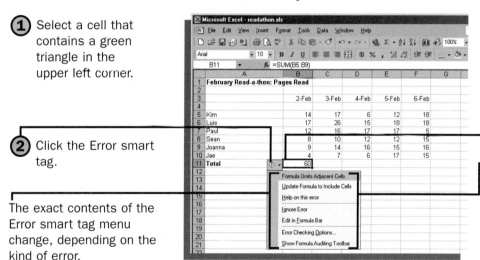

A green triangle signals a possible error.

(2) Click the Error smart tag.

The exact contents of the Error smart tag menu change, depending on the kind of error.

(3) Use the menu options to troubleshoot the error:

- To have Excel correct the error, choose Update Formula. (This option is not available for all error messages, and has different wording depending on the error.)

- To understand more about the error, choose Help On This Error.

- To remove the error alert for the cell, choose Ignore Error.

- To correct the error manually, choose Edit In Formula Bar, and type your changes in the Formula Bar.

> **! TIP: Excel can walk you through the possible errors it found, so that you don't have to pore over the worksheet hunting for green triangles. To do this, choose Error Checking from the Tools menu, and review the information shown in the Error Checking dialog box. This dialog box shows you each error Excel has found, explains the problem, and helps you fix it.**

Review a Cell Formula Using Audit Tools ⊕ NEW FEATURE

(1) Select the cell that contains the formula.

! TIP: To see which formulas use a certain cell, click the Trace Dependents button on the Formula Auditing toolbar.

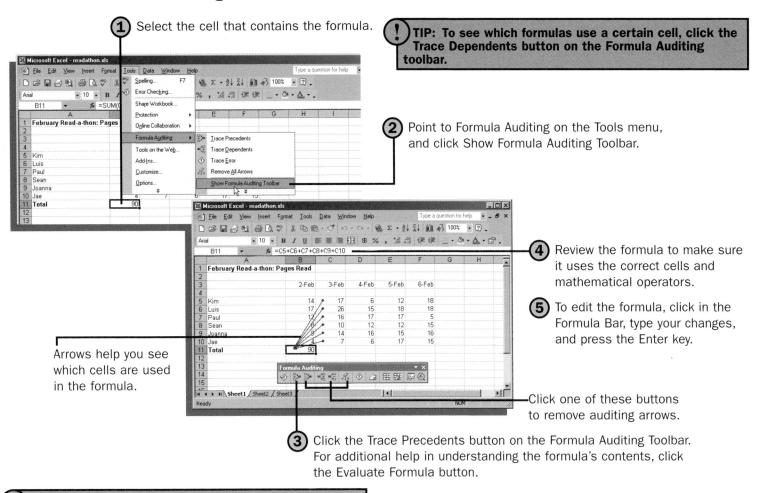

(2) Point to Formula Auditing on the Tools menu, and click Show Formula Auditing Toolbar.

(4) Review the formula to make sure it uses the correct cells and mathematical operators.

(5) To edit the formula, click in the Formula Bar, type your changes, and press the Enter key.

Arrows help you see which cells are used in the formula.

Click one of these buttons to remove auditing arrows.

(3) Click the Trace Precedents button on the Formula Auditing Toolbar. For additional help in understanding the formula's contents, click the Evaluate Formula button.

! TIP: Excel offers spelling checking, which works much like spelling checking in other Microsoft Office programs. To check the spelling of a word, select a cell, and then click the Spelling button on the Standard toolbar. Excel will go through the worksheet and show you any spelling errors.

! TIP: To hide the Formula Auditing toolbar, click the Close button in the upper right corner of the toolbar.

Working with Large Workbooks

Large workbooks with many complex worksheets can challenge your efficiency (and, possibly, your sanity). Their sheer size makes it hard to see and remember everything they contain.

Excel offers techniques that display large workbooks, or several workbooks, in ways that make it easier to get your work done. *Freezing* panes keeps certain rows or columns visible at all times as you scroll through the worksheet, so that you can see the data's identifying labels. *Splitting* a worksheet lets you display different parts of a worksheet side by side. *Tiling* workbooks displays two or more workbooks at once, so that you can more easily create cell references across workbooks.

Freeze a Worksheet's Rows and Columns

(1) Scroll through your worksheet until the rows you want to see at all times appear at the top of the display area, and the columns you want to see appear at the far left.

(2) Select the areas you want to freeze:
- To freeze certain rows at the top of the display area, select the entire row that appears immediately below the rows you want to display.
- To freeze certain columns at the left of the display area, select the entire column that appears to the right of the columns you want to display.

> **CAUTION: Freezing rows or columns doesn't affect the way your worksheet will be printed. If you want certain rows or columns to appear on all pages when you print your worksheet, choose Page Setup from the File menu, and click the Sheet tab. In the Print Titles area, specify which rows or columns should appear on all printed pages.**

> **! TIP:** *Splitting* **is another technique for displaying your worksheet. Use it to show different parts of your worksheet side by side. Select an entire row or column, and choose Split from the Window menu. You can scroll through one of the areas without changing what's displayed in the other areas. (To remove a split, double-click on the bar that appears between worksheet areas.)**

> **! TIP: To "unfreeze" the panes, choose Unfreeze Panes from the Window menu.**

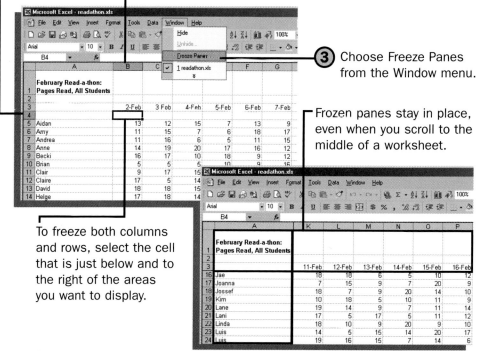

(3) Choose Freeze Panes from the Window menu.

Frozen panes stay in place, even when you scroll to the middle of a worksheet.

To freeze both columns and rows, select the cell that is just below and to the right of the areas you want to display.

Arrange Several Workbooks on the Screen

① Open each workbook you want to display.

② Choose Arrange from the Window menu.

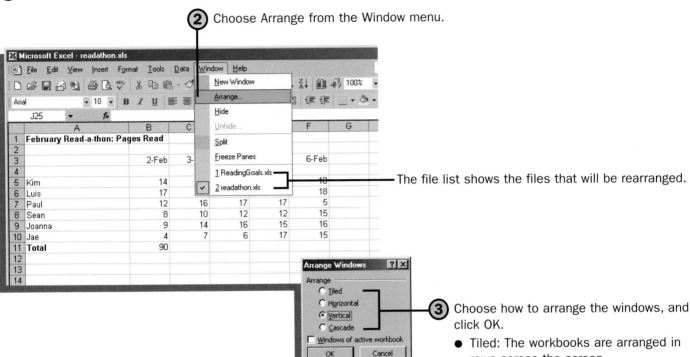

The file list shows the files that will be rearranged.

③ Choose how to arrange the windows, and click OK.

- Tiled: The workbooks are arranged in rows across the screen.
- Horizontal: The workbooks appear one above each other.
- Vertical: The workbooks appear next to each other.
- Cascade: The workbooks are layered, so that you see only the title bar for each workbook.

> **⚠ TIP: To view more than one worksheet from a single workbook at the same time, click a worksheet in the workbook, and choose New Window from the Window menu. In the new window, click the tab for the worksheet you want to view. You can then use the Arrange options to display both worksheets at once.**

Adding Notes to a Worksheet Using Comments

Comments are like electronic sticky notes for your worksheet—a way to keep track of an idea or add a note, without actually displaying it in the worksheet itself. By adding a comment to a cell, you can explain calculations, cite data sources, or comment on a colleague's work.

But unlike sticky notes, you can tuck comments out of the way until you need them. Excel hides a cell's comment until you place the pointer over the cell. The cell's comment will then appear in a box that seems to hover over the worksheet, near the cell.

Add Comments to a Cell

(1) Right-click the cell, and choose Insert Comment from the shortcut menu.

(2) Type the comment.

TIP: To edit or delete a comment, right-click the cell containing the comment, and click either Edit Comment or Delete Comment.

(3) To close the comment, click anywhere on the worksheet.

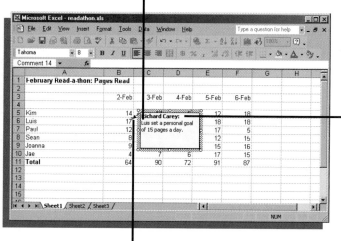

Your name is inserted at the beginning of the comment.

A red triangle signals that a cell has an attached comment.

TIP: To display all comments on a worksheet, choose Comments from the View menu. Do the same thing to hide them.

TRY THIS: If you have a long comment and want to see all the text at once, you can enlarge the comment area. To do so, right-click the cell containing the comment, and click Edit Comment. Position the mouse pointer over one of the *sizing handles* (the circles that appear on the sides and corners of the comment area). When the mouse pointer changes to a double-headed arrow, drag the sizing handle to enlarge the comment area and see the entire comment.

9 Charting and Analyzing Data

After you've entered your data, made your calculations, and set up your formats, you might feel like you know everything about your numbers—except what they mean. Fortunately, Microsoft Excel's charting and data summary features let you step back and find the broader patterns hiding in your worksheets.

- **Charts** help you and your audience understand your data at a glance. Tailor your charts to fit your needs by choosing a particular type of chart—maybe a bar chart to display monthly sales data over time or a pie chart to show how the parts make up the whole. Then use chart enhancements, such as titles, legends and labels, to clarify your chart.

- **Sorts, filters, and subtotals** help you organize your information. Set up your data as an Excel list, then sort it into the groups you care about, or use filters to zoom in on just a few rows—say, the 10 top-selling products or the sales figures for a certain salesperson. If you need to create subtotals or averages for different groups of data, a sorted list is the fastest, easiest way.

As with most Microsoft Office XP tools, the basic charts and data summary techniques will cover most of your requirements. As you learn your way around, though, start investigating the different options tucked into the dialog boxes and menus. You'll find the basics can stretch to accommodate your trickiest needs.

Showing Data in a Chart

Charts are the simplest way to show your audience what your numbers are saying, and Excel's Chart Wizard helps you create them with a few clicks. The core of an Excel chart is the *plot area,* the area that displays your data graphically. The plot area is surrounded by optional chart contents, such as titles, legends, or labels, which you can use to help explain exactly what the plot area is showing.

Until you become comfortable with creating charts, use Step 1 of the wizard to set up a basic chart that you can modify later. After you know your way around the chart process, though, you can use Steps 2, 3, and 4 to make your own tweaks before you create the chart.

TIP: Does your chart seem backwards, somehow? It might show data from your worksheet's rows when it should show the columns, or vice versa. To see whether this is the problem, click the chart, click the Chart Wizard button, and then click Next. On the Data Range tab, click the unmarked option in the Series In area. The preview area of the tab displays how the chart will look. You can click the original option again if you decide you liked the chart better the first time.

SEE ALSO: For more information about how to select data ranges, see "Working with Cells and Ranges" on page 100.

Create a Basic Excel Chart

1 Select the range(s) you want to appear in the chart, including any cells you want to use as labels in the chart.

2 Click the Chart Wizard button on the Standard toolbar.

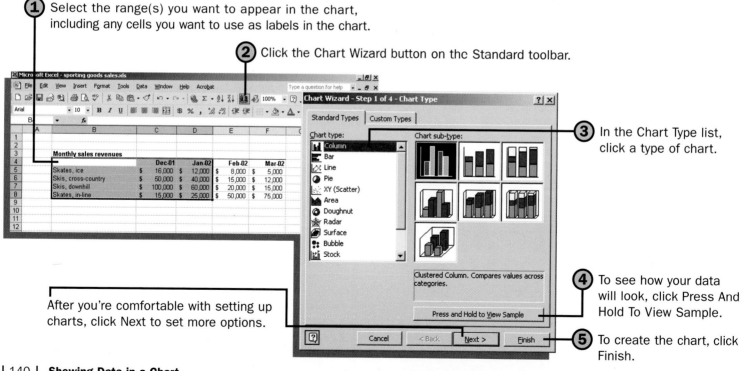

3 In the Chart Type list, click a type of chart.

After you're comfortable with setting up charts, click Next to set more options.

4 To see how your data will look, click Press And Hold To View Sample.

5 To create the chart, click Finish.

Working Efficiently with Charts

Creating an Excel chart is never very complicated, but if you expect to create charts regularly, you'll discover that a little worksheet organization and a handy Excel shortcut will make the process even speedier. Follow these guidelines for developing worksheets that can be transformed into charts almost effortlessly. (And as a bonus, you'll discover that your worksheets become easier to read and work with!)

Organize the Worksheet

> **TIP:** Sometimes you won't be able to create a graph out of a single range. You can still work faster and smarter by getting comfortable with selecting multiple ranges using your mouse and by naming ranges that you plan to graph frequently.

Use text labels at the top of every column and to the left of every row. When you select the data in those columns or rows for a chart, select the labels as well and they'll become part of your chart.

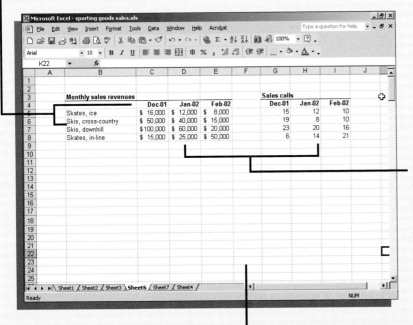

Group similar kinds of information. If you're tracking sales data, put each month's sales data in the column or row after the previous month's data. Then, when you want to show a trend, your numbers will be in a single range, ready for charting.

Use blank rows or columns to help structure your worksheet, but don't interrupt groups of related data with empty cells. Empty cells can make your charts harder to read.

Edit with Colored Outlines

If your chart is based on a single data range, Excel provides a special shortcut for working with the chart data. When you select the plot area, Excel shows you its data by outlining the numbers and labels on your worksheet in color-coded boxes. Use these boxes to make fast changes to the data included in your chart.

Shift to a different data range by moving the pointer to the side of the outline. When you drag the side of the outline, the box will move, but not change shape. Move the box to include the information you want.

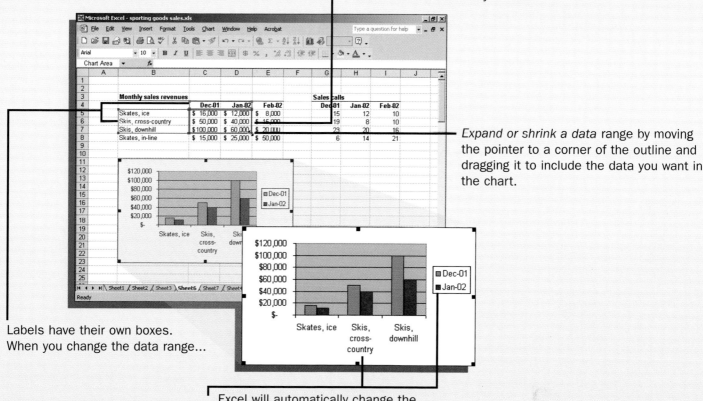

Expand or shrink a data range by moving the pointer to a corner of the outline and dragging it to include the data you want in the chart.

Labels have their own boxes. When you change the data range...

...Excel will automatically change the labels to match the new selection.

Adding Text or Special Formats to Charts

If a chart needs context in order to tell its story clearly, use Excel tools to add text helpers such as titles, legends, and data labels. Another way to add clarity is to emphasize your most important numbers by changing their formatting in the chart. You can give special treatment to a *data series* (that is, a set of data the chart displays together in a single color) or even to a single number.

Modify Elements that Apply to the Entire Chart

1 Right-click in the blank area surrounding the chart, and click Chart Options.

!TIP: After you've added a title to your chart, you can edit it just by clicking it and making your changes.

2 To add a title above the chart or labels for the chart's margins, click the Titles tab.

To modify other elements, click the appropriate tab.

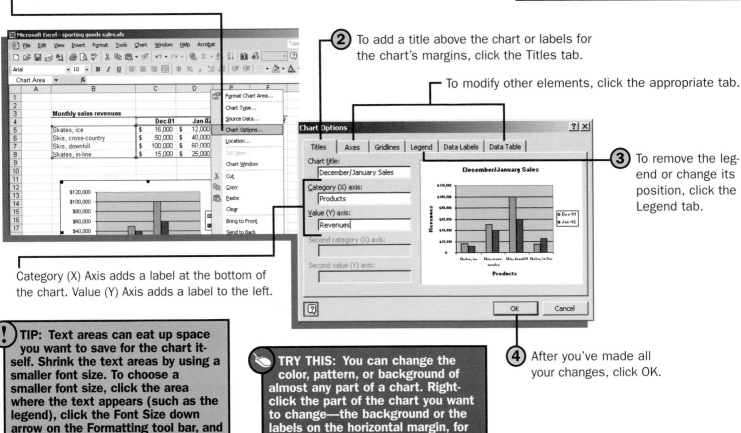

3 To remove the legend or change its position, click the Legend tab.

Category (X) Axis adds a label at the bottom of the chart. Value (Y) Axis adds a label to the left.

4 After you've made all your changes, click OK.

!TIP: Text areas can eat up space you want to save for the chart itself. Shrink the text areas by using a smaller font size. To choose a smaller font size, click the area where the text appears (such as the legend), click the Font Size down arrow on the Formatting tool bar, and then click the font size you want.

TRY THIS: You can change the color, pattern, or background of almost any part of a chart. Right-click the part of the chart you want to change—the background or the labels on the horizontal margin, for example—and click Format.

Modify Text or Appearance for a Data Series

1 To select the entire series, right-click any data point in the data series, and click Format Data Series.

! **TIP: To change the format of a single data point and not the entire data series, click anywhere in the data series, and then click the** *data marker* **that appears over the data point you want to change. Then right-click the data point, click Format Data Point, and make your choices as you would for a data series.**

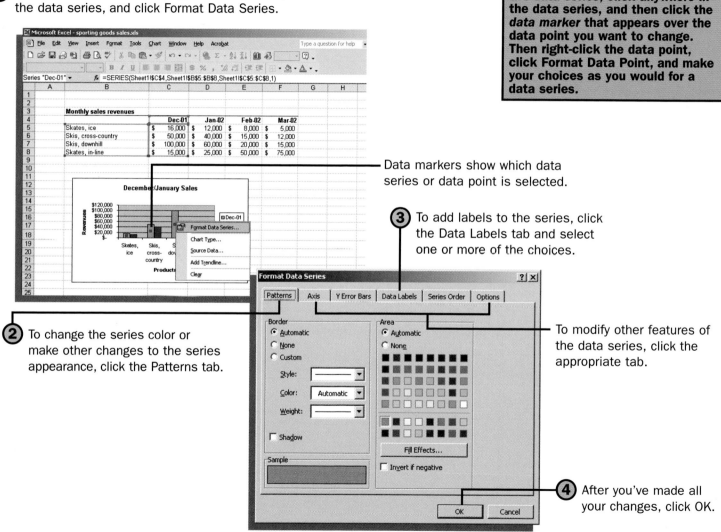

Data markers show which data series or data point is selected.

3 To add labels to the series, click the Data Labels tab and select one or more of the choices.

2 To change the series color or make other changes to the series appearance, click the Patterns tab.

To modify other features of the data series, click the appropriate tab.

4 After you've made all your changes, click OK.

Modifying Data in a Chart

It's a good bet that sooner or later, you'll need to change the data reflected in your chart. You might want to expand the chart to include new data you've added to your worksheet, add a few more points to the data series your chart already shows, or delete data that doesn't matter any more. You won't need to modify the chart if you change a number in a worksheet cell, though—Excel automatically updates the chart to reflect the new value.

> **CAUTION: Depending on how your data and chart are set up, it might be difficult to insert chart data from worksheet cells that are either above or to the left of the data that is already in the chart. If you have trouble adding data, try setting up a new chart that includes all the data you want to display.**

Add Data to an Existing Chart

(1) In the worksheet containing the data, select the range with the data you want to add (including any labels, if you want to display them on the chart).

(2) Right-click the selected range, and click Copy.

(3) Right-click in the blank area surrounding the plot area, and click Paste.

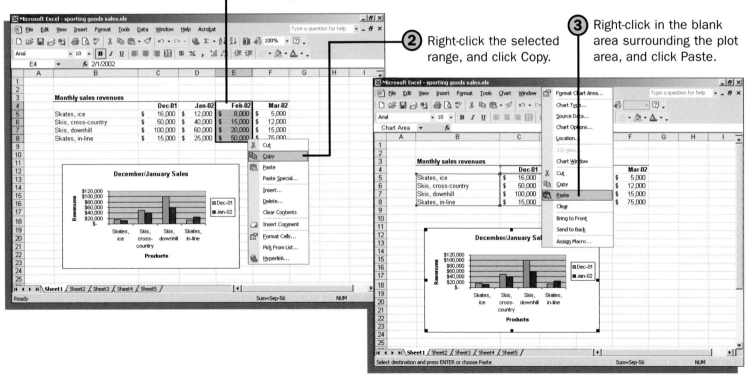

Remove a Data Series from a Chart

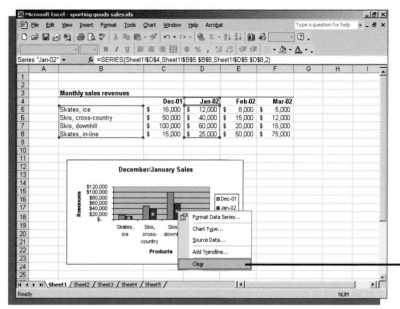

① On the chart, right-click a data point in the series, and click Clear.

✋ **CAUTION:** After you add or remove data, make sure the chart's title (if you've added one) still matches your picture! Excel updates most parts of your chart when you make a data change, but it won't change titles.

✓ **SEE ALSO:** For more information about how to modify data using the colored outline that might appear on your worksheet, see "Working Efficiently with Charts" on page 141.

❗ **TIP:** If you want to keep your original chart as well as a new version, make a copy: right-click the blank area surrounding the original chart and click Copy, and then right-click a worksheet cell and click Paste. Be sure to do your editing in the copy, not in the original.

✋ **CAUTION:** Don't remove a data series from a pie chart. Because pie charts are made up of just one data series (a row or column), removing the series will delete the entire chart. To change data in a pie chart, right-click the chart, and then place your pointer over the colored outline that appears around the data on the worksheet. Move the outline to include the new data.

Creating Excel Lists: Why and How

Excel *lists* streamline the work involved in creating subtotals, averages, and other calculations that help you summarize your information. They also make it easy to sort data and use *filters*, which let you concentrate on certain rows by temporarily hiding the others. If you don't use lists, you'll need to sort, combine, and pull out data manually, a process that eats up time and patience.

A list is just a set of rows of data, where every row has the same kind of data in the same order. In fact, lists look a lot like any other set of data in Excel, but they have to follow a few rules. To use list-based tools on your data, be sure your set of data matches the requirements illustrated here:

Use a *header row* (a row that contains text labeling each column), and don't skip a row between the header row and the first row of data.

The first few columns should hold information you'll use to organize your data—for example, here, the worksheet owner could decide to sort by product, salesperson, or region (or a combination).

CAUTION: Excel is very literal, so make sure you're consistent in spelling and punctuation for rows that have text. Otherwise, "NE" will end up separated from "N.E.," for example.

TIP: To learn more about the specific format requirements for lists, click in the Ask A Question box in the upper right corner of the window. **Type** guidelines for lists, **and then press the Enter key.**

Microsoft Excel - sporting goods sales.xls

File Edit View Insert Format Tools Data Window Help Acrobat

	Product	Rep	Region	Dec-01	Jan-02	Feb-02	Mar-02
2	Monthly sales revenues						
3	Product	Rep	Region	Dec-01	Jan-02	Feb-02	Mar-02
4	Skates, in-line	Mitchell	SE	$ 23,000	$ 27,000	$ 41,000	$ 53,000
5	Skates, in-line	O'Hara	NE	$ 20,000	$ 36,000	$ 59,000	$ 72,000
6	Skates, ice	Rothenberg	NE	$ 17,000	$ 15,000	$ 9,000	$ 4,000
7	Skis, cross-country	Anderson	SE	$ 75,000	$ 55,000	$ 40,000	$ 22,000
8	Skis, cross-country	Rothenberg	NE	$ 12,000	$ 14,000	$ 12,000	$ 10,000
9	Skis, downhill	Perera	NE	$ 47,000	$ 33,000	$ 25,000	$ 14,000
10	Skis, downhill	Tibbott	NE	$ 37,000	$ 30,000	$ 18,000	$ 12,000
11	Skates, ice	Anderson	SE	$ 22,000	$ 22,000	$ 8,000	$ 4,000
12	Skis, downhill	Mitchell	SE	$ 52,000	$ 32,000	$ 27,000	$ 25,000
13	Skates, in-line	Perera	NE	$ 15,000	$ 26,000	$ 42,000	$ 58,000
14	Skates, ice	Perera	NE	$ 19,000	$ 14,000	$ 11,000	$ 5,000
15	Skis, downhill	Rothenberg	NE	$ 78,000	$ 74,000	$ 50,000	$ 35,000
16	Skis, downhill	Dalal	SE	$ 100,000	$ 60,000	$ 20,000	$ 15,000
17	Skis, downhill	O'Hara	NE	$ 22,000	$ 18,000	$ 14,000	$ 9,000
18	Skates, in-line	Rothenberg	NE	$ 10,000	$ 15,000	$ 27,000	$ 38,000
19	Skates, ice	Tibbott	SE	$ 16,000	$ 8,000	$ 8,000	$ 3,000
20	Skates, ice	O'Hara	NE	$ 25,000	$ 20,000	$ 14,000	$ 9,000
26	Team Assignments						

Sheet1 Sheet2 **Sheet3** Sheet4 Sheet5 Sheet6

Ready

NUM

Don't leave any rows or columns blank; Excel will think they signal the end of the list.

Put your list on a worksheet by itself, if possible. If you have to put both a list and other data on a single worksheet, put a few blank rows or columns between the list and the other data.

Sorting and Filtering Data in a List

After you've set up your data as a list, you can *sort* to see all your data, organized by certain criteria you set, or *filter* to see only the rows with values matching requirements you choose. Sorting changes the worksheet by rearranging the rows in the list, grouping similar data together. In contrast, filtering doesn't change how the list is organized; it just hides certain rows temporarily. For example, you can use filtering to see sales figures for a certain salesperson or to show the top-selling products, and then remove the filter to see all the rows again.

If you plan to use Excel tools to figure subtotals, averages, or other calculations for groups in your data, you must sort the list first. For example, if you'll want average sales by salesperson, sort your data by salesperson.

Sort an Excel List

1 Click a cell in the list.

2 Choose Sort from the Data menu.

CAUTION: Because sorting actually changes the order of the rows, don't sort lists that you use as data sources for charts. If you need to sort a list you've used as the basis for a chart, copy the list to a blank worksheet and sort the copy.

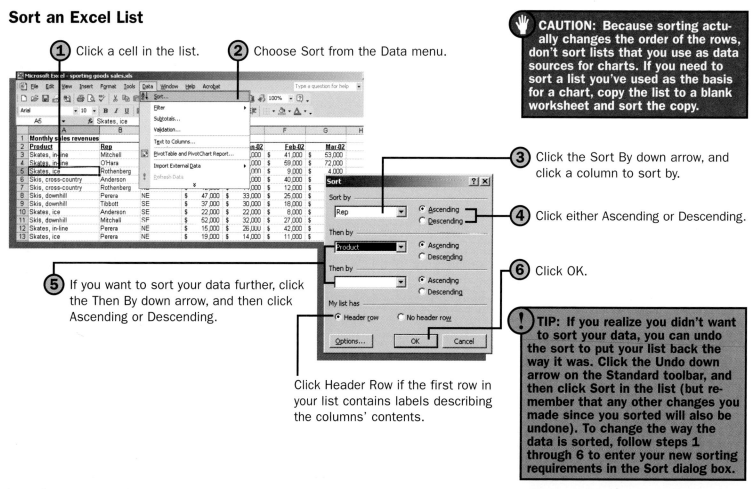

3 Click the Sort By down arrow, and click a column to sort by.

4 Click either Ascending or Descending.

5 If you want to sort your data further, click the Then By down arrow, and then click Ascending or Descending.

6 Click OK.

Click Header Row if the first row in your list contains labels describing the columns' contents.

TIP: If you realize you didn't want to sort your data, you can undo the sort to put your list back the way it was. Click the Undo down arrow on the Standard toolbar, and then click Sort in the list (but remember that any other changes you made since you sorted will also be undone). To change the way the data is sorted, follow steps 1 through 6 to enter your new sorting requirements in the Sort dialog box.

Filter an Excel List

✋ **CAUTION: AutoFilter assumes that a list starts with a header row of labels, so make sure that you put a header row at the top of your list.**

① Click a cell in the list.

② Point to Filter on the Data menu, and click AutoFilter.

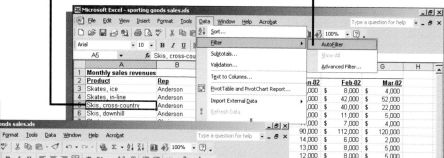

⑥ To see all your data again, remove each filter you've set by clicking each column's down arrow and clicking All.

⑤ To filter the data further, click the down arrow of the column that contains the next set of information you want to use as a filter, and click an entry in the drop-down list.

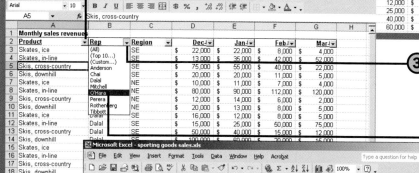

③ Click the down arrow of the column that contains the information you'll use as a filter (such as name).

④ To specify which rows to display, click an entry in the drop-down list.

The down arrow for each column you've used as a filter is blue.

⚠️ **TIP: To remove all the filters and the filter arrows, choose Filter from the Data menu, and click AutoFilter to uncheck it.**

The filtered list shows only rows that match the filter choice.

🖱️ **TRY THIS: Click Custom in the filter drop-down list to set up specialized or more flexible filters. In the Custom AutoFilter dialog box, click Begins With to see all entries that start with the same few letters, for example, or click And to see all items that match two requirements (instead of just one).**

Creating Subtotals and Other Information for Groups of Numbers

Often, knowing your data's big picture (such as February's sales total) leads to questions about the little details. Which product had greater sales—skates or skis? Which region had the highest average sales per salesperson?

Answer questions like these quickly by sorting your data, and then using Excel tools to analyze the sorted data. You can add subtotals, calculate averages, find the largest or smallest value in a group, and more. Excel displays these calculations in rows it adds to your worksheet, but the new rows won't disrupt charts or formulas that use your data.

SEE ALSO: For more information about sorting your data, see "Sort and Filtering Data in a List" on page 148.

TIP: To learn more about subtotal calculations and ways you can use them in charts and reports, click in the Ask A Question box in the upper right corner of the window. Type about subtotals, and then press the Enter key.

CAUTION: Make sure your list begins with a header row that labels the columns. If it doesn't, you won't be able to use the Subtotals tool.

Analyze Sorted Data

1 Click a cell in a sorted list.

2 Choose Subtotals from the Data menu.

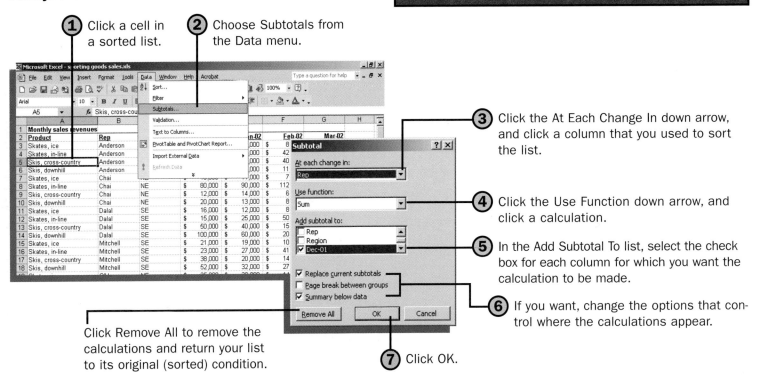

3 Click the At Each Change In down arrow, and click a column that you used to sort the list.

4 Click the Use Function down arrow, and click a calculation.

5 In the Add Subtotal To list, select the check box for each column for which you want the calculation to be made.

6 If you want, change the options that control where the calculations appear.

Click Remove All to remove the calculations and return your list to its original (sorted) condition.

7 Click OK.

10 Using Outlook for E-Mail

As in previous versions, you can rely on Microsoft Outlook to transmit your messages faithfully; but Outlook 2002 has new powers. Now you can add e-mail accounts right from within Outlook so you can switch from your work account to your personal account, for example. You can also take advantage of more accessible tools for keeping your mailbox small and fending off junk mail.

Outlook starts out with a basic framework of folders to help you manage your e-mail messages:

● **Inbox.** The Inbox folder is home to incoming messages and is mission central for the Outlook e-mail system.

● **Sent Items.** Outlook stores a copy here of every e-mail message you send.

● **Deleted Items.** Delete any message and it goes into this folder, where it awaits more permanent deletion from the hard disk when you empty the Deleted Items folder.

● **Drafts.** Outlook stores any messages here that you saved before sending or that you were crafting when your computer shut down unexpectedly.

Setting Up an E-Mail Account for the First Time ⊛ NEW FEATURE

The instructions on these two pages paint in broad strokes the steps you'll follow to set up your Outlook e-mail account. The first time you start Outlook, you might see screens like the ones that follow; you might see an introductory screen or two before you see them; or, you might not see any screens at all!

Furthermore, the screens you see depend on the type of account you set up. (Our example shows the steps to set up a POP3 account.) We suggest that you contact your Internet service provider (ISP) or system administrator before you begin, using the graphics that follow as a guide for what you'll need to know to set up your account.

Setting Up an E-Mail Account for the First Time ⊛ NEW FEATURE

① Choose E-Mail Accounts from the Tools menu.

② Click Add A New E-Mail Account, and click Next.

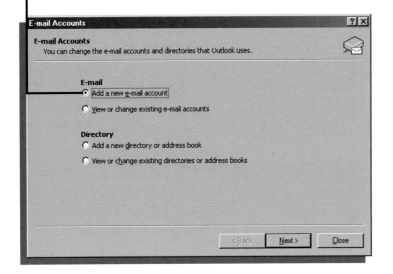

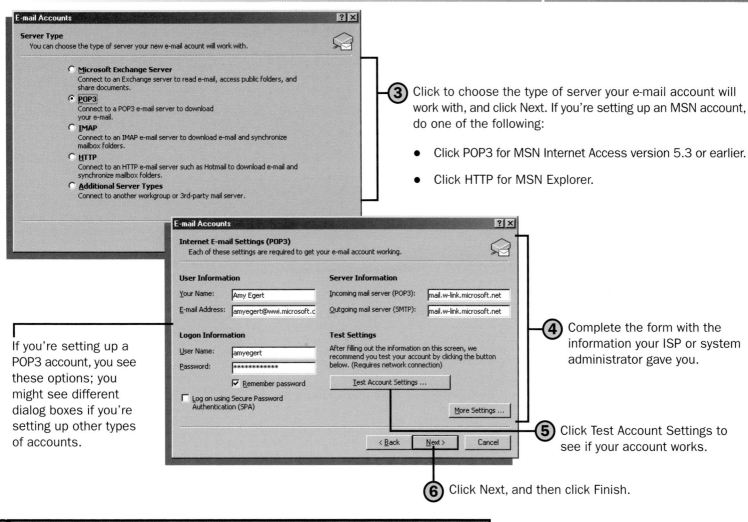

③ Click to choose the type of server your e-mail account will work with, and click Next. If you're setting up an MSN account, do one of the following:

● Click POP3 for MSN Internet Access version 5.3 or earlier.

● Click HTTP for MSN Explorer.

If you're setting up a POP3 account, you see these options; you might see different dialog boxes if you're setting up other types of accounts.

④ Complete the form with the information your ISP or system administrator gave you.

⑤ Click Test Account Settings to see if your account works.

⑥ Click Next, and then click Finish.

TRY THIS: Still unsure if your new e-mail account is working? Send an e-mail message to yourself; if you get it, your account is working! If you run into further problems setting up your account, however, Outlook offers help. Click in the Ask A Question box in the upper right corner of the window. Type trouble-shoot e-mail accounts, **and then press the Enter key. Click Troubleshoot E-Mail Accounts, and scan the list for your problem.**

Composing and Sending an E-Mail Message

Because e-mail addresses must be letter-perfect in order for your mail to reach the intended destination, Outlook lets you choose them from a list or type a few letters of the person's name in the *To* and *Cc* (for carbon copy) lines and then automatically supplies the full address.

To protect the privacy of your recipients' e-mail addresses, type the recipients' names in the *Bcc* (blind carbon copy) line. Names and e-mail addresses in the Bcc line are invisible to every-

one who receives your message. This is the polite way to send e-mail to a large group of people—change of e-mail address, a joke, and so on.

You can write a message and send it off right away; or you can compose a draft and return to it later to finish and send. Outlook also automatically saves messages as you write them, so if your computer shuts down unexpectedly, your messages will be waiting for you in the Drafts folder.

Write an E-Mail Message, Send It Now

> ! TIP: If you want to send e-mail to someone whose name isn't in your Contacts list, you can type it into the To line. Capitalization doesn't matter, and there should be no spaces in the address.

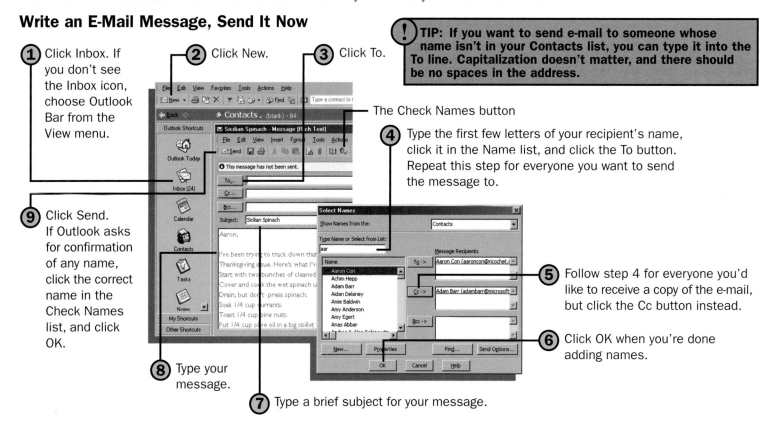

(1) Click Inbox. If you don't see the Inbox icon, choose Outlook Bar from the View menu.

(2) Click New.

(3) Click To.

The Check Names button

(4) Type the first few letters of your recipient's name, click it in the Name list, and click the To button. Repeat this step for everyone you want to send the message to.

(9) Click Send. If Outlook asks for confirmation of any name, click the correct name in the Check Names list, and click OK.

(5) Follow step 4 for everyone you'd like to receive a copy of the e-mail, but click the Cc button instead.

(6) Click OK when you're done adding names.

(8) Type your message.

(7) Type a brief subject for your message.

Get Help Entering Names

⊕ NEW FEATURE

(1) Type the first few letters of your recipient's name in the To, Cc, or Bcc box, and then let Outlook help you with one of the following:

- If Outlook starts filling in the correct name, press the Enter key.

- If Outlook offers a choice of one or more names on a tiny list, use the arrow keys to choose the correct name, and then press the Enter key.

- If Outlook offers nothing, click the Check Names button, click a name on the list, and then click OK.

! TIP: If you have any problem at all sending e-mail, Outlook has a ready-made troubleshooter standing by to help. Click in the Ask A Question box in the upper right corner of the window. Type troubleshoot e-mail, and then press the Enter key. Scan the list for your problem, and click it to read the solution.

! TIP: You can have Outlook check your spelling before you send a message simply by choosing Spelling from the Tools menu. You can also have Outlook automatically check for spelling errors in every message. To do this, choose Options from the Tools menu, click the Spelling tab, and then select the Always Check Spelling Before Sending check box.

Write an E-Mail Message, Send It Later

(1) Compose as much of an e-mail message as you want, following the steps in "Write an E-mail Message, Send It Now."

(2) Click Save.

(3) Click Close.

(4) When you're ready to finish and send the message, look for it in the Drafts folder of your Inbox. If you don't see the Drafts folder, choose Folder List from the View menu.

! TIP: To send blind copies, follow the steps in "Write an E-Mail Message, Send It Now." In step 3, click the Bcc button. Follow step 4, but click the BCC button instead of the To button. Then follow the remaining steps starting with step 6. When a recipient opens the message, only the sender's name appears (in the From line). If you don't see the Bcc button in your message, choose Bcc Field from the View menu.

Checking E-Mail and Responding to Messages

To check your e-mail, go directly to your Inbox. There, Outlook tells you a lot about your messages before you even open them. For example, as you scan messages, it's easy to see those you haven't read (they're still highlighted in bold), which messages are high priority (look for the red exclamation point), and so on. The Preview Pane comes in handy—you can scroll to read an entire message without actually opening it. Or, if you use AutoPreview, you can see the first few lines of a message. You can capitalize on Outlook's organizational strengths by opening e-mail from all your accounts—personal, Hotmail, work, and so on—right in Outlook.

Set Up Your View of the Inbox

(1) Click Inbox. If you don't see the Inbox icon, choose Outlook Bar from the View menu.

(2) Choose either Folder List, Preview Pane, or AutoPreview from the View menu.

This mail has not been opened.

This mail has been opened.

This e-mail has been responded to.

AutoPreview

Paper clip indicates attachments.

Preview Pane

Folder List   High priority mail

> **CAUTION: Be cautious about opening e-mail. Opening certain messages, even sometimes those from people you know, can propagate a destructive virus in your e-mail system, the electronic-mail equivalent of a letter bomb. In general, though, if you don't open e-mail from senders you don't recognize or messages without a name in the From column, your system should remain safe.**
>
> **Another security tactic is not to open e-mail at all, but instead use the Preview Pane or AutoPreview to view your e-mail. To show as many messages as possible, we recommend choosing one of these features, but not both.**

> **TIP: High priority mail (marked with a red exclamation point) doesn't get to you (or your recipient, if you send it) any faster. The exclamation point is simply a flag to the reader that the sender considers the contents of the message to be important.**

> **SEE ALSO: For information about how to protect your e-mail account further, see "Subduing Junk E-Mail" on page 166.**

Read and Reply to E-Mail

② Depending on how you want to reply, do one of the following:
- Click Reply to send the message just to the person who wrote you.
- Click Reply All to send the message to the person who wrote you and everyone who received the e-mail (except those on the Bcc line).
- Click Forward to send the message and the original to someone who hasn't received it yet.

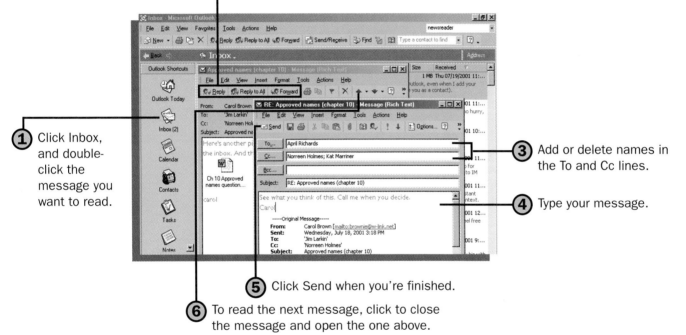

① Click Inbox, and double-click the message you want to read.

③ Add or delete names in the To and Cc lines.

④ Type your message.

⑤ Click Send when you're finished.

⑥ To read the next message, click to close the message and open the one above.

> **TIP:** If your company is set up on Microsoft Exchange Server, Outlook can reply automatically to messages when you're out of the office for any period of time, from hours to weeks. To use this service, choose Out Of Office Assistant from the Tools menu, and then click I Am Currently Out Of The Office. In the AutoReply Only Once To Each Sender With The Following Text area, type the message you want everyone to receive while you're out, and then click OK.

> **TIP:** If you have added more than one e-mail account to Outlook, you can choose to send and receive mail from just one account—or all accounts. Choose Tools, point to Send/Receive, and click the individual account you want to check, or click All Accounts to check them all.

Sending and Receiving E-Mail Attachments

It's easy, and often efficient, to attach files to e-mail—a picture of the new baby, the paper you're coauthoring, your tax file for the accountant, or a favorite song.

Attach a File to an E-Mail Message

① Compose the e-mail message.

② Click Insert File.

! TIP: To forward an e-mail message containing an attached file to someone else, click the Forward button. If you click the Reply button, Outlook will not include the attachment.

③ Browse to locate the file you want to attach in the Insert File box, and select the file.

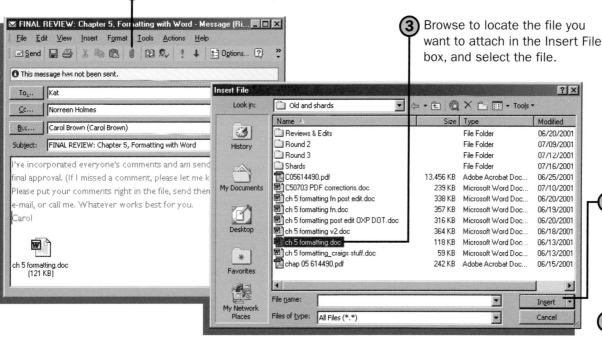

④ Click Insert. Repeat steps 2 through 4 if you want to attach more than one file.

⑤ Click Send.

Open an Attached File

(1) Open the e-mail message that contains the attachment.

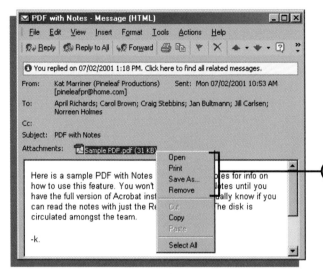

(2) Right-click the attachment, and do one of the following:

- Click Open to open the file.
- Click Print to open the attachment and print it instantly.
- Click Save As if you have *any* doubt about the reliability of the file. In the Save As dialog box, find the folder where you want to store the file, and click Save.
- Click Remove to delete the attachment without viewing or saving it.

Creating an E-Mail Signature

One advantage of the letterhead on most business papers is that you don't have to repeat information—name, address, phone numbers, logo—on every piece of correspondence. You can duplicate that advantage in e-mail by creating a special signature that doubles as letterhead and signature, and can even include your company logo.

Outlook can then append that signature automatically to new messages and use a different one (or none at all) for responses (figuring that people know who you are by then!). Or, you can delete the automatic signature and sign each e-mail individually.

Create a Personal Signature

(1) Choose Options from the Tools menu.

(2) Click the Mail Format tab, click Signatures in the Signature area, and then click New in the Create Signatures dialog box.

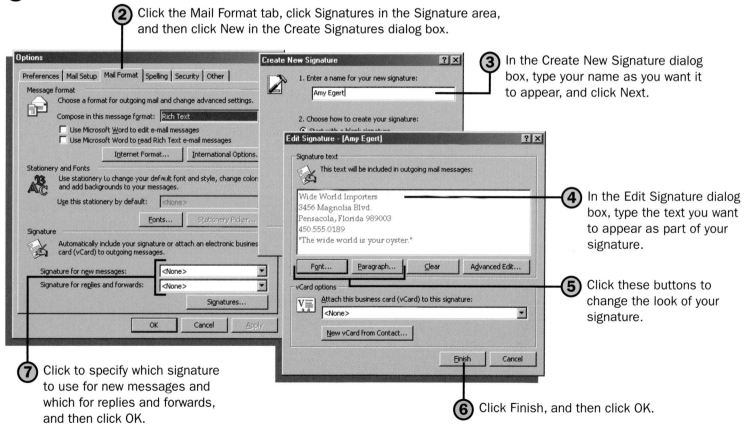

(3) In the Create New Signature dialog box, type your name as you want it to appear, and click Next.

(4) In the Edit Signature dialog box, type the text you want to appear as part of your signature.

(5) Click these buttons to change the look of your signature.

(7) Click to specify which signature to use for new messages and which for replies and forwards, and then click OK.

(6) Click Finish, and then click OK.

Add Your Signature as You Go

1 Compose your e-mail message.

2 When you're ready to sign it, point to Signature on the Insert menu, and click the signature you want.

> **(!) TIP:** To personalize an e-mail message using colored backgrounds and images, point to New Mail Message Using on the Actions menu, and then click More Stationery. Browse through the list for the look you want, and then click OK. Images and backgrounds can slow the transmission of your messages, however, so you might want to reserve them for special occasions, such as selling your baby grand piano or hosting an impromptu party.

> **(!) TIP:** To attach a logo or other image to your signature, create your entire signature in a file—in Microsoft Word, for example. Then choose Save As from the File menu, and click the Save As Type down arrow. Click Rich Text Format (*.rtf) in the list, and click Save. To add the signature to Outlook, follow steps 1 through 3 in "Create a Personal Signature." Then, in the Create New Signature dialog box, click Use This File As A Template, and browse to find your signature file. When you've found it, click Next, and follow the remaining steps.

Organizing E-Mail Messages

In addition to the file folders Outlook provides, you can build your own e-mail filing system. All Outlook folders behave just as they do in Microsoft Windows Explorer, so you'll have no trouble storing messages and deleting them, as well as creating and moving folders.

After you've set up your filing system, Outlook can help you retrieve any message from it. Your search can be as simple as looking for one word anywhere in a message or as complex as finding only messages with attachments sent from a certain person within a specified time frame.

Create a Folder

1 If the list of folders isn't open, choose Folder List from the View menu.

2 Right-click the folder in which you want to create a new folder, and click New Folder.

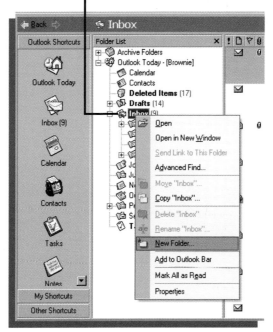

3 Type a name for the new folder, and click OK.

Find a Message ⊕ NEW FEATURE

(1) Click Find.

Click here to clear the message area and your search criteria.

Click here to fine-tune your search with Advanced Find options.

Find bar

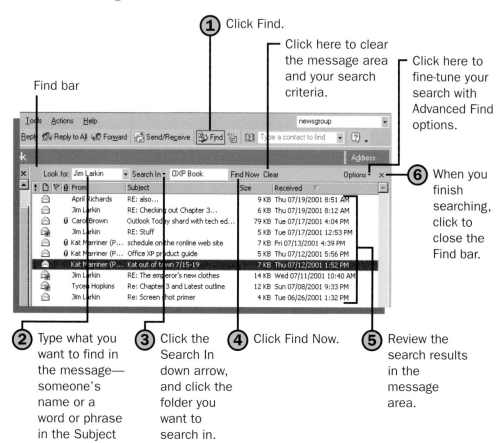

(2) Type what you want to find in the message— someone's name or a word or phrase in the Subject line or body of the message.

(3) Click the Search In down arrow, and click the folder you want to search in.

(4) Click Find Now.

(5) Review the search results in the message area.

(6) When you finish searching, click to close the Find bar.

Move Messages to Another Folder

(1) Make sure you see the destination folder in the Folder List.

(2) Click the folder that contains the messages you want to move.

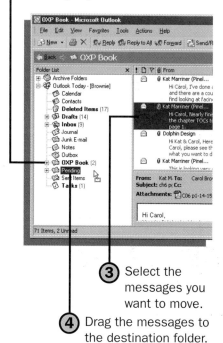

(3) Select the messages you want to move.

(4) Drag the messages to the destination folder.

> **!** **TIP:** You can use these same in- structions to move a folder, too— but only one folder at a time.

Managing Your Mailbox Size

If you get lots of e-mail, those messages can gobble up disk space, so enlist Outlook's help in keeping your mailbox trim. The first line of defense is deleting messages, a two-step process to prevent you from removing an important message too hastily. When you jettison a message or a folder, it makes its way to the Deleted Items folder. There it awaits more permanent deletion, which ordinarily happens when you exit Outlook. Next, Outlook offers a mailbox cleaning service that helps you identify the size of folders and offers you the option of deleting messages or *archiving* (that is, storing) them for future reference.

Temporarily Delete a Message or Folder

① Select the folder in the Folder List or the message you want to delete.

② Click Delete.

③ If you change your mind, click the Deleted Items folder to retrieve the folder or messages you deleted.

Delete a Message or Folder Permanently

(1) Choose Options from the Tools menu.

(2) Click the Other tab.

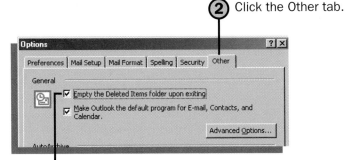

(3) Make sure the Empty The Deleted Items Folder Upon Exiting box is selected, and then click OK. When you quit Outlook, Outlook might ask if you're sure you want to delete these items permanently. Click Yes.

Clean Up Your Mailbox ⊚ NEW FEATURE

(1) Choose Mailbox Cleanup from the Tools menu.

(2) In the Mailbox Cleanup dialog box, click to see the size of your entire mailbox and each folder in it.

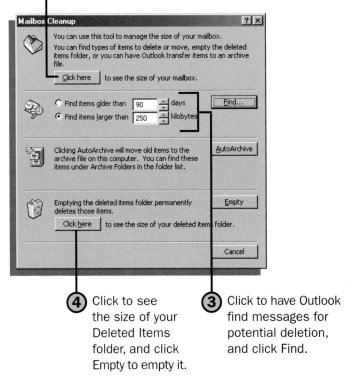

(4) Click to see the size of your Deleted Items folder, and click Empty to empty it.

(3) Click to have Outlook find messages for potential deletion, and click Find.

CAUTION: When you click AutoArchive in the Mailbox Cleanup dialog box, Outlook plunges right into archiving items according to its rules. Before you click this button, specify how you want Outlook to archive your folders. To do this, choose Options from the Tools menu, and click the Other tab. Then click AutoArchive, select the Run AutoArchive Every X Days check box, and specify archiving requirements.

TIP: To read up on AutoArchiving, click in the Ask A Question box in the upper right corner of the window. Type archiving, and then press the Enter key. Click About Archiving Items Using AutoArchive in the list of topics that appears.

Subduing Junk E-Mail

Outlook is a worthy ally in your battle against junk mail (popularly known as *spam*). Outlook can sort through incoming messages that meet criteria you set and will either mark the offending messages with the color of your choice or move them to the Junk E-Mail folder that Outlook sets up for this purpose. But how does Outlook know what to move? Outlook filters e-mail, applying certain rules—for example, it identifies e-mail with "money back" or "extra income" in the body of the message as junk and "must be 18" or "over 21" as adult content.

Manage Junk E-Mail

1 Click Organize.

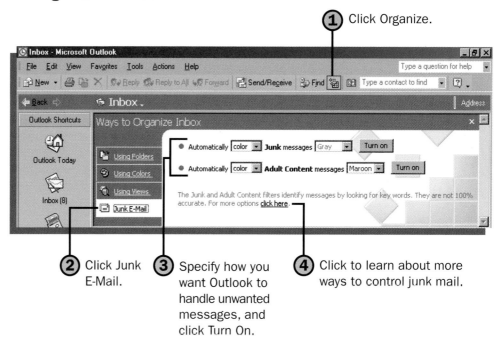

2 Click Junk E-Mail.

3 Specify how you want Outlook to handle unwanted messages, and click Turn On.

4 Click to learn about more ways to control junk mail.

CAUTION: Never respond to a *spammer* (someone who sends spam e-mail), even with the promise of being removed from a list. A response just confirms that your e-mail address is a viable one, and spawns even more spam.

TIP: To find out exactly what rules Outlook uses to filter undesirable e-mail, open this file on your hard disk: C:\Program Files\Microsoft Office\Office10\ 1033\Filters.txt.

Scheduling with Outlook

❋ NEW FEATURE

The Microsoft Outlook Calendar does what a day planner does for you—and a lot more. The Calendar can help you schedule meetings with others based on the times they're available; set up and schedule reminders for recurring appointments, meetings, or events; and choose how you view your calendar (using the standard daily, weekly, and monthly views; as a list of appointments or recurring events; or using other specialized ways of viewing upcoming happenings).

Outlook makes a distinction between appointments, meetings, and events:

● **Appointments** are those occurrences that don't involve inviting other people to a meeting and coordinating schedules.

● **Meetings** are appointments that require coordinating schedules with one or more people. Outlook provides tools to quickly invite others to a meeting via e-mail, coordinate schedules to determine the best meeting time, and reserve resources such as meeting rooms.

● **Events** are occurrences that last a whole day or longer, but that don't necessarily require all of your time. For example, a trade show might occur over several days, but you might also schedule meetings and appointments on those days as well.

With a few important exceptions, you work with all three in the same way, and we refer to them generically as *calendar items*.

Scheduling Appointments, Meetings, and Events

The simplest way to add a calendar item (an appointment, meeting, or event) is to type it directly into the calendar page. Calendar items you create in this way are automatically added as appointments, but you can quickly change an appointment into a meeting or event.

Add an Appointment, Meeting, or Event to Your Schedule

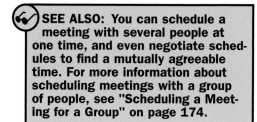

SEE ALSO: You can schedule a meeting with several people at one time, and even negotiate schedules to find a mutually agreeable time. For more information about scheduling meetings with a group of people, see "Scheduling a Meeting for a Group" on page 174.

(1) To change to Calendar view, click Calendar.

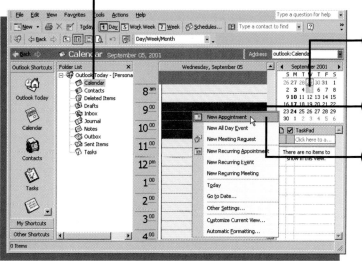

(2) To view the month you want, click the left or right arrow, and click the day you want.

(3) Drag the pointer to reserve the time you need.

(4) Right-click and choose New Appointment, New All Day Event, or New Meeting Request from the shortcut menu.

TIP: When you need to remind yourself to do something that isn't really an appointment—respond to an e-mail message or make a phone call, for instance—you can set a reminder for it as well. Reminders don't appear on your calendar, but you can schedule them much like you schedule appointments. For more information about scheduling tasks, see the Try This on page 171.

TRY THIS: The Outlook Calendar provides lots of options for categorizing, labeling, and otherwise customizing your view. Right-click the various buttons and labels in the window for a brief description of what each option does.

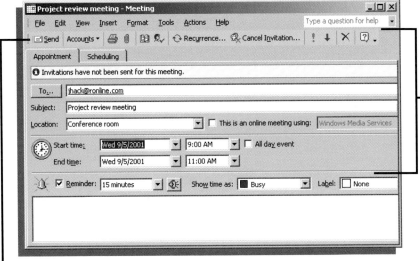

⑤ Type information and select options about the calendar item:

- Type a subject and location for the item as you want it to appear in your schedule.
- Click to make the item a recurring one.
- Click to set a reminder and choose how early you want to be reminded.
- If the item is a meeting, in the To box type in the e-mail addresses of those you want to invite to the meeting.

⑥ Click Send to schedule your meeting (or click Save And Close, if you're scheduling an appointment or event).

Changing Appointments, Meetings, and Events

Schedules change, and when they do, you can quickly update your calendar using a couple of techniques. If the time or date of an existing calendar item changes, you can simply drag the item to the new time or day. You also can edit details about an item, including its time and place, by double-clicking it, making your changes, and updating your calendar.

Drag an Appointment to a New Time or Day

(1) To change to Calendar view, click Calendar.

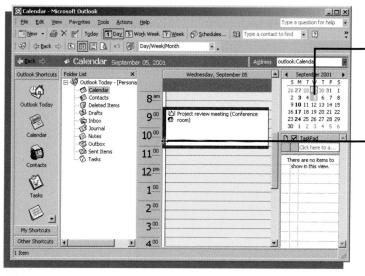

(2) Click the date on which the calendar item is currently scheduled.

(3) Position the mouse pointer over the left edge of the calendar item, until it changes to a four-headed arrow.

> **TIP:** You can quickly remove a calendar item from your schedule. Just click the item and press Delete.

> **TRY THIS:** Color labels for your calendar items can help you quickly differentiate high-priority entries on a busy schedule. To apply a color label, right-click a calendar item, choose Label from the shortcut menu, and click a label.

> **TIP:** If you're rescheduling calendar items from one day to another, you might find it helpful to display more days on the calendar. To do this, click the Work Week, Week, or Month button on the Standard toolbar. You can then easily drag calendar items from one day to another.

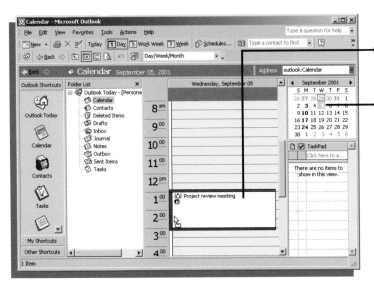

④ To change the calendar item to a new time on the same day, drag it to the new time.

⑤ To change the calendar item to the same time on a different day, drag it to the new day.

! **TIP:** If you have many calendar items, you might find it useful to categorize them by type. To do this, right-click a calendar item and choose **Categories** from the shortcut menu. In the Categories dialog box, check all the categories to which the calendar item belongs, and click **OK**. You can then view your calendar events sorted by category by choosing **By Category** from the Current View list.

TRY THIS: To remind yourself to prepare for an important appointment, meeting, or event, drag a copy of the item to the TaskPad list in the lower right corner of your calendar. Be sure to drag the item to the list itself, not to the TaskPad heading above the list. When you're finished, click **Save And Close**. To cross the item off the list, select the check box next to the occurrence.

! **TIP:** You can make a calendar item extend over multiple days. To do this, click the **Work Week** or **Week** button to change the view. Then, drag the upper or lower border of the item across the border separating the days.

Viewing and Printing a Calendar

With Outlook, you can change the way you view your calendar. The shortest view—one day—is the default, but you can also get a quick view of your week, work week, or month. You can also change how calendar items are listed—for example, you can have Outlook list your calendar items for either a week or a month. Of course, you can then print a daily schedule, a weekly or monthly calendar, or a list of calendar items to carry with you. When you print a calendar, Outlook prints whatever the current view displays—the day, week, month, or the list.

Change a Calendar Format

1 To change to Calendar view, click Calendar.

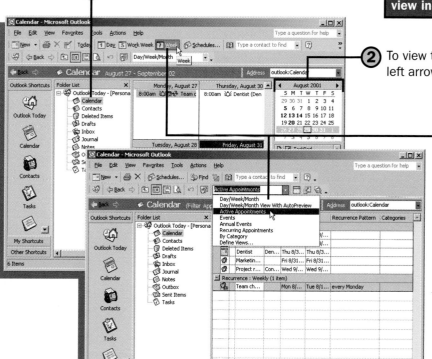

> **TRY THIS:** You can also drag to select only certain days in the Month task pane—for example, just the next three days or the next two weeks—that you want to view in the Schedule task pane.

2 To view the month you want, click the right or left arrow, and then click the day you want.

3 Specify the Calendar view:
- To change the number of days displayed, click the appropriate button on the Standard toolbar.
- To change the current Calendar view, click the option you want in the Current View list on the Advanced toolbar. (If this toolbar is not already open, point to Toolbars on the View menu, and click Advanced.)

Print a Calendar

① Make sure Outlook is displaying the view of your calendar that you want to print.

② Click the Print button.

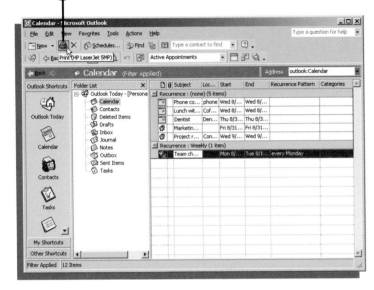

③ Click a print style, and confirm the date range or number of lines (depending on the calendar view) to print.

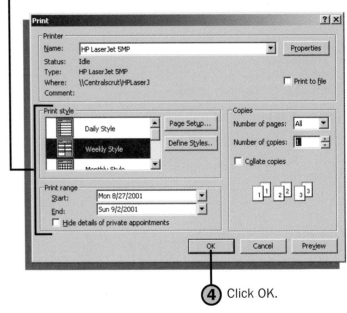

④ Click OK.

> ⚠ **TIP:** You can preview your calendar before printing it by clicking Preview in the lower right corner of the Print dialog box.

> ⚠ **TIP:** Like the calendar in your kitchen, the Outlook Calendar can be a handy reference for past events. For example, scheduling your billable work time can make filling out a timesheet or an invoice a snap—you just review your calendar at the end of the billing period.

Scheduling a Meeting for a Group

With only a little direction from you, Outlook can handle many of the routine tasks of inviting and negotiating times when a group of people can convene. You can use Outlook to send a special type of e-mail message—a meeting request—to as many people as you want to invite to a meeting; they can then accept, decline, or propose another time. When invitees respond to invitations, their answers are automatically logged in and placed on the calendar. If your organization uses Microsoft Exchange Server, you can share information about your schedule with others or, if your organization doesn't use Exchange Server, you can use the free Microsoft Office Internet Free/Busy Service instead.

Schedule a Group Meeting

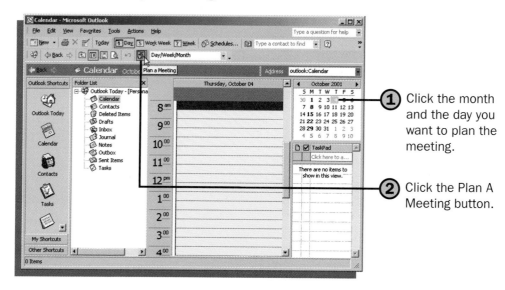

① Click the month and the day you want to plan the meeting.

② Click the Plan A Meeting button.

⚠ **TIP:** If resources such as meeting rooms have e-mail addresses on your Exchange Server, you can schedule these resources just like you schedule meetings with people. Check with your e-mail administrator to determine if this is the case.

⚠ **TIP:** You can set Outlook to automatically accept meeting requests or automatically decline conflicting or recurring meeting requests. To do this, choose Tools from the Options menu. Then click Calendar Options, and click Resource Scheduling.

⚠ **TIP:** If you regularly invite the same group of people to a meeting, you can set up a group schedule. To do this, click Schedules, and click New in the Group Schedules dialog box. Then name the group, and add members to it.

✓ **SEE ALSO:** For more information about the Microsoft Office Internet Free/Busy Service, see "Using the Microsoft Office Internet Free/Busy Service" on page 176.

3 Type e-mail addresses for the people you are inviting to the meeting, one for each line. Or click Add Others to select addresses from the Outlook Address book.

4 To set the meeting start and end times, do one of the following:
- Drag the green and red bars to set the meeting start and end times.
- Type in the times.
- If you have either Exchange Server or have set up the Free/Busy Service, you can click AutoPick Next to find the next time that everyone in your list is available.

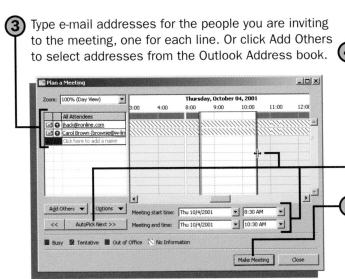

5 Click Make Meeting when you are satisfied with the meeting time.

6 Fill out the details for the meeting:
- Type a subject and location for the meeting.
- To make the meeting an all-day event, select the All Day Event check box.
- To make the meeting a recurring one, click Recurrence, click the options you want, and click OK.
- Select this check box if the meeting is online; you must have Microsoft NetMeeting (which is included in Microsoft Windows 2000, or available for free download from Microsoft for earlier versions of Windows); Microsoft Windows Media Services; or Microsoft Exchange Server to use this feature. Click the down arrow, and click the service you have.

7 Click Send when you are satisfied with the options you've chosen.

8 Click Close.

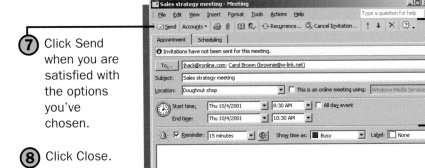

Using the Microsoft Office Internet Free/Busy Service ⊕ NEW FEATURE

Scheduling meetings is a lot easier when everyone's schedule information is available to everyone else in an organization. If your organization uses Microsoft Exchange Server, you probably already have access to schedule information. If your organization doesn't use Exchange Server, you can still share schedule information using the Free/Busy Service. (You can use both methods to share schedule information if you want.) After you set up the Free/Busy Service on your computer, Outlook automatically publishes information about your free and busy times. Only those to whom you have given access to this information—and who have set up the Free/Busy Service on their computers—can view your schedule.

If you try to schedule a meeting and your organization doesn't use Exchange Server, Outlook offers to help you set up the Free/Busy Service. Click Join to connect to the Free/Busy Internet site, and follow the instructions.

> ⚠ TIP: The first time you use the Free/Busy Service, Outlook might need to install files from your Office CD. Outlook will prompt you if it needs to install files.

Manage Free/Busy Options

① Choose Options from the Tools menu.

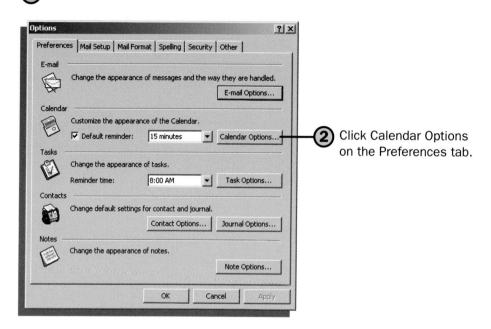

② Click Calendar Options on the Preferences tab.

> ⚠ TIP: To allow people using programs other than Outlook to schedule meetings, make sure the When Sending Meeting Requests Over The Internet, Use iCalendar Format check box is selected in the Calendar Options dialog box.

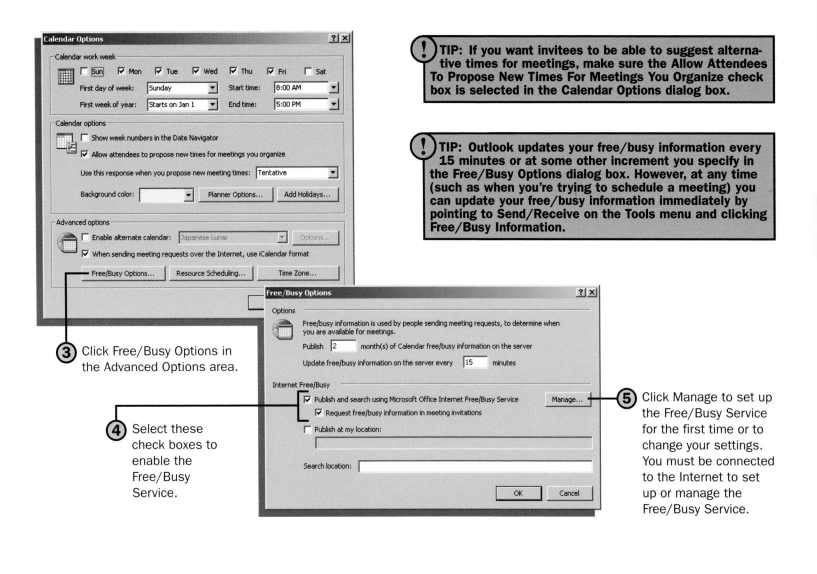

TIP: If you want invitees to be able to suggest alternative times for meetings, make sure the Allow Attendees To Propose New Times For Meetings You Organize check box is selected in the Calendar Options dialog box.

TIP: Outlook updates your free/busy information every 15 minutes or at some other increment you specify in the Free/Busy Options dialog box. However, at any time (such as when you're trying to schedule a meeting) you can update your free/busy information immediately by pointing to Send/Receive on the Tools menu and clicking Free/Busy Information.

③ Click Free/Busy Options in the Advanced Options area.

④ Select these check boxes to enable the Free/Busy Service.

⑤ Click Manage to set up the Free/Busy Service for the first time or to change your settings. You must be connected to the Internet to set up or manage the Free/Busy Service.

Personalizing Your Calendar

Like all Microsoft Office programs, Outlook provides options to change the way your calendar looks and works. Your choices include when (and if) the Calendar reminds you of appointments, which days to include in your work week, and what appearance your calendar will have.

Change Calendar Options

TRY THIS: You can also change the appearance of your calendar simply by dragging the borders between areas in the Outlook window. For example, to make the daily schedule wider, drag either of its vertical borders toward the edge of the Outlook window.

① Choose Options from the Tools menu.

② Select the Default Reminder check box to change the amount of time before an appointment that Outlook will display a reminder message, or clear this check box to turn off the reminder.

③ For more choices, click Calendar Options.

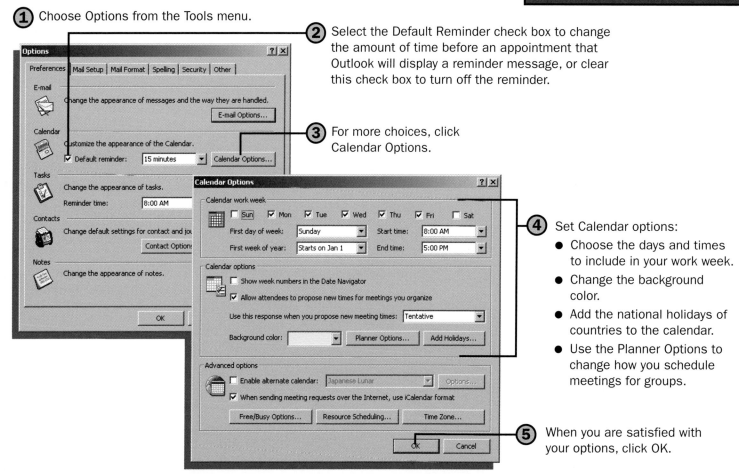

④ Set Calendar options:
- Choose the days and times to include in your work week.
- Change the background color.
- Add the national holidays of countries to the calendar.
- Use the Planner Options to change how you schedule meetings for groups.

⑤ When you are satisfied with your options, click OK.

Managing Personal Information Using Outlook

Microsoft Outlook, the Microsoft Office electronic day planner, helps you communicate through e-mail, schedule and track your daily activities, and maintain your address book and calendar. Folders organize and store the information these activities generate. Each folder also serves as a home base or the place you go to conduct the business at hand—compose e-mail in the Inbox, refer to your address book in Contacts, and so on. (You can only access these folders from within Outlook, however, so don't look for them on your hard disk.)

● **Outlook Today** presents your day (or more) at a glance—schedule, tasks, and the number of unread e-mail messages awaiting you.

● The **Inbox** is mission central for Outlook's e-mail system.

● The **Deleted Items** folder holds any Outlook entry you delete while it awaits more permanent deletion when you empty the folder.

● Use the **Calendar** to schedule and track meetings.

● **Contacts** serve as your online address book.

● The **Tasks** folder provides a spot for you to note the things you have to do and then helps you monitor your progress.

● The **Journal** stores information about events you want to track.

● **Notes** are the electronic equivalent of sticky notes.

Previewing Your Day's Work

Outlook Today gives you a glimpse of your upcoming day—your schedule, the things you need to accomplish, and the number of unread e-mail messages waiting in your e-mail box. Want to see more than a day at a time? Or only the tasks due today? No problem—it's easy to customize Outlook Today.

Get a Bird's-Eye View of Your Workday

① Click Outlook Today.
If you don't see Outlook Today, choose Outlook Bar from the View menu.

② Click any entry to see details.

Address box

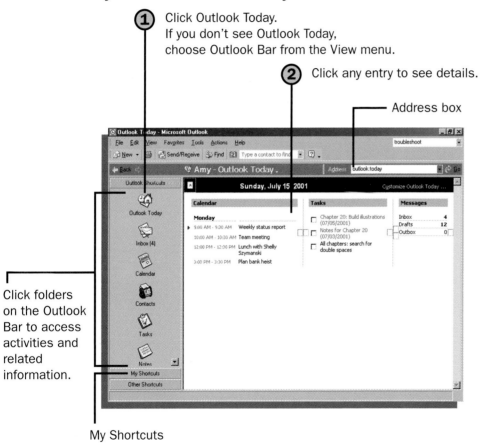

Click folders on the Outlook Bar to access activities and related information.

My Shortcuts

TIP: To return to Outlook Today after you open a Messages folder, just click the Outlook Today shortcut on the Outlook Bar.

TRY THIS: You can add a Web link to My Shortcuts at the bottom of the Outlook bar—for example, to your company's home page or to a favored portal. Enter the Web address in the Address box in the upper right corner of the Outlook Today window, and then press the Enter key. When the Web page opens, click the New down arrow on the Outlook toolbar, and then click Outlook Bar Shortcut To Web Page.

Personalize Outlook Today

① Click Outlook Today.

② Click Customize Outlook Today.

④ Click Save Changes.

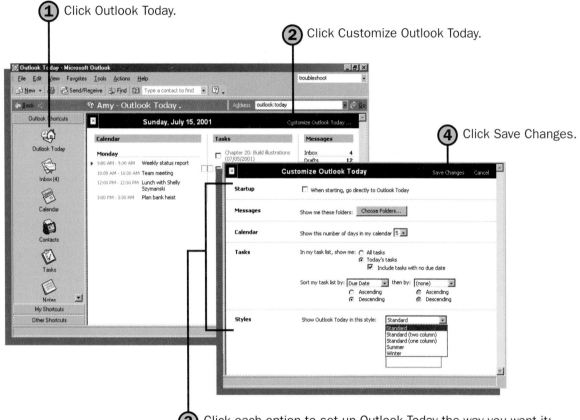

③ Click each option to set up Outlook Today the way you want it:

- Set Outlook Today as your home page.
- Choose the e-mail folders you want to see.
- Choose how many days you want to see at a time.
- Indicate which tasks you want to see on your to-do list and in what order.
- Choose the style that suits you best.

Creating an Online Address Book

You can say goodbye forever to marked-up, dog-eared address books with the Outlook Address Book, a collection of address books whose offerings vary depending on your setup. For example, if you're a corporate employee, you'll likely have access to the corporate-wide address book set up by your system administrator, the Global Address List.

Outlook's primary address book, however, is the Outlook Address Book, best known as *Contacts*. This is the most powerful and flexible of all the address books, with a reach that lets you use its information in other Office products—for example, making an

address available for correspondence in Microsoft Word. The Contacts list contains all the details you could want to store on someone (and then some)—from name, address, and up to 19 phone numbers (for the truly connected) to birthdays and nicknames.

If there's a group of people you e-mail frequently—say, the parents in your child's class or your soccer team—you can gather all their names together under one entry (and name)—*Parents* or *Soccer Team,* for example. You can then send e-mail to everyone on the distribution list simply by typing that name.

Create a New Contact

1 Click the New down arrow, and click Contact.

2 Type the information you want in the Contact form.

Find A Contact box

After you type the full name, Outlook automatically enters the last name first so you can search for either name.

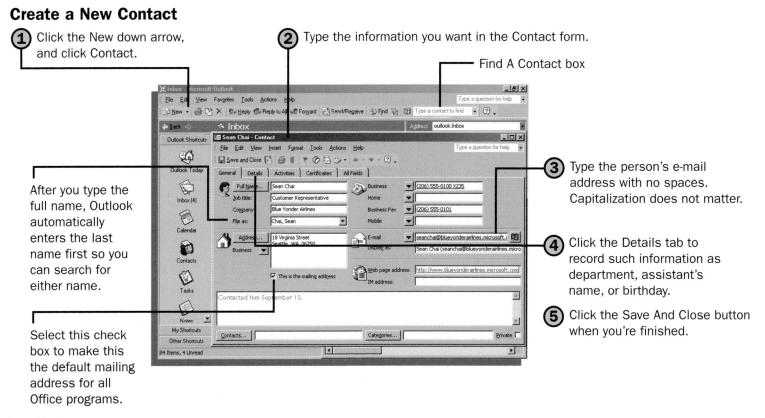

3 Type the person's e-mail address with no spaces. Capitalization does not matter.

4 Click the Details tab to record such information as department, assistant's name, or birthday.

5 Click the Save And Close button when you're finished.

Select this check box to make this the default mailing address for all Office programs.

Open the Contacts Folder

1 Choose Outlook Bar from the View menu, and click the Contacts shortcut.

Create One Contact for a Group of People

1 Click the New down arrow, and click Distribution List.

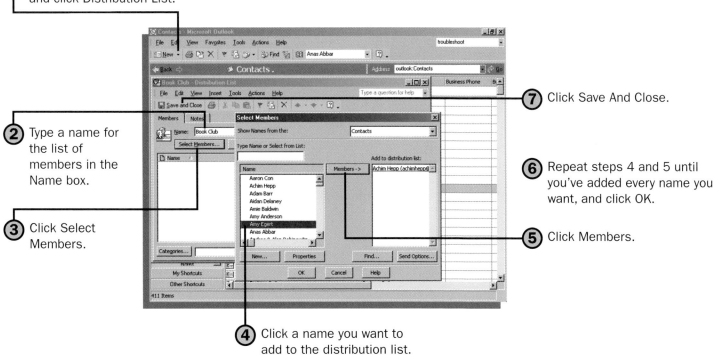

2 Type a name for the list of members in the Name box.

3 Click Select Members.

4 Click a name you want to add to the distribution list.

5 Click Members.

6 Repeat steps 4 and 5 until you've added every name you want, and click OK.

7 Click Save And Close.

Building on Your Address Book

We live in a culture of constant flux. People switch jobs and names, are assigned new area codes, buy cell phones, or swap Internet service providers (ISPs) and e-mail addresses with mind-blowing frequency. Outlook was designed to handle this sort of change, making it easy for you to update or copy information about a person into your address book.

Copy a Contact from an E-Mail Message

1 In the Inbox, double-click an e-mail message that contains the address you want to copy.

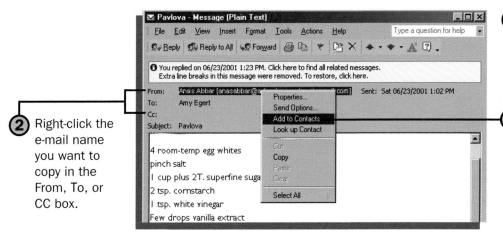

2 Right-click the e-mail name you want to copy in the From, To, or CC box.

3 Click Add To Contacts.

4 Review the Contact form, adding any information you want, and then click the Save And Close button.

Update an Existing Contact

1 Type the name you want to update in the Find A Contact box, and press the Enter key.

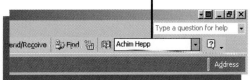

2 Change the information you want on the Contact form, and click the Save And Close button.

> **! TIP:** If you have more than one person from the same company to add to your Contacts list, you can make short work of it. Follow step 1 in "Update an Existing Contact" to open the contact. Choose New Contact From Same Company from the Actions menu in the Contact form. Outlook creates the new contact and copies all the business-related data; you only need fill in the person's name and other personal details.

Creating an Online To-Do List

Unlike a list posted on your fridge or tucked into your day planner, Outlook's Tasks list never gets lost. It also never deletes an undone task until you actually mark it as done. Furthermore, if you tend to be forgetful, Outlook can send you a reminder of the things you need to do.

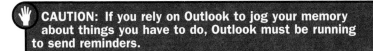

CAUTION: If you rely on Outlook to jog your memory about things you have to do, Outlook must be running to send reminders.

Create a New Task

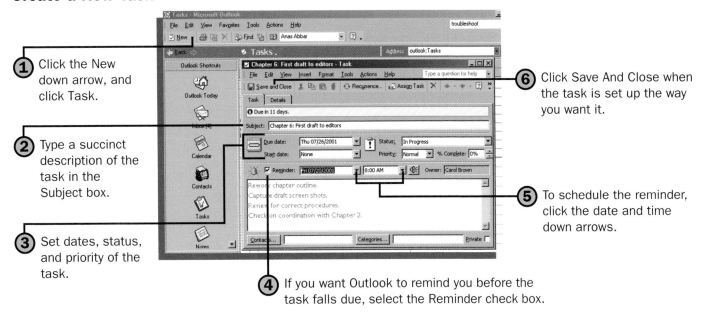

① Click the New down arrow, and click Task.

② Type a succinct description of the task in the Subject box.

③ Set dates, status, and priority of the task.

④ If you want Outlook to remind you before the task falls due, select the Reminder check box.

⑥ Click Save And Close when the task is set up the way you want it.

⑤ To schedule the reminder, click the date and time down arrows.

TIP: The fastest way to add a task (and due date) to the list is to type the task name in the Click Here To Add A New Task box. (That box is below Subject at the top of the Tasks window.) Then click the box just below Due Date, and click the down arrow. Choose a date from the calendar, and press the Enter key. You can always add reminders or change the status of the task later by double-clicking it on the Tasks list.

Managing Your Online To-Do List

In addition to using your Outlook to-do list to track things you do just once, you can make short work of tracking tasks that come up regularly, like planning a weekly meeting or cleaning the gutters on your house. You can even enlist Outlook's help in delegating your work.

When you're ready to remove a completed task from the list, you delete tasks just as you would e-mail—the task goes to the Deleted Items folder, a protective stop along the way to permanent deletion.

Mark a Task As Complete or Delete It

4 To delete the task, click Delete.

3 To mark the task as complete, select the check box in this column. Outlook makes it gray and draws a line through it.

2 Select the task you want to work with.

1 Click Tasks.

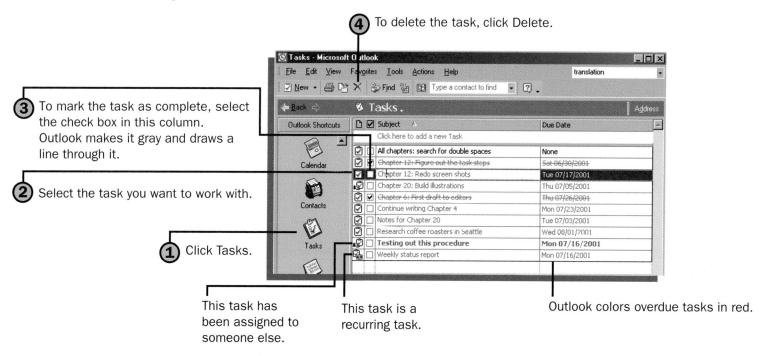

This task has been assigned to someone else.

This task is a recurring task.

Outlook colors overdue tasks in red.

> **TIP:** If you change your mind after deleting a task, press Ctrl+Z to restore the task to the list.

> **TIP:** You can shuffle tasks on the list simply by dragging them. Before you can do this, however, point to Current View on the View menu, and click Customize Current View. In the View Summary dialog box, click Sort, click Clear All, and then click OK twice. *Now* you're ready to drag tasks around.

Create a Recurring Task

(1) Click the New down arrow, and click Task.

(2) Type a description of the task in the Subject box.

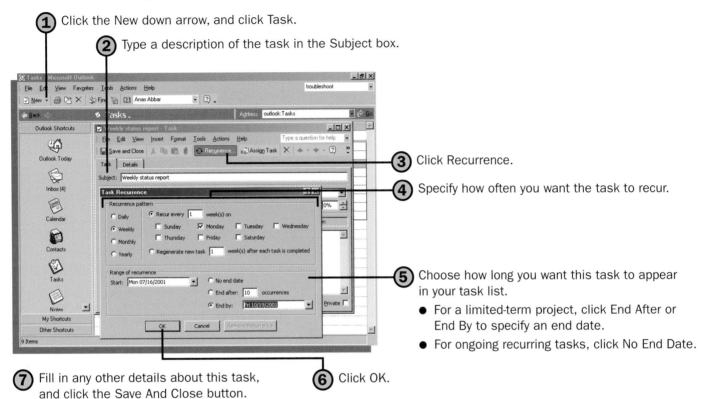

(3) Click Recurrence.

(4) Specify how often you want the task to recur.

(5) Choose how long you want this task to appear in your task list.

- For a limited-term project, click End After or End By to specify an end date.
- For ongoing recurring tasks, click No End Date.

(7) Fill in any other details about this task, and click the Save And Close button.

(6) Click OK.

TIP: Problems with tasks? Click in the Ask A Question box in the upper right corner of the window. Type troubleshoot**, and then press the Enter key. Then click Troubleshoot Tasks in the list and look for a description of your problem. Click a topic to read the solution.**

TRY THIS: Let others help you out—assign a task to someone else. Click the New down arrow, and click Task Request. On the Task tab, type the name of the person you're delegating to and a description of the task. Set the due date, indicate how you want to keep tabs on progress, and then click Send. The person can accept your assignment or not—but you'll get an e-mail message either way letting you know.

Keeping a Journal

Have you ever gotten to the end of a busy day and wondered, "What *did* I do today"? Well, Outlook's Journal can help answer that question. The Journal stores information on events you want to track, such as telephone calls you make or letters and e-mail messages you write. It creates some journal entries automatically—for instance, e-mail messages you send and receive or certain Office documents you open. You can also create a journal entry manually and record pretty much anything else you do—telephone calls made, meetings attended, and so on.

Use this feature judiciously, however. If you're over-enthusiastic about recording too much, you can slow Outlook's response time. So, for example, it might be a more efficient use of system resources to direct Outlook to sift through all your e-mail, notes, and upcoming appointments than to use the Journal to track this. And finally, to keep the size of your Journal folder in check, save and then store the journal entries (that is, *archive* it) frequently.

Set the Journal to Record Activities Automatically

1 Choose Options from the Tools menu.

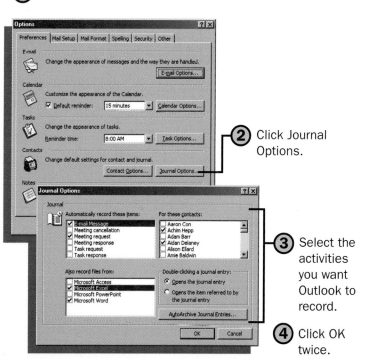

2 Click Journal Options.

3 Select the activities you want Outlook to record.

4 Click OK twice.

! **TIP:** To archive your Journal, choose Options from the Tools menu. Click Journal Options on the Preferences tab, and click AutoArchive Journal Entries. In the Journal Properties dialog box, specify how you want to archive your journal entries, and then click OK twice.

! **TIP:** To stop automatic journaling, retrace the steps you took to start it. Choose Options from the Tools menu, and then click Journal Options. In the Journal Options dialog box, clear all the check boxes or select individually the ones you want to clear, and then click OK twice.

! **TIP:** To track down activity with someone whose name is in your address book, start by opening the contact information. In the Find A Contact box at the top of the window, type the name of the contact, and press the Enter key. Then click the Activities tab. While Outlook starts looking for *all* activity with this person, click the Show down arrow. Choose the type of activity to narrow Outlook's search, and press the Enter key. This might take a few minutes. Click the Save And Close button when you've found what you wanted.

Record an Activity Manually As You Work

② Type a brief, but memorable, description of the activity.

① Click the New down arrow, and click Journal Entry.

③ Click the Entry Type down arrow, and click the most appropriate activity type in the list.

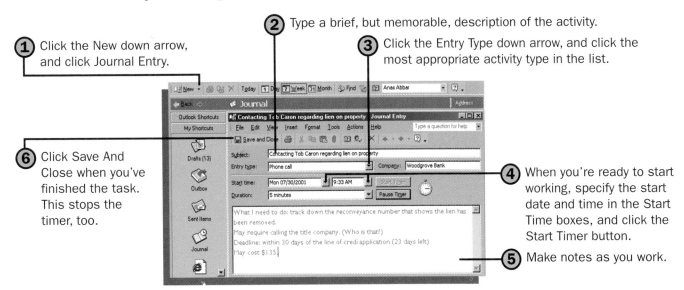

⑥ Click Save And Close when you've finished the task. This stops the timer, too.

④ When you're ready to start working, specify the start date and time in the Start Time boxes, and click the Start Timer button.

⑤ Make notes as you work.

Review a Journal Entry

② Click the Entry Type plus sign (+) to see the details of that entry.

Click to change your view of the timeline.

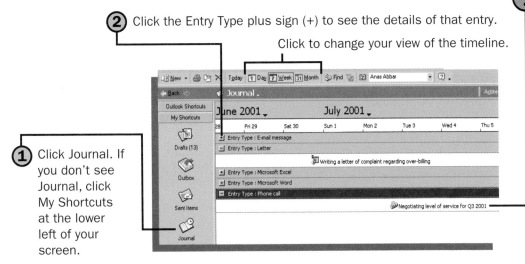

① Click Journal. If you don't see Journal, click My Shortcuts at the lower left of your screen.

③ Double-click the expanded journal entry to open it.

TIP: You can also return to the Journal and record something you did after the fact. Create a new entry as you did in "Record an Activity Manually As You Work": follow steps 1 through 4, but do not start the timer in step 4. Instead, type the time the activity took in the Duration box, and then transcribe your notes in the box below to store them.

Making Notes to Yourself

Outlook furnishes an endless supply of electronic sticky notes that stick with you. Easy to create. Easy to sort. Easy to delete. Virtually impossible to lose.

Use Notes in Outlook to scribble an idea or reminder, save shards of text for later use, or record a Web link. You can color-code notes to organize them—for example, pink for Web links, green for reminders, blue for a certain project. Outlook also saves your notes automatically so you don't have to think about it.

Write Yourself a Note

③ Type your note.

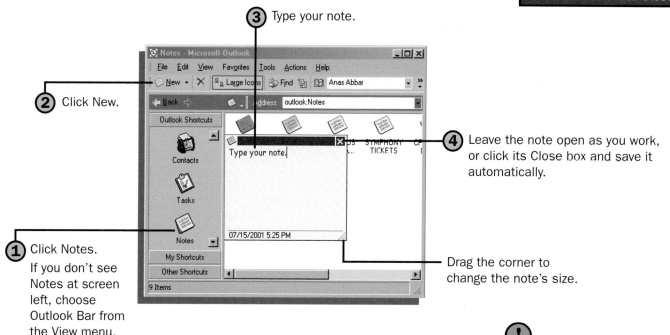

② Click New.

④ Leave the note open as you work, or click its Close box and save it automatically.

① Click Notes.

If you don't see Notes at screen left, choose Outlook Bar from the View menu.

Drag the corner to change the note's size.

TRY THIS: Today a note; tomorrow a task or appointment. Simply drag the note onto the Calendar or Tasks shortcuts on the Outlook Bar, and Outlook will open the appropriate dialog box to put it on your calendar or to-do list. You just need to fill in the details, and then click the Save And Close button.

TIP: If your note is extra long, you can scroll through it using the Page Up and Page Down keys. Or give in to verbosity, and drag the lower right corner of the note to make it big enough so you can see it all at once.

Open a Note

(1) Click Notes on the Outlook Bar.

(2) Double-click the note you want to open.

Change the Color of a Note

(2) Double-click the note you want to color.

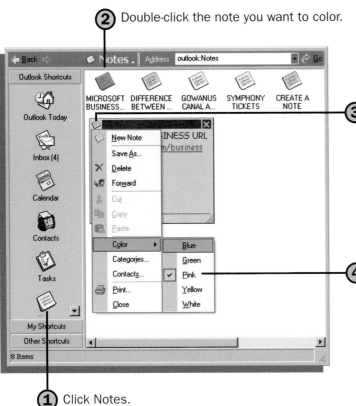

(1) Click Notes.

Delete a Note

(1) Right-click the note you want to delete, and choose Delete from the shortcut menu.

> **TRY THIS:** You can change the default yellow note color, font, and font size. To do this, choose Options from the Tools menu. In the Options dialog box under Notes, click Note Options. Make the changes you want, and then click OK twice.

(3) Click the Note icon, and point to Color on the shortcut menu.

(4) Click the color you want.

> **SEE ALSO:** For information about how to sort notes, see "Sorting and Filtering Data in a List" on page 148.

Sorting and Filtering Contacts, Tasks, and Other Outlook Entries

Every folder in Outlook (Contacts, Tasks, Inbox, and so on) provides half a dozen ways or more to view its entries, with each folder offering different choices.

In some views, Outlook *sorts* (rearranges) *all* the entries—for example, if you create a phone list from your contact list, Outlook sorts all the entries to create a list in alphabetical order. Other views actually *filter* out all but those entries that satisfy certain criteria—making a list, for example, of only tasks that are overdue or of e-mail messages just from the last seven days.

In some views, Outlook displays column headings. Look closely and you'll see they actually do double duty as buttons. These buttons work like light switches: click to sort entries in ascending order (low to high, A to Z, most recent to oldest); click again to sort entries in descending order (high to low, Z to A, oldest to most recent).

Sort or Filter Entries Using Outlook's Criteria

① Point to Current View on the View menu.

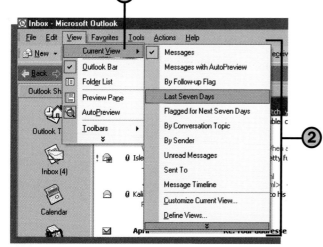

② Click the view you want.

TRY THIS: Outlook also lets you find specific items using your own criteria—every address in a certain postal code or just the tasks you've delegated, for example. Point to Current View on the View menu, and then click Customize Current View. Click the Filter button in the View Summary dialog box, and then make your choices on any of the tabs to narrow the search. Then click OK twice.

To return to your view of all items, retrace your steps: point to Current View on the View menu, and then click Customize Current View. Click the Filter button, click Clear All, and click OK twice.

TIP: Outlook clues you in when your choice of view will sort or filter the list: if you see the word "by", meaning "By Sender" or "By Company," Outlook will sort the list; otherwise it will filter the list.

Sort Entries Quickly

Before sorting: tasks are listed in alphabetical order.

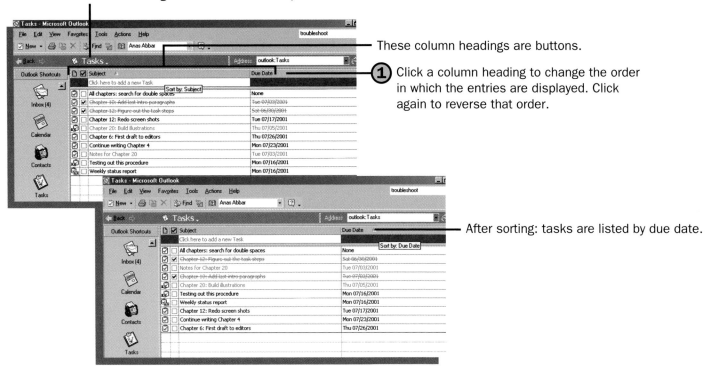

These column headings are buttons.

(1) Click a column heading to change the order in which the entries are displayed. Click again to reverse that order.

After sorting: tasks are listed by due date.

Remove a Sort Order

(1) Point to Current View on the View menu, and click Customize Current View.

(2) Click Sort.

(3) Click the Sort Items By down arrow, click None, and then click OK.

Printing from Outlook

In Outlook, you can print almost everything—from one contact or note to a list of all the e-mail messages in your Inbox or a portable list of every contact in your address book. (One note: you cannot print a Journal timeline.) Depending on the view, Outlook offers different printing options. For example, if you print from the Inbox, you'll get different printing options than if you print an open e-mail message. The illustration below shows printing from the Contacts folder.

Print Outlook Entries or Lists

(1) Switch to the folder you want to print from.

(2) Point to Current View on the View menu, and click the view you want to print.

> **CAUTION:** Unlike printing in other Office programs, it's not a good idea to print in Outlook using the Print button on the Standard toolbar because the printed results depend so much on how you display the information. For best results, use the steps in "Print Outlook Entries or Lists" as your guide.

(4) Choose Print from the File menu.

(3) If you want to print one or just a few entries, select the entry (or entries) you want to print:
- Click to select one entry.
- To select more than one entry, hold down the Ctrl key while you click each entry.

(5) In the Print Style area, click the style you want to print.

Outlook offers these printing choices if you've selected a few contacts in the Address Card view of Contacts.

(6) Make other printing choices as needed.

Click to Preview what you're printing.

In this case, Outlook lets you specify whether to print all or just selected contacts.

(7) Click OK when you're ready to print.

Collaborating Using Office

In a team environment, the process of creating a document—which typically includes planning and conceptualizing, outlining, drafting, editing, reviewing, revising, and publishing—is almost always shared among a number of people. Whether you're in an academic, a personal, or a business environment, chances are you'll have others working with your documents. Often the people who contribute to your documents are not physically nearby; instead, you communicate with collaborators via marked-up hard copy, telephone, e-mail, and Web sites.

Collaboration can be vital to creating a high-quality document. However, *managing* collaboration—tracking changes made by various writers, editors, and managers, or even just among a few colleagues—can be difficult. Microsoft Office XP solves this problem by using a combination of e-mail and collaboration features such as in-document comments, markup for tracking changes, file sharing, and online meetings, allowing you to effectively communicate with other team members and to coordinate your group's efforts.

In the following tasks, we'll show you how to work effectively with others using Office XP's standard collaboration features, allowing you to take full advantage of change tracking, e-mail, the Web, and other communication and workgroup tools.

Sending Out Documents for Review

Editors, managers, and other writers can help you ensure your document is clear and as free from errors as possible. Giving friends and colleagues copies to review is easy if you're in the same office, but if your collaborators are miles away, or even on different continents, handing out printouts by the water cooler isn't an option.

E-mail is a great way to distribute documents back and forth among reviewers, whether they're right next door or on the other side of the world. If you have an e-mail program (such as Microsoft Outlook) set up on your computer, you can e-mail your documents for review directly from the Microsoft Word, Microsoft PowerPoint, or Microsoft Excel window you're editing them in.

Use E-Mail to Send Out Documents for Review ⊕ NEW FEATURE

1 Point to Send To on the Word, Excel, or PowerPoint File menu, and click Mail Recipient (For Review).

2 Type the e-mail addresses of your reviewers.

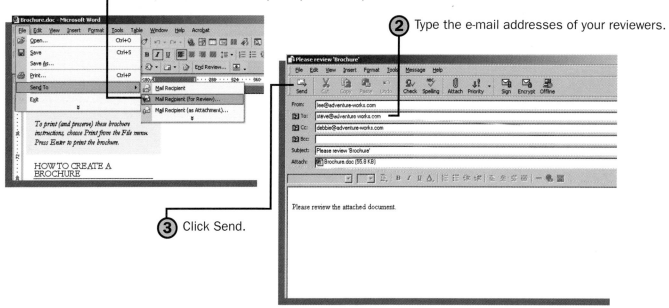

3 Click Send.

> ⚠ **TIP:** When sending out a document for review, you can attach additional documents to the outgoing e-mail message, add text to the message body, and make any other changes you would with a normal e-mail message.

Adding Comments

When collaborating on a document as an author, reviewer, or editor, you need a way to take notes, which can include reminders to yourself or brief comments to others—questions, corrections, or explanations. Inserting comments in a Word document, Excel spreadsheet, or PowerPoint presentation allows you to place your notes where other team members can see them as they work.

Insert a Comment into a Document

1 Choose Comment from the Insert menu.

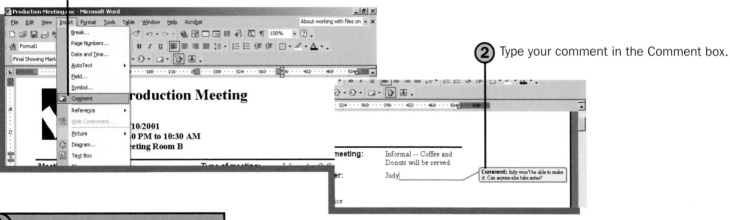

2 Type your comment in the Comment box.

> **TIP:** Pausing the mouse pointer over a comment or the text the comment refers to will show you additional information about the comment. In Word, it will show who made the comment and when they made it; in Excel, it will show who made the comment and its text; and in PowerPoint, it shows the comment's creator, time, and text.

> **TIP:** When printing, you can choose how (and if) comments are printed by clicking one of the options in the Print What list in the Print dialog box.

> **TRY THIS:** To see all the comments in your documents, click the Show down arrow on the Reviewing toolbar, and click Reviewing Pane.

Tracking Changes

When you've distributed a document for others to comment on or edit, you need to track who's making what changes. It's also nice to be able to review changes, and go back to the original version if the edits remove or distort important information. Office XP documents allow you to track all changes proposed by others, and then selectively accept or reject their suggestions.

Enable Change Tracking in Word

1 Choose Track Changes from the Tools menu.

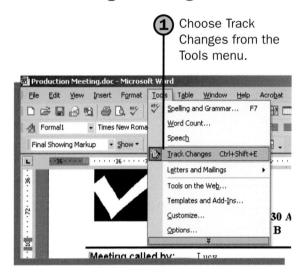

Enable Change Tracking in Excel

1 Point to Track Changes on the Tools menu, and click Highlight Changes.

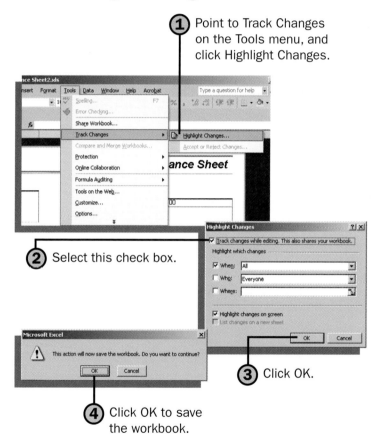

2 Select this check box.

3 Click OK.

4 Click OK to save the workbook.

Accept or Reject a Change in Word

(1) Right-click a change, and click Accept or Reject.

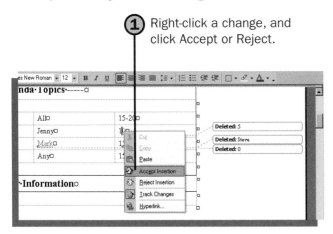

Accept or Reject a Change in Excel

(1) Point to Track Changes on the Tools menu, and click Accept Or Reject Changes.

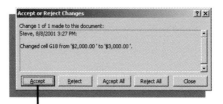

(2) Click OK.

(3) Click Accept or Reject to accept or reject the changes in the highlighted cell and go on to the next change.

(!) **TIP:** Word can display changes a number of ways. By default, changes appear inline with text in Normal view. In Print Preview view, insertions are kept inline with the rest of the document's text, while deletions and format changes are displayed as callouts on the right side of the page.

TRY THIS: To accept or reject all changes in a Word document, click Accept Change (or Reject Change/Delete Comment) on the Reviewing toolbar, and select Accept All Changes In Document (or Reject All Changes In Document).

TRY THIS: In Excel, you can limit change tracking to particular parts of the spreadsheet, and also allow yourself free rein to edit while tracking everyone else's changes. In the Highlight Changes dialog box, select the Who or Where check box, click the Who or Where down arrow, and then click the options you want.

Discussing a Document On Line ⊛ NEW FEATURE

Discussing a document through e-mail can be difficult when you have to wait for the next set of comments to know what other people think or have changed. If you're working on a document in a time-critical situation, for example, if you have a presentation to give later in the day, you may need a more interactive editing process. If your system administrator or Internet service provider (ISP) has set up a discussion server, you can discuss documents on line, which lets you send messages back and forth between collaborators while you edit the document at the same time.

> **SEE ALSO:** For more information about having online discussions with team members, see "Creating and Working with a SharePoint Team Web Site" on page 319.

Set Up Discussions in a Document

(1) Point to Online Collaboration on the Word, Excel, or PowerPoint Tools menu, and click Web Discussions.

(2) Click the Discussions down arrow on the Discussions toolbar, and click Discussion Options.

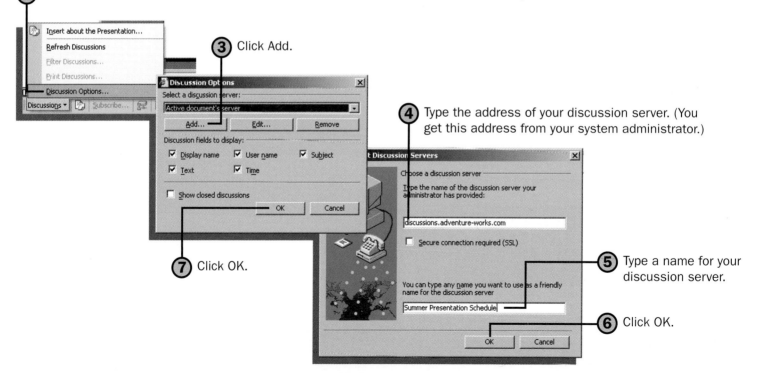

(3) Click Add.

(4) Type the address of your discussion server. (You get this address from your system administrator.)

(5) Type a name for your discussion server.

(6) Click OK.

(7) Click OK.

Add a New Discussion

① Click Insert Discussion on the Discussions toolbar.

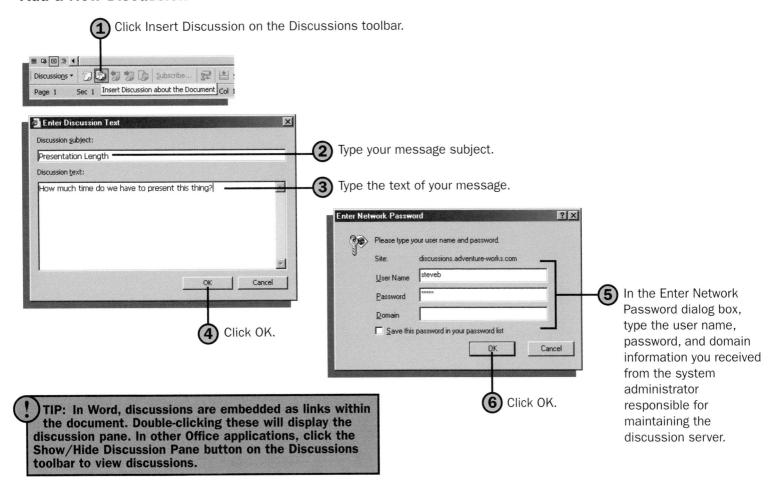

② Type your message subject.

③ Type the text of your message.

④ Click OK.

⑤ In the Enter Network Password dialog box, type the user name, password, and domain information you received from the system administrator responsible for maintaining the discussion server.

⑥ Click OK.

TIP: In Word, discussions are embedded as links within the document. Double-clicking these will display the discussion pane. In other Office applications, click the Show/Hide Discussion Pane button on the Discussions toolbar to view discussions.

Comparing and Merging Changes and Comments

It's not always possible for members of a team to work on a document sequentially. For situations in which two or more people are reviewing a document—and inserting revisions and comments—simultaneously, Word, Excel, and PowerPoint let you merge all the edits from multiple reviewers into a single document, so you can check reviewers' comments and changes in a single pass. Document merging keeps track of who made additions, deletions, and comments, which you can approve or reject just like in other forms of change tracking in Office.

SEE ALSO: For document merging to work in Excel, change tracking must be turned on. For more information about tracking changes in Excel, see "Tracking Changes" on page 198.

Merge Two Documents

 Depending on which application you're running, do one of the following:

- In Word, choose Compare And Merge Documents from the Tools menu.
- In PowerPoint, choose Compare And Merge Presentations from the Tools menu.
- In Excel, choose Compare And Merge Worksheets from the Tools menu.

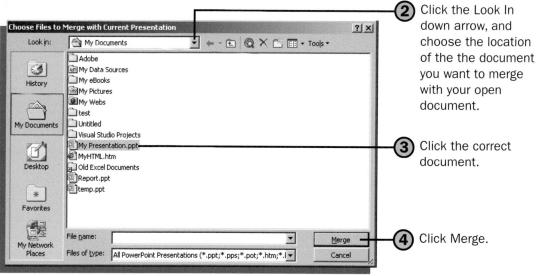

② Click the Look In down arrow, and choose the location of the the document you want to merge with your open document.

③ Click the correct document.

④ Click Merge.

Sharing Information Among Programs

Each of the programs in Office XP is designed to copy and share information between different Office XP programs. For example, you can copy raw financial data from a Microsoft Access database to create a chart in Excel showing profit trends over the past six months. You can then use the chart in a report you create with Word, and in a PowerPoint presentation describing quarterly profits.

Paste an Excel Chart in Word

① Open an Excel workbook containing the chart you want to copy, and select the chart.

② Choose Copy from the Edit menu.

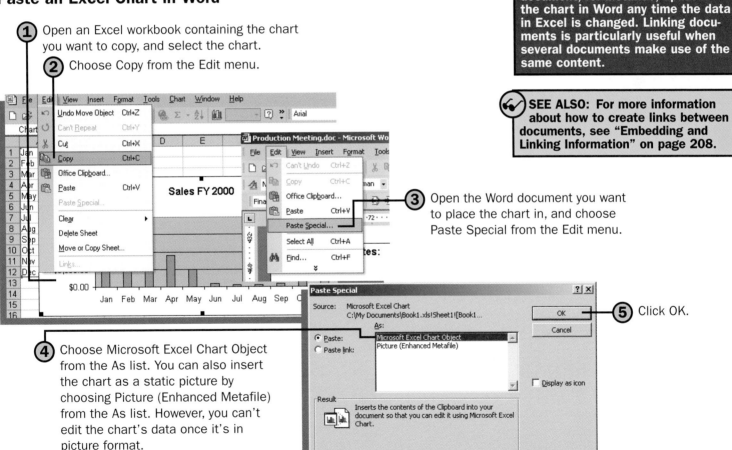

③ Open the Word document you want to place the chart in, and choose Paste Special from the Edit menu.

④ Choose Microsoft Excel Chart Object from the As list. You can also insert the chart as a static picture by choosing Picture (Enhanced Metafile) from the As list. However, you can't edit the chart's data once it's in picture format.

⑤ Click OK.

TRY THIS: By default, Office makes a copy of the content you're sharing between Office applications; however, you can also create *linked* information, or information in a document that is stored in a different document. Linking an Excel chart to a Word document, for instance, updates the chart in Word any time the data in Excel is changed. Linking documents is particularly useful when several documents make use of the same content.

SEE ALSO: For more information about how to create links between documents, see "Embedding and Linking Information" on page 208.

Getting Documents from the Internet

When collaborating with a team of colleagues or coworkers, you can use the Internet as an excellent way to organize documents. Team Web sites are becoming increasingly common, and using them to distribute templates, drafts, schedules, and other information related to a project can streamline the document production process. Having documents available through the Web gives you flexibility in how you and your team get work done, allowing writers and editors to work from home, on the road, or anywhere else they've got a connection to the Internet.

There are a number of ways to access documents stored on a Web site. You can navigate to a document and open it directly using your browser. This opens up a copy of Word, PowerPoint, or Excel (depending on what type of file you're trying to view) that runs inside your browser. Another option is to save the document on your hard disk by right-clicking it and clicking Save Target As. If you know the exact Internet address of the document (for instance, *http://docs.adventure-works.com/docs/mydocument.doc*), you can choose Open from the File menu to open the document from its Web location. The My Network Folders feature (Called Web Folders in Windows 98 and Windows NT 4.0) also lets you keep a list of Web sites that you commonly retrieve documents from.

Most Web sites, however, allow *read-only* access to their document, which means you can't edit or save these documents on the site. An FTP (File Transfer Protocol) site doesn't have this limitation, because it can be set up for users to both download and upload files. Accessing files from an FTP server can work the same way as accessing documents through a Web page; however, you also have the option of saving your documents directly on your FTP server instead of on your hard disk.

SEE ALSO: For more information about working with team Web sites, see "Creating and Working with a SharePoint Team Web Site" on page 319.

Importing and Exporting Files

Office XP programs share files among themselves, but they also allow you to import and work with files created in other programs or to export files that other programs can use. Word, for example, can import an HTML (HyperText Markup Language) file that you save from a Web page; and Excel can export spreadsheets as text files for use with an accounting program. Most Office programs can also import and export files from earlier versions of Office, so you can work with others who haven't upgraded. Simply put, Office XP's extensive import and export formats extend the ways in which you can collaborate with other people and programs.

Open a Non-Office File in Word

1 Choose Open from the File menu.

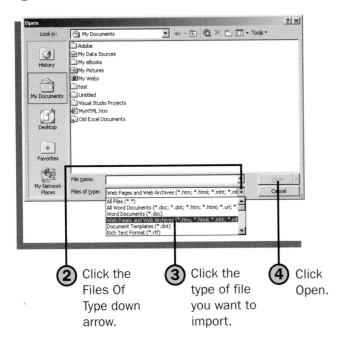

2 Click the Files Of Type down arrow.

3 Click the type of file you want to import.

4 Click Open.

Save an Excel Workbook in Another Format

1 Choose Save As from the File Menu.

2 Click the Save As Type down arrow.

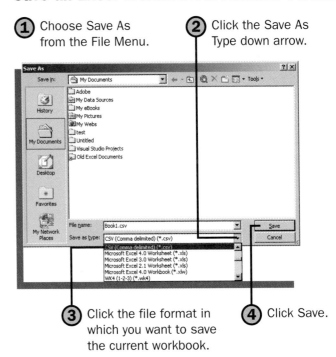

3 Click the file format in which you want to save the current workbook.

4 Click Save.

> ✋ **CAUTION:** Not all file formats can store the same type of information. For instance, versions of Office before Office 97 don't have the newer change-tracking and comment capabilities, so by saving in older formats you may lose information. You should always save copies of documents as standard Office XP files to keep all of your information safe.

> ❗ **TIP:** If your Word document needs to be used by people using different operating systems or word processing programs, RTF (Rich Text Format) is a good general-purpose file format. RTF files are platform independent, and they support almost all of the Office document features.

Holding an Online Meeting

When your collaborators are located in different cities or countries, having a face-to-face meeting can be inconvenient, expensive, and often simply impossible. While e-mail is useful, it's limited in the types of information it can display. Microsoft NetMeeting is an application that allows you to meet via the Internet using text-based chat or, if you have a Web camera, you can video conference with your collaborators. You can access NetMeeting in Word, Excel, and PowerPoint to discuss issues, share files, and even sketch ideas out using the built-in whiteboard.

Schedule an Online Meeting

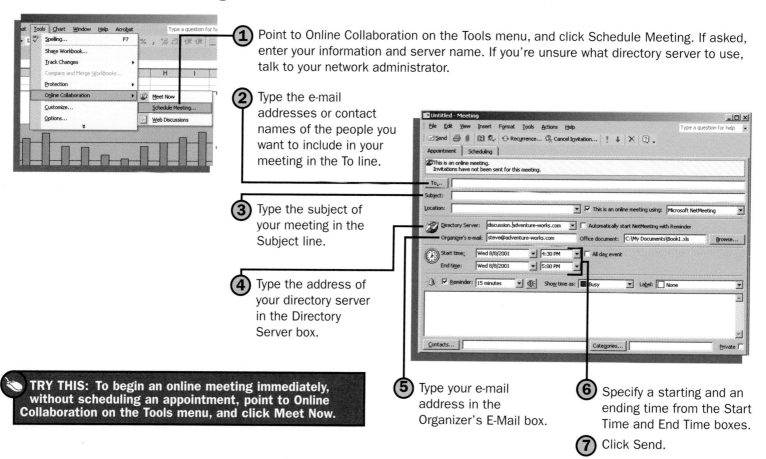

(1) Point to Online Collaboration on the Tools menu, and click Schedule Meeting. If asked, enter your information and server name. If you're unsure what directory server to use, talk to your network administrator.

(2) Type the e-mail addresses or contact names of the people you want to include in your meeting in the To line.

(3) Type the subject of your meeting in the Subject line.

(4) Type the address of your directory server in the Directory Server box.

TRY THIS: To begin an online meeting immediately, without scheduling an appointment, point to Online Collaboration on the Tools menu, and click Meet Now.

(5) Type your e-mail address in the Organizer's E-Mail box.

(6) Specify a starting and an ending time from the Start Time and End Time boxes.

(7) Click Send.

Accept an Invitation to a Meeting

① In Outlook, open the meeting invitation e-mail from your Inbox.

② Click Accept to let the meeting organizer know that you will attend the meeting.

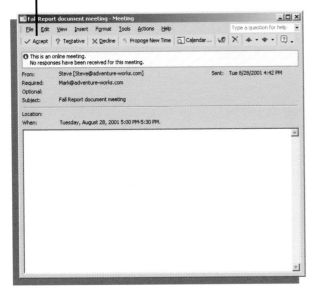

Join an Online Meeting

① When the meeting reminder appears, click Start NetMeeting.

> **①** TIP: When viewing a meeting invitation, you can do more than simply accept a meeting time. By clicking the Calendar button, you can view all of your existing appointments to make sure nothing conflicts with the meeting. If you're unsure whether you'll be able to join the meeting, click the Tentative button to let the meeting organizer know that you might have a conflict. If there is a conflict, the Propose New Time button allows you to suggest a new time to everyone who was invited. You can click Decline if you just can't join.

> **①** TIP: You need to have Outlook running for meeting reminders to appear. These reminders are set to appear 15 minutes before an event by default. You can have Outlook remind you again later by clicking the Snooze button.

Embedding and Linking Information

Updating data used across multiple documents can be a daunting and frustrating task. Office XP allows you to maintain links between information in different documents. This means that when the underlying data in, say, an Access database or an Excel spreadsheet changes, these changes are automatically reflected in all the documents where you linked data from your original. Not only do you save work, but you also avoid potentially costly errors due to outdated data. Office also allows you to embed data within a document, allowing you to take a snapshot of the information you want, without linking to the original data source.

> **TIP:** If you're in a situation where you don't have access to the file a document is linked to, you'll need to break the links between the documents and create copies of the most up-to-date versions of the linked content. To break links and create a static copy of linked content, select a linked object, choose Links from the Edit menu, and click Break Link.

Link Access Data to an Excel Worksheet

(1) In Access, right-click the table you want to include in the Excel worksheet and select Copy.

(2) Open the Excel worksheet, and choose Paste Special from the Edit menu.

(3) Click the Paste Link option in the Paste Special dialog box.

(4) Click OK.

Embed an Excel Worksheet in a PowerPoint Presentation

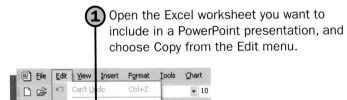

① Open the Excel worksheet you want to include in a PowerPoint presentation, and choose Copy from the Edit menu.

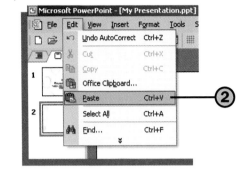

② Open the PowerPoint presentation, and choose Paste from the Edit menu.

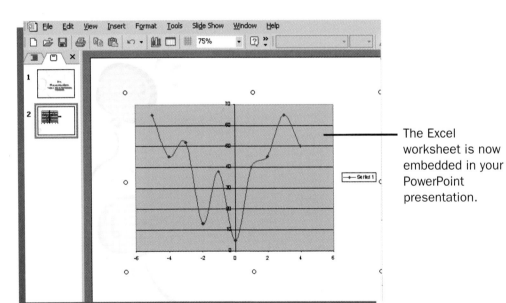

The Excel worksheet is now embedded in your PowerPoint presentation.

! **TIP:** You can double-click an embedded object to edit it in the program that it was created in.

Protecting Your Excel Data

When you're sharing information stored in an Excel spreadsheet, such as a schedule, you'll probably want only a few people to be able to make changes in it, and many people to be able to view it without making changes. *Password-protecting* the document can ensure that everyone on your team can see information stored in a spreadsheet, but that only authorized people who know the password, such as project managers, can edit the information.

Password-Protect an Excel Worksheet

TIP: Word also allows you to protect documents. To do this, choose Protect Document from the Tools menu. In the Protect Document dialog box, click Tracked Changes to allow reviewers to make tracked edits in the document, or click Comments to allow them to comment only. Enter the password you want to use to unlock the document, and click OK.

1 Point to Protection on the Tools menu, and click Protect Sheet.

2 Type the password you want to use to unlock the worksheet.

3 Click OK.

4 Retype the password.

5 Click OK.

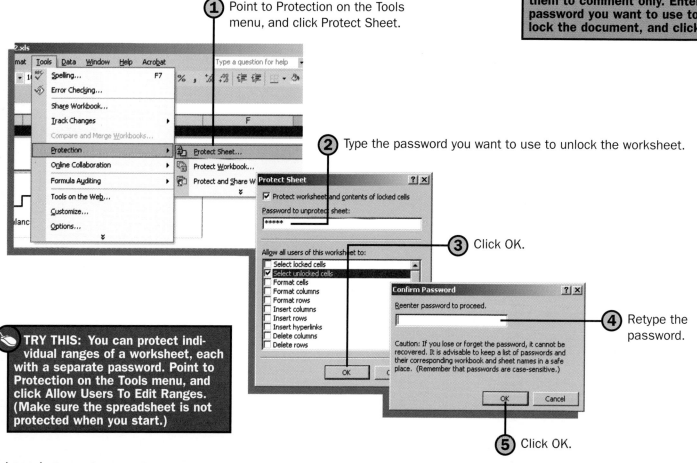

TRY THIS: You can protect individual ranges of a worksheet, each with a separate password. Point to Protection on the Tools menu, and click Allow Users To Edit Ranges. (Make sure the spreadsheet is not protected when you start.)

14 Creating a PowerPoint Presentation

If you've attended a conference or corporate meeting in the last several years, you've probably seen a Microsoft PowerPoint presentation. You can easily create your own presentation, which is a file that contains one or more slides that you can display in a variety of ways. With PowerPoint, you can prepare all the information you need to deliver a great presentation, including a thorough outline, detailed speaker's notes, and audience handouts.

There are several ways you can create a presentation in PowerPoint, including starting from scratch. However, PowerPoint offers convenient wizards that help you assemble slides—text and all—as well as many attractive designs, called *templates*, that you can use to create a polished, consistent look for all the slides. With built-in color schemes and automatic text layout and formatting, PowerPoint presentations come together quickly.

Depending on how you plan to deliver your presentation, you have even more options. Will you be delivering your presentation from a computer? You can include exciting visual elements, such as animation that helps keep your audience's attention. In addition, charts and clip art add visual interest to slides of any type.

This section introduces PowerPoint and shows you several ways to get started, organize your ideas, and create slides that you can preview and print.

Creating a Presentation from Scratch

When you first start PowerPoint, a new, blank slide appears in *Normal* view so that you can create a presentation from scratch. Even a blank slide, though, includes some design elements. For example, slides feature *placeholder* boxes that show you where to type text and insert other content, such as clip art, charts, or other images.

When you work in Normal view, the New Presentation task pane appears on the right. A miniature picture (called a *thumbnail*) appears on the Slides tab on the left.

! TIP: A blank presentation is really a presentation based on the Default Design template. For more information about templates in PowerPoint, see "Creating a Presentation Using a Template" on page 213.

Create a New, Blank Presentation

① Start PowerPoint.

② Click in a placeholder box, and type the text you want.

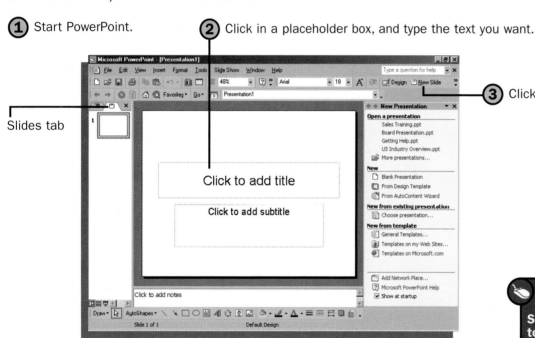

Slides tab

③ Click New Slide to insert the next slide.

✎ TRY THIS: To change the appearance of the slide shown, choose Slide Layout from the Format menu to display the Slide Layout task pane, and then click a layout.

! TIP: Each slide is based on a master that controls the attributes of the slide, including the position of elements on the slide. To make changes to all slides based on a master, point to Master on the View menu and click Slide Master. Any changes you make will be reflected on all the slides based on that master.

! TIP: To increase the size of the thumbnails shown on the Slides tab, drag the vertical splitter bar (which separates the tab from the Slides pane) to the right.

Creating a Presentation Using a Template

To give your presentation the most professional look, you'll probably want to base it on one of the many predesigned *templates* that PowerPoint provides. A template applies a coordinated set of colors and fonts in a range of designs from formal to fun. The Slide Design task pane displays thumbnails of all the available templates. To change the look of the presentation, you simply select the design you want.

TRY THIS: You can change the look of a presentation at any time by applying a new design template. First display the Slide Design task pane by choosing Slide Design from the Format menu. Then click the design you want to use.

Start a Presentation with a Design Template

(1) Choose New from the File menu.

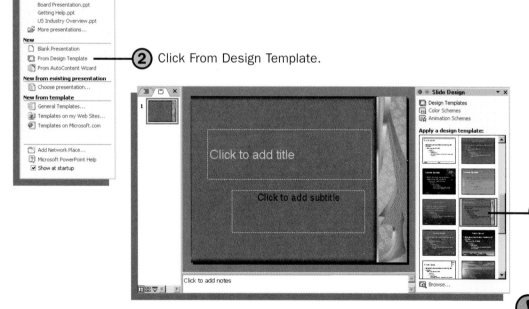

(2) Click From Design Template.

(3) Click the design you want to apply to your presentation.

!)TIP: The same design template can take on a fresh look with a different color scheme. To change a template's colors, click Color Schemes in the Slide Design task pane, and then click the scheme you want.

Creating a Presentation Using Sample Content

If you need a jump-start on your next presentation, you can start with the AutoContent Wizard, which creates a complete presentation—text and all. The wizard can create many types of common presentations, such as product overviews or marketing strategies. You choose the type of presentation you're giving and the delivery method, and then the wizard does the rest, inserting predesigned slides with suggested text that you can customize.

Use the AutoContent Wizard

① Choose New from the File menu.

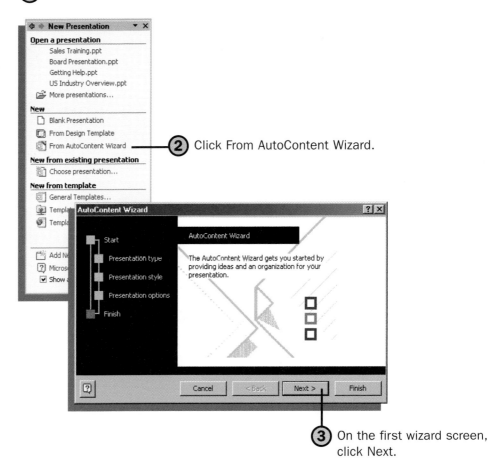

② Click From AutoContent Wizard.

③ On the first wizard screen, click Next.

⬛ **TIP: If you don't see the New Presentation task pane on the right side of the PowerPoint window, choose Task Pane from the View menu.**

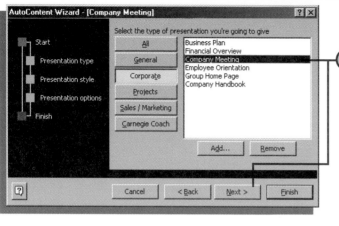

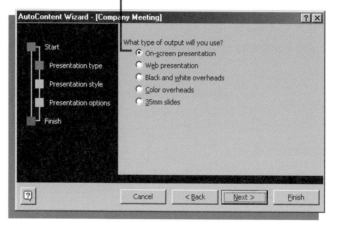

④ Click a presentation category, click the specific presentation type, and click Next.

⑤ Click an option to specify how you want your presentation displayed, and click Next.

⑥ Type a title and footer text, if necessary.

⑦ If you do not want PowerPoint to display the date and slide number on each slide, clear the appropriate check box.

⑧ Click Next.

⑨ Click Finish.

> ⚠ **TIP:** The AutoContent Wizard applies a predesigned template to the presentation based on the presentation type you specify on the second screen. If you prefer a different template, click Slide Design on the Format menu and click the template you want.

Using a Word Outline to Start a Presentation

If you have an existing Microsoft Word document, you can import its outline to create a new PowerPoint presentation. PowerPoint creates a new slide for every paragraph in the Word document that is formatted with a top-level heading—that is, the Heading 1 style. PowerPoint creates bullets for each item under this heading (that is, formatted with the Heading 2 style), and so on for each level of items in the Word document.

Create a Presentation from a Word Outline

CAUTION: Be sure to close the Word document containing the outline you want to insert in PowerPoint. Otherwise, PowerPoint displays a dialog box saying that it can't open the file. If this happens, click OK in the box, close the Word document, and then repeat the procedure.

TIP: You can also create a new presentation based on an outline that you created in Microsoft Excel or any program that can create a text file (.txt) or Web page (.htm or .html). To see all the formats that you can insert, in the Insert Outline dialog box, click the Files Of Type down arrow.

(1) Choose Slides From Outline from the Insert menu.

(2) Click the Look In down arrow to browse to the location of your Word document.

(3) Click the document you want to insert.

SEE ALSO: For more information about ways to copy information between Word and PowerPoint, see "Editing More Than One Document at a Time" on page 11.

(4) Click Insert.

Viewing PowerPoint Slides in Different Ways

In PowerPoint, most of the time you work in Normal view, which displays one slide at a time and lists all the slides in your presentation on the Slides tab. To see more of your presentation at once, you can display Slide Sorter view, which shows thumbnails of each slide in order. Slide Sorter view also makes it easy to reorganize your presentation, because you can change slide order simply by dragging a slide to a new position.

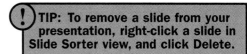
TIP: To remove a slide from your presentation, right-click a slide in Slide Sorter view, and click Delete.

Display Slides in Slide Sorter View

1 Click the Slide Sorter View button.

2 To change the number of slides displayed at once, click the Zoom down arrow, and click a new percentage.

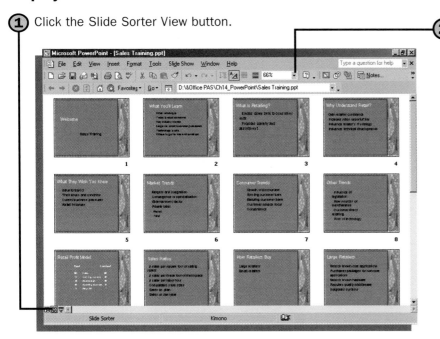

TRY THIS: : To start PowerPoint with the same view every time, choose Options from the Tools menu. On the View tab, select the view in the Default View area that you want PowerPoint to always open.

Outlining a Presentation

To quickly organize your presentation without worrying about the design, you can use the Outline tab in Normal view. The Outline tab displays just your slide text in outline form, making it easy to rearrange topics and ideas. To add text to a new slide or edit existing text, you can type on the Outline tab. In addition, by changing text indents on the Outline tab, you change the level of a bullet, which automatically changes the font and bullet style displayed on the slide.

> **! TIP:** When the insertion point (the blinking vertical line) is at the end of a bullet and you press the Enter key, PowerPoint inserts a new bullet on the next line. When the insertion point is at the end of a slide title and you press the Enter key, PowerPoint inserts a new slide.

Type Outline Text for a Slide

1 Click the Normal View button.

2 Click the Outline tab.

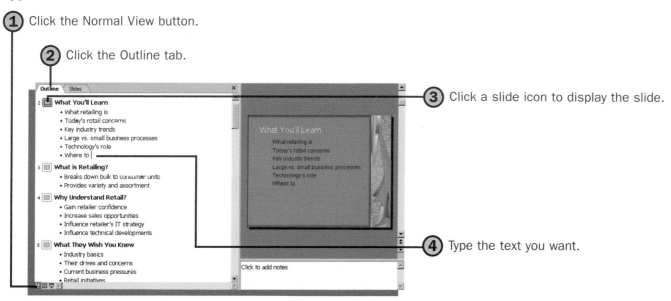

3 Click a slide icon to display the slide.

4 Type the text you want.

> **! TIP:** Sometimes the Outline tab is labeled "Outline" and sometimes the tab displays only an icon. The size of the left pane determines whether PowerPoint displays the text label or the Icon.

Reorder Slides on the Outline Tab

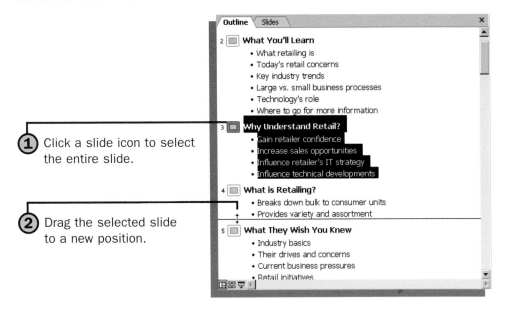

1 Click a slide icon to select the entire slide.

2 Drag the selected slide to a new position.

TRY THIS: To collapse the text on the Outline tab so that only slide titles are visible, click the Expand All button on the Standard toolbar. To restore the full text, click the Expand All button again.

Move Bulleted Text

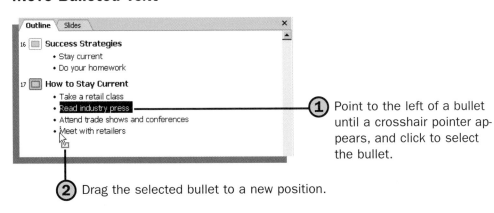

1 Point to the left of a bullet until a crosshair pointer appears, and click to select the bullet.

2 Drag the selected bullet to a new position.

TIP: To indent a bullet, click anywhere in the bulleted text, and press the Tab key. To *promote*, or "outdent," a bullet, click anywhere in the bulleted text, and press Shift+Tab. When you promote a top-level bullet, PowerPoint creates a new slide. If the Formatting toolbar is visible, you can also use the Increase Indent and Decrease Indent buttons.

Adding Slides

When you have more to say in a presentation, you can insert a new slide. Whether you work in Normal view or Slide Sorter view, it's a simple matter to add a blank slide.

Although PowerPoint slides often consist of a title and several bullets, you might want to display a chart or add clip art for variety. Depending on what you want a slide to contain, you can choose from many different predesigned blank slides, called *slide layouts*, in the task pane. PowerPoint includes text-only slide layouts as well as balanced designs that include many combinations of text and images. When you insert a new slide, PowerPoint displays the Slide Layout task pane automatically.

Insert a Blank Slide in Normal View

1 Click the Normal View button.

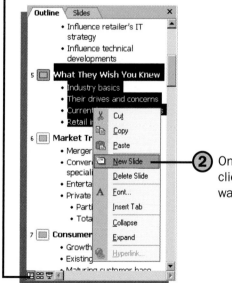

2 On the Slides tab or the Outline tab, right-click the slide that precedes the one you want to insert, and click New Slide.

TIP: When you use the New Slide command on the shortcut menu, the new slide features the same layout as the preceding slide.

TRY THIS: If you want to insert a particular style of slide, you can use the Slide Layout task pane to specify a layout and insert a slide in one step. To do this, point to the layout you want in the Slide Layout task pane to display an arrow button on the thumbnail. Click the arrow, and then click Insert New Slide.

Insert a Blank Slide in Slide Sorter View

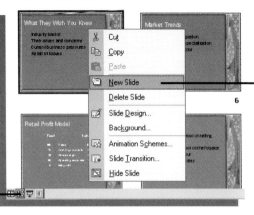

1 Click the Slide Sorter View button.

2 Right-click the slide that precedes the one you want to insert, and click New Slide.

> **! TIP:** If the Slide Layout task pane is not visible, choose Slide Layout from the Format menu.

> **! TIP:** You can change the layout of a slide whether you're working on the Slides or Outline tab in Normal view as well as in Slide Sorter view.

Change a Slide's Layout

1 Click to select the slide you want to change.

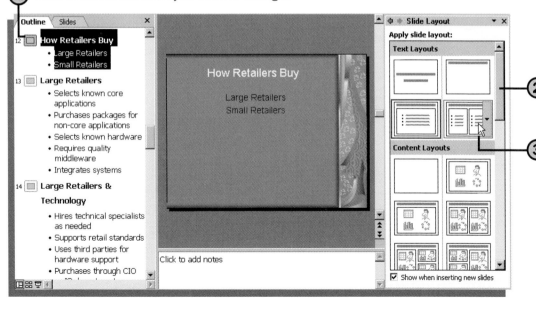

2 Use the scroll bar to view all the slide layouts until you see the one you want.

3 Click a slide layout.

Adding Slides from Other Presentations

What if you created a great set of slides for an earlier presentation, and now want to add them to a new presentation? PowerPoint can list the slides contained in a separate presentation file so that you can choose the ones you want to add to the current presentation. When you insert slides from another presentation, you can choose whether to retain the slide's original formatting or have the inserted slides adopt the current presentation's design.

⟨✓⟩ **SEE ALSO:** For more information about inserting slides based on an outline you create in Word, see "Using a Word Outline to Start a Presentation" on page 216.

Insert Slides from Another PowerPoint File

① Choose Slides From Files from the Insert menu.

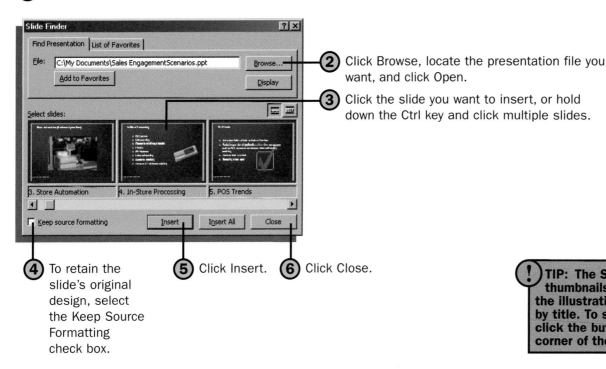

② Click Browse, locate the presentation file you want, and click Open.

③ Click the slide you want to insert, or hold down the Ctrl key and click multiple slides.

④ To retain the slide's original design, select the Keep Source Formatting check box.

⑤ Click Insert.

⑥ Click Close.

⟨!⟩ **TIP:** The Slide Finder can display thumbnails in a scrolling list, as the illustration shows, or list slides by title. To switch between views, click the buttons in the upper right corner of the Select Slides area.

Adding Text

You can add text where you want it on any slide by creating a text box and typing in it. Unlike placeholder text, the text you type in a text box does not appear on the Outline tab. You add the text box and type its text directly on the slide in Normal view. This type of text is particularly useful when you want to add a label to call attention to a picture or to a chart on your slide or to emphasize a special word or phrase with a border, fill, shadow, or 3-D effect.

> **! TIP: If the Drawing toolbar is not visible, point to Toolbars on the View menu, and click Drawing.**

Create a Text Box with Text

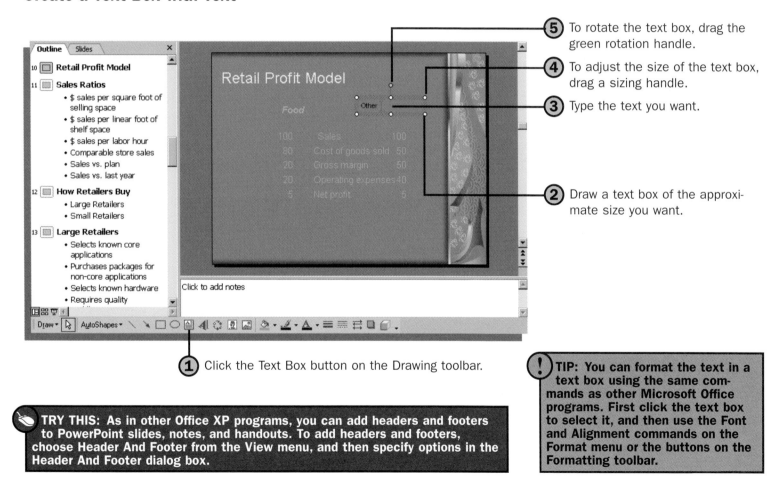

⑤ To rotate the text box, drag the green rotation handle.

④ To adjust the size of the text box, drag a sizing handle.

③ Type the text you want.

② Draw a text box of the approximate size you want.

① Click the Text Box button on the Drawing toolbar.

> **✎ TRY THIS: As in other Office XP programs, you can add headers and footers to PowerPoint slides, notes, and handouts. To add headers and footers, choose Header And Footer from the View menu, and then specify options in the Header And Footer dialog box.**

> **! TIP: You can format the text in a text box using the same commands as other Microsoft Office programs. First click the text box to select it, and then use the Font and Alignment commands on the Format menu or the buttons on the Formatting toolbar.**

Previewing Your Presentation

Whether you plan to deliver your presentation from a computer, as overhead transparencies, as 35mm slides, on paper, or through another method, you preview it from your desktop first. Slide Show view in PowerPoint puts the presentation on your computer's screen just as it will appear when you deliver it. In Slide Show view, no toolbars or windows appear; you see only your slides. To move from one slide to the next, you can use your mouse or the keyboard.

Preview a Presentation as a Slide Show

(1) In the lower left corner of the PowerPoint window, click the Slide Show (From Current Slide) button, or press the F5 key.

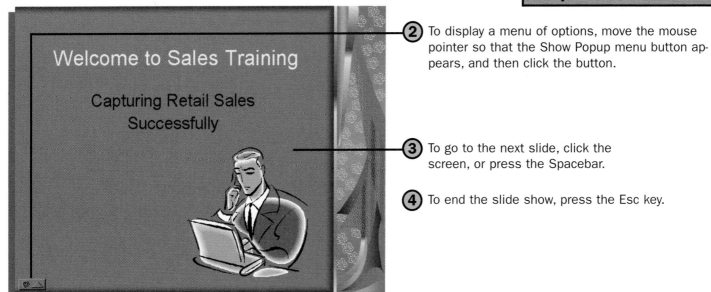

Welcome to Sales Training

Capturing Retail Sales
Successfully

(2) To display a menu of options, move the mouse pointer so that the Show Popup menu button appears, and then click the button.

(3) To go to the next slide, click the screen, or press the Spacebar.

(4) To end the slide show, press the Esc key.

TRY THIS: In Slide Show view, you can draw on a slide to call attention to something important. To do so, right-click a slide, point to Pointer Options, click Pen, and then draw on the slide.

TIP: To display a particular slide, use the Slide Navigator. Right-click a slide, point to Go, and then click Slide Navigator. In the Slide Navigator box, double-click the slide you want to view.

SEE ALSO: For more information about giving your presentation, see "Setting Up a Slide Show" on page 244, and see "Presenting a Slide Show" on page 247.

Printing from PowerPoint

Whether you plan to deliver your presentation on paper or simply want a portable version, you can print some or all the slides. Depending on the capabilities of your printer, the printed slides can be as colorful as they appear on the screen in PowerPoint or appear in shades of gray, called *grayscale*. For quickest turnaround, you can print using only black and white.

If your goal is to verify your presentation's content on paper, you can print just the outline. If the Outline tab is expanded to show all text, PowerPoint prints everything. If the view is collapsed, PowerPoint prints only slide titles.

> **!** **TIP:** For a description of the other options in the Print dialog box, click the Help button (the question mark) in the upper right corner, and then click an option.

Print a Presentation or Its Outline

1 Choose Print from the File menu.

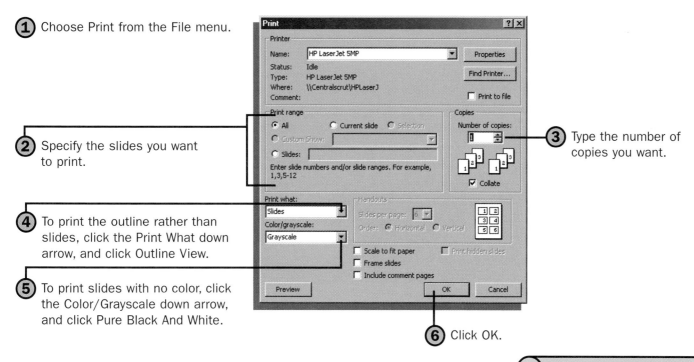

2 Specify the slides you want to print.

3 Type the number of copies you want.

4 To print the outline rather than slides, click the Print What down arrow, and click Outline View.

5 To print slides with no color, click the Color/Grayscale down arrow, and click Pure Black And White.

6 Click OK.

> **✓** **SEE ALSO:** For more information about speaker notes and audience handouts, see "Preparing Notes and Handouts" on page 240.

15 Enhancing a PowerPoint Presentation

When you want to make a presentation move, Microsoft PowerPoint provides the ways. Not only does PowerPoint give you almost complete control over the appearance and behavior of your slides, it also provides a large array of well-designed color schemes, transitions from one slide to the next, and animation schemes for how your text appears on a slide.

You make things move in PowerPoint in three primary ways:

Slide transitions determine how one slide replaces the previous slide. The simplest transition, of course, is no transition—the next slide just appears. Transitions apply to the entire slide.

Animation schemes control how the slide elements appear on the slide. They allow you to manage the flow of your presentation—for example, should bullet points fade in all at once, or fly in individually?

Custom animations let you manipulate any visual element on the slide—text, graphics, imported images, and even imported video clips.

A slide can contain any or all of these effects.

In addition to movement, you may want sound—that is, narration that you record to accompany each slide, such as when you're making a self-running presentation for a kiosk. You can add a pre-recorded audio clip to a slide as you would any other media element, but you can also record your narration in real time as you deliver it. The narration is saved with the presentation, and PowerPoint does the work of matching up your narration with the appropriate slides.

Creating Impact with Color

Each design template includes choices about colors to use for various elements on your slides—the background, text, graphic elements, bullets, and links, for example. You can modify these color schemes for an individual slide or for all slides in a presentation by assigning another pre-existing color scheme, copying a scheme from one slide to another, or even creating a custom color scheme. The choices you make should be dictated by your slide show and how it will be presented. In general, light colors on dark backgrounds are best for projecting from a computer, whereas dark colors on light backgrounds are better for printing on paper or transparencies.

Change a Color Scheme

① Click Design.

② Click Color Schemes.

③ Click a color scheme.

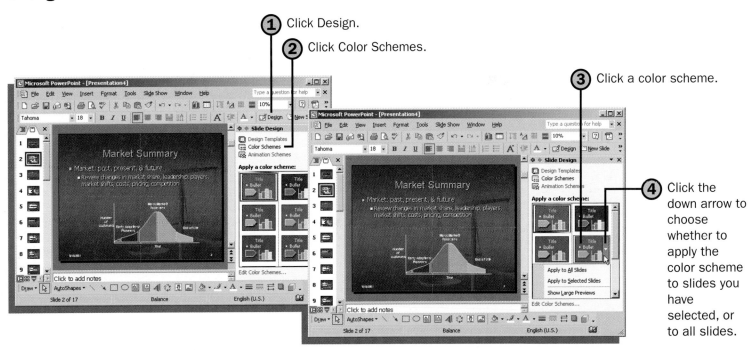

④ Click the down arrow to choose whether to apply the color scheme to slides you have selected, or to all slides.

> **! TIP:** You can select slides for which you want to change the color scheme by holding down the Ctrl key and clicking the slide in the Slides tab at the left.

Create a Custom Color Scheme

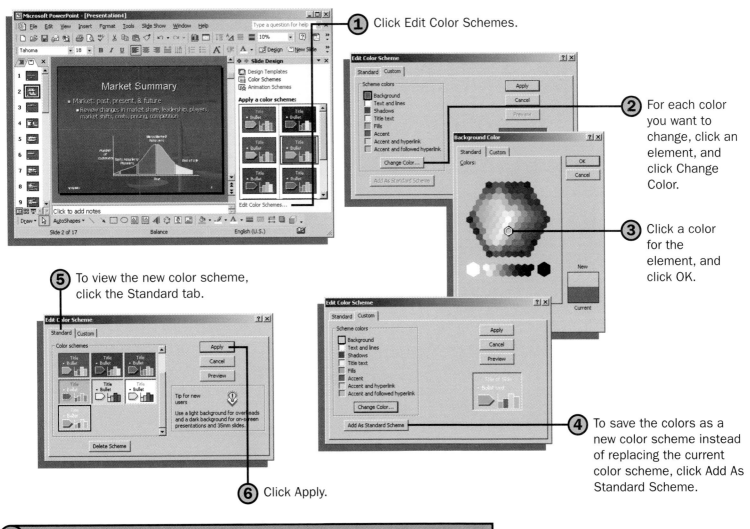

1 Click Edit Color Schemes.

2 For each color you want to change, click an element, and click Change Color.

3 Click a color for the element, and click OK.

5 To view the new color scheme, click the Standard tab.

4 To save the colors as a new color scheme instead of replacing the current color scheme, click Add As Standard Scheme.

6 Click Apply.

! **TIP:** Most design templates include at least one color scheme in black and white. Use this scheme—temporarily, at least—if the background colors make text hard to read when you print your presentation on a black-and-white printer.

Animating Slide Transitions

While spiffy transitions between slides may not add anything to the substantive content of your presentation, they can serve to signal changes to your audience—a gentle admonition to take a look, something new is happening. Don't get carried away, however. Even though transitions are fun to play with, content rules; although you could while away a rainy afternoon experimenting with transitions, it's probably one of the last little tweaks you'll make after your slide show is substantively complete.

Add an Animated Transition

1 Choose Slide Transition from the Slide Show menu.

2 In either Normal or Slide Sorter view, click one or more slides for which you want to add a transition.

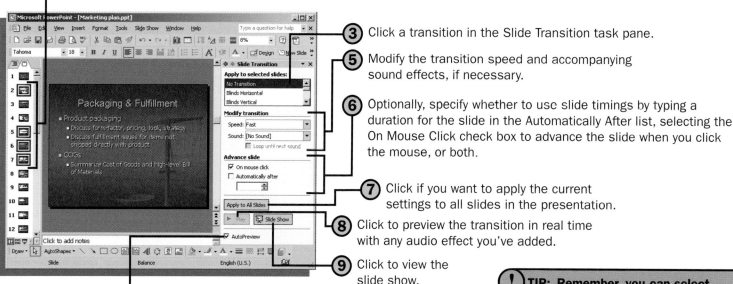

3 Click a transition in the Slide Transition task pane.

5 Modify the transition speed and accompanying sound effects, if necessary.

6 Optionally, specify whether to use slide timings by typing a duration for the slide in the Automatically After list, selecting the On Mouse Click check box to advance the slide when you click the mouse, or both.

7 Click if you want to apply the current settings to all slides in the presentation.

8 Click to preview the transition in real time with any audio effect you've added.

9 Click to view the slide show.

4 If you want to preview the transition on the current slide, make sure the AutoPreview check box is selected.

✋ **CAUTION:** Make sure only the slides you want to modify are selected when you add transitions. Your transition choices will affect all the selected slides, including those for which you previously set other transition settings.

❗**TIP:** Remember, you can select multiple individual slides by pressing the Ctrl key as you click each slide, or select a range of slides by pressing the Shift key as you click the first and last slide in the range you want. Select all the slides in a presentation by pressing Ctrl+A.

Animating a Presentation

You can achieve a lot of visual impact with very little work by adding an animation scheme to a presentation. Animation schemes control how your text becomes visible on the slide; by default, your text simply appears. You can pick an animation scheme that is subtle and stately, or one that bounces the text onto the screen. For important or formal presentations, particularly, be judicious in your choice of which scheme and how many different schemes you use. Just because you can choose a different scheme for each slide doesn't mean that you should.

Apply an Animation Scheme to a Slide

(1) Choose Animation Schemes from the Slide Show menu.

(2) If you want to add a scheme only to one or more specific slides, click one or more slides in either Normal or Slide Sorter view.

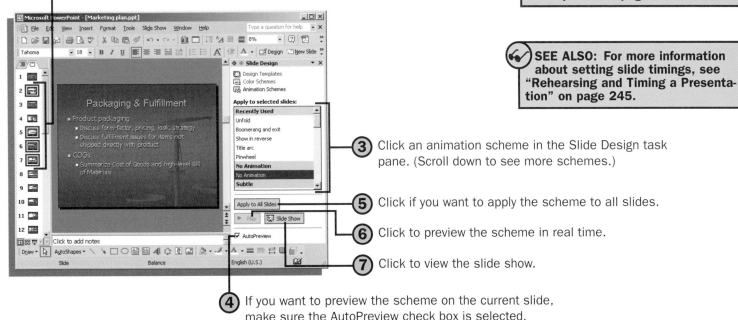

(3) Click an animation scheme in the Slide Design task pane. (Scroll down to see more schemes.)

(5) Click if you want to apply the scheme to all slides.

(6) Click to preview the scheme in real time.

(7) Click to view the slide show.

(4) If you want to preview the scheme on the current slide, make sure the AutoPreview check box is selected.

> **TIP:** If you apply an animation scheme to a master slide, the animation scheme will become the default for all slides in the presentations that use that master. To edit the master for the current slide, point to Master on the View menu and click Slide Master.

> **SEE ALSO:** For more information about saving design templates, see "Creating a Presentation Using a Template" on page 213.

> **SEE ALSO:** For more information about setting slide timings, see "Rehearsing and Timing a Presentation" on page 245.

Recording Narration for a Presentation

Recording a narration can help you in three ways: First, you can create either a self-running version of your presentation for a kiosk or for the Web. Second, recording and replaying your narration is a great way to practice a presentation that you will deliver live. Third, because PowerPoint records the timings of the narrations, it's a great way to establish realistic timings for self-running slide shows, even if you won't use the recorded narration in the final presentation.

Record a Narration

1 Navigate to the slide on which you want to start the narration, and choose Record Narration from the Slide Show menu.

2 To set the recording level, click Set Microphone Level.

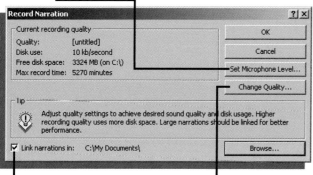

6 To store narration files outside of the PowerPoint presentation file for better performance, select the Link Narrations In check box, and type a location for the files.

4 To change the quality of the recording, click Change Quality.

7 Click OK. When the presentation plays, record your narration, advancing through the presentation just as you would otherwise—by clicking the mouse. To stop, press the Esc key. When you're finished, PowerPoint will ask whether you want to save the slide timings that you just recorded.

3 Read the text in the Microphone Check dialog box, and PowerPoint will adjust the level automatically. Click OK. If the meter does not respond to your reading, your microphone may be incorrectly connected or set up— check your microphone connection.

5 Click an option in either the Name or Attributes list, and click OK.

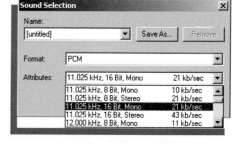

> **!** **TIP: The higher you set sound quality, the larger the audio files will be. If you're recording for formal presentation, use a higher-level quality. The 11,025 Hz, 16-bit, mono setting will sound a lot better than the default setting (11,025 Hz, 8-bit, mono), and the audio file sizes will still be quite small. Use at least 22,050 Hz, 16-bit, mono for audio that will be played on a kiosk or amplified in a meeting room or hall. In most cases, avoid any stereo setting—it doubles the file size without improving the quality of your mono recording.**

Power Tips for PowerPoint

PowerPoint provides a great deal of flexibility in creating sophisticated animation effects, as you'll see in the following pages in this section. If you create presentations regularly, it's worth your time to experiment with these options so that you understand them thoroughly. Among the most useful tips for budding power users:

- If you apply an animation scheme to a slide or slideshow, you can modify the settings applied by the scheme on an individual slide. The effects applied by the animation scheme appear in the effects list in the task pane, along with any other effects you've applied. You can select and modify them, change the order, or remove them as you would any effect.

- You can combine two or more effects to play simultaneously—for example, to move an element on a motion path at the same time an Emphasis effect is playing, or to make a sound file play at the same time a visual effect plays. Apply each effect you want to an object, and make sure the effects are arranged sequentially in the effect list. Then click the second effect (and any subsequent effects), click the down arrow next to the effect, and click Start With Previous.

- You might be able to animate sub-elements of graphics like charts and graphs, such as an individual bar or pie slice to which you want to apply an Emphasis effect: click to select the sub-element and apply an effect, just as you would any other element on the slide. If you want to animate individual elements of a chart imported from Microsoft Excel, the chart must be converted to a PowerPoint chart. To convert an imported Excel chart, right-click the chart, point to Chart Object on the shortcut menu, and click Convert.

- When you preview a slide containing animation effects, a timeline appears at the bottom of the effects list that shows the length of the effects as they're played. Click the down arrow next to the effect, and click Show Advanced Timeline. A timeline appears in the list next to each effect as it's previewed to let you know which effect is currently playing. You can drag the sides of timelines in the list to adjust the timing for the effect.

- Group elements that you want to animate together. Grouping makes it easier to work with the elements all together. To group objects, select them, right-click, point to Grouping on the shortcut menu, and click Group.

- To change an existing effect applied to an object, you don't need to remove the effect—just choose the object and click a new effect. (The Add Effect button becomes the Change button.)

Animating Text and Other Objects

Animating individual objects is a great way to control the flow of information in a presentation—demonstrate sequences of events, show relationships, emphasize a particular point on a graphic, or just lend visual interest to your presentation. You can animate virtually all visual elements on a slide—text, graphics, imported images, charts, or media files. You can animate elements on a slide from scratch, or you can modify effects applied to a slide as part of an animation scheme. You can also make an element move along a predefined path that you choose, edit the path, or create one of your own. Because PowerPoint provides many options for custom animation, to get the most out of this feature you'll need to spend some time experimenting.

Create and Modify an Animation Effect

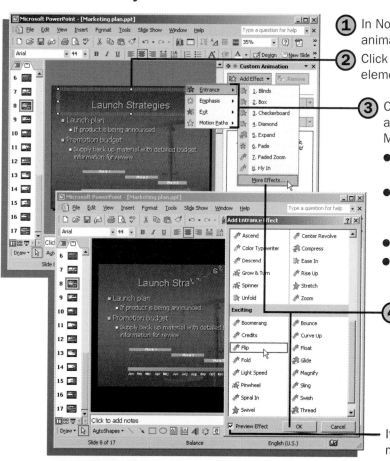

(1) In Normal view, click the slide that contains elements you want to animate, and choose Custom Animation from the Slide Show menu.

(2) Click an element, or hold down the Shift key and click multiple elements, to which you want to apply an animation effect.

(3) Click the Add Effect down arrow, point to a category of effect, and either click the effect you want, or click More Effects (or More Motion Paths) to view the entire list of available effects.

- **Entrance:** Controls how an element first appears on the slide.
- **Emphasis:** Lets you add effects for elements already visible on the slide. Emphasis effects don't change the size or position of an element.
- **Exit:** Controls how an element disappears from the slide.
- **Motion Paths:** Lets you specify a movement for an element by selecting a predefined path or by drawing your own path.

(4) If you chose More Effects (or More Motion Paths), click an effect and click OK to apply the selected effect.

If you want to preview the effect on the current slide, make sure the Preview Effect check box is selected.

CAUTION: Apply any animation schemes that you intend to apply to the entire slide show before you add custom effects to individual slides. Applying an animation scheme can override custom entrance effects you applied to text. For more information about adding an animation scheme, see "Animating a Presentation" on page 231.

SEE ALSO: For more information about motion paths, see "Modifying Motion Path Animation" on page 236.

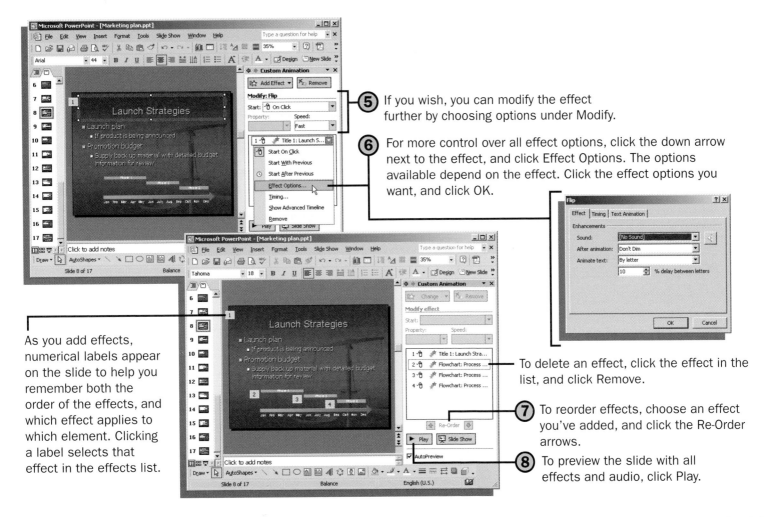

(5) If you wish, you can modify the effect further by choosing options under Modify.

(6) For more control over all effect options, click the down arrow next to the effect, and click Effect Options. The options available depend on the effect. Click the effect options you want, and click OK.

As you add effects, numerical labels appear on the slide to help you remember both the order of the effects, and which effect applies to which element. Clicking a label selects that effect in the effects list.

To delete an effect, click the effect in the list, and click Remove.

(7) To reorder effects, choose an effect you've added, and click the Re-Order arrows.

(8) To preview the slide with all effects and audio, click Play.

Modifying Motion Path Animation ❂ NEW FEATURE

A motion path is a special kind of animation that gives you complete control over how an element moves in two-dimensional space. You apply a predefined motion path to an object just as you apply any other effect. After you've applied a predefined effect, however, you can modify its behavior by scaling, rotating, or changing the path. You can also create your own path from scratch using the tools PowerPoint provides.

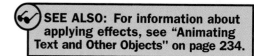

SEE ALSO: For information about applying effects, see "Animating Text and Other Objects" on page 234.

Modify a Predefined Motion Path

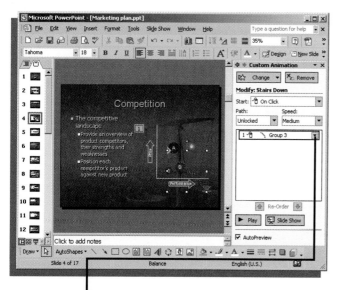

① In the effects list, select a motion path that you've applied.

- To scale the path, drag one of the side or corner points. To scale proportionally, press the Shift key as you drag a corner point.
- To rotate the path, drag the rotation handle.
- To change the path, click the Path down arrow, click Edit Points, and drag individual points.
- To reverse the path direction, click the Path down arrow, and click Reverse Path Direction.
- To change either the beginning point or the end point location, move the mouse pointer over the point until it changes to a double-headed arrow. Then drag the end of the path to a new location.
- To move a path, drag the path to a new location.

② To view and modify other options available for the motion path, click the down arrow next to the effect, and click Effect Options or Timing.

Apply a Custom Path

(1) Choose the object you want to move along a path.

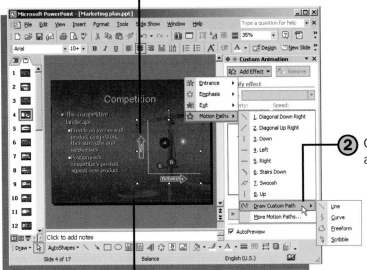

TRY THIS: To make an element disappear at the end of a motion path, click the effect, click the down arrow next to the effect in the Modify: Custom Path task pane, click Effect Options, click the After Animation down arrow, and then click Hide After Animation.

(2) Click Add Effect, point to Motion Paths, point to Draw Custom Path, and click the type of custom path you want.

(3) Move the pointer over the slide where you want the path to begin. Depending on the type of motion path you selected, the pointer works slightly differently:

- Line: Click and drag. Release the mouse button to end the path.
- Curve: Click and release, then move. Each time you click, PowerPoint places an invisible anchor point for the curve. Double-click to end the path.
- Freeform: Click and drag or click and release. Drag between clicks to draw freeform path segments; release between clicks to draw straight line segments. Double-click to end the path.
- Scribble: Click and drag. Release the mouse button to end the path.

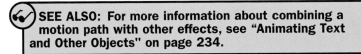

SEE ALSO: For more information about combining a motion path with other effects, see "Animating Text and Other Objects" on page 234.

Delivering a PowerPoint Presentation

Delivering a Microsoft PowerPoint presentation is where all your preparation pays off—provided you know the ins and outs of delivering a presentation successfully. This section shows you how to set up a slide show in PowerPoint and how to deliver it using the most common method: an electronic slide show in front of an audience. You'll also learn how to deliver a live broadcast of your slide show over the Internet, and save the broadcast for later viewing.

Two other methods of presenting a slide show—exporting the presentation as a series of Web pages and producing a slide show as 35mm transparencies or overheads—are covered elsewhere. For more information about exporting to the Web, see "Saving a Presentation as a Web Page" on page 294. Producing your slide show as transparencies or slides is similar to printing them; for more information about printing a presentation, see "Printing from PowerPoint" on page 225.

Preparing Notes and Handouts

Both notes (sometimes called *speaker notes*) and handouts can be a great help to you and your audience. Speaker notes are optional notes that you create to accompany each slide. The notes don't appear on your slides during the presentation, but you can print the speaker notes and refer to them during the presentation. Each notes page typically contains information supporting its respective slide—text, a table, a chart, or a diagram—that you can use to make the slide more informative. You might even want to distribute notes pages to your audience, or use them to rehearse your presentation or to solicit feedback from colleagues.

Handouts are pages that contain thumbnail images of your slides, as well as space for your audience to take their own notes.

Add Notes to a Slide

1 In Normal view, click the slide to which you want to add a note.

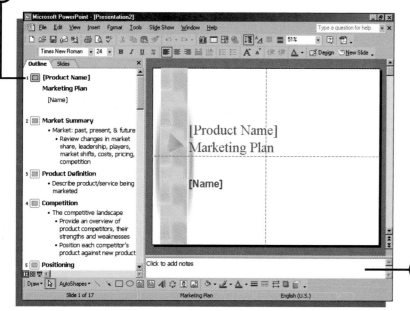

2 Type your notes.

! **TIP:** For longer notes, or if you want to add graphics or other objects to the notes page, you can switch to the notes page for the slide to enter your text by choosing Notes Page from the View menu.

TRY THIS: You can quickly add notes while delivering your presentation—when someone asks a question or makes a point that you want to remember, for example—by choosing Slide Show from the View menu, right-clicking the slide, and choosing Speaker Notes from the shortcut menu.

Format Notes Pages

 1 Point to Master on the View menu, and click Notes Master.

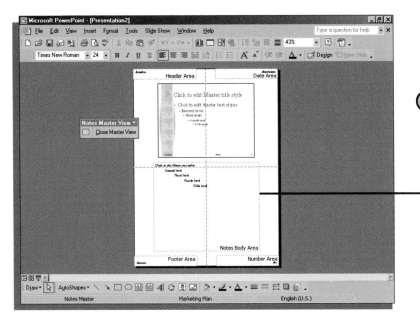

2 To change the attributes, size, or position of a placeholder, or to delete it, click the placeholder and do any of the following:

- To change the size, point to a sizing handle. When the pointer changes to a double-headed arrow, drag the handle.
- To change the position, point to the placeholder. When the pointer changes to a crosshair pointer, drag the placeholder to a new position.
- To remove any placeholder you don't want (such as the date, headers, and footers), click the placeholder, and press the Delete key.
- To change the default text formatting, select a text placeholder, choose Fonts from the Format menu, and specify text attributes.
- To change fill and line attributes, choose Placeholder from the Format menu, and, in the Format Placeholder dialog box, click the options you want.

TIP: If you delete a placeholder on the notes or handouts master page and later want to reinsert it, switch to Master view, choose Notes Master Layout or Handouts Master Layout from the Format menu, and, in the dialog box that appears, select the placeholder you want to reinsert.

TIP: You can insert any kind of object on a notes page, such as graphics, charts, and tables, just as you insert them on a slide. (But don't bother inserting media elements such as animations or audio—they won't play on a printed page and won't appear in your presentation.)

Format Handout Page

① Point to Master on the View menu, and click Handout Master.

② To change the attributes, size, or position of a placeholder, or to delete it, click the placeholder and do any of the following:

- To change the size, point to a sizing handle. When the pointer changes to a double-headed arrow, drag the handle.

- To change the position, point to the placeholder. When the pointer changes to a crosshair pointer, drag the placeholder to a new position.

- To remove any placeholder you don't want (such as the date, headers, and footers), click the placeholder, and press the Delete key.

- To change the default text formatting, select a text placeholder, choose Fonts from the Format menu, and specify text attributes.

- To change fill and line attributes, choose Handout Background from the Format menu, and, in the Handout Background dialog box, click the options you want.

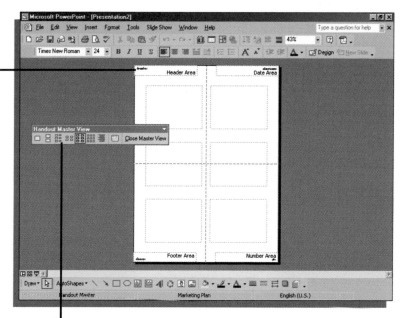

③ To specify the handout layout you want, click one of the buttons on the Handout Master View toolbar.

 SEE ALSO: For more information about formatting text, see "Adding Text" on page 223.

TIP: Although changes you make on a master page apply to all notes or handout pages in the presentation, you can always override the changes on any individual page—for example, to reduce the size of a slide on a single notes page to accommodate a particularly long set of notes. To do this, choose Notes Page from the View menu, go to the notes page you want to change, and then make your changes.

Customizing a Slide Show for a Particular Audience

You can set up any number of custom shows using a single presentation by choosing which slides in a presentation you want to present to a particular audience, and in what order you want to present them.

TIP: You can modify a show you've already created by clicking it and clicking Edit. You can delete the show by clicking Remove, or you can click Copy to create a new custom show based on an existing one.

Create a Custom Slide Show

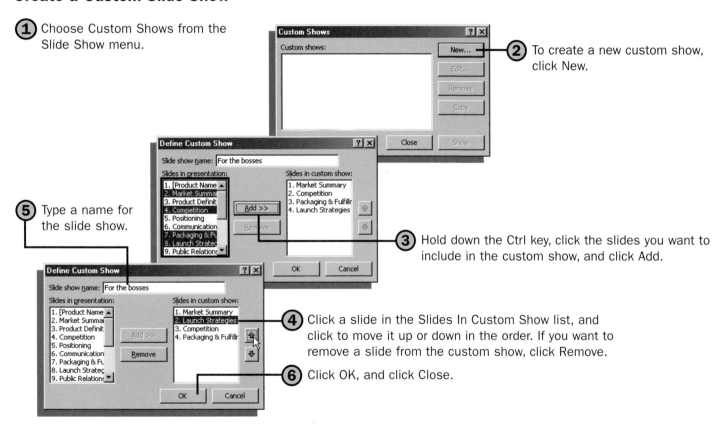

1 Choose Custom Shows from the Slide Show menu.

2 To create a new custom show, click New.

5 Type a name for the slide show.

3 Hold down the Ctrl key, click the slides you want to include in the custom show, and click Add.

4 Click a slide in the Slides In Custom Show list, and click to move it up or down in the order. If you want to remove a slide from the custom show, click Remove.

6 Click OK, and click Close.

Setting Up a Slide Show

You might use any given slide show in a variety of situations—presented before a large or small audience, self-running in a kiosk, timed to fit in a particular time slot, and narrated or not—or even show just some of the slides in a presentation. PowerPoint lets you set up these options in advance, so you're ready with the right show for the situation.

Set Up a Show

(2) Specify one of following Show Type options:

- Click Presented By A Speaker (Full Screen) to present the slide show in full-screen view.
- Click Browsed By An Individual (Window) to view slides one window at a time.
- Click Browsed At A Kiosk (Full Screen) to present the slide show in full-screen view while it loops continuously using slide timings.

(4) Use the rest of the settings in the dialog box to refine your show:

- In the Show Options area, select a check box to make the presentation loop continuously (if you've added slide timings), by-pass narration (so you can deliver live narration), or skip animations (useful if you're using a slow computer).
- In the Show Options area, click the Pen Color down arrow to select a color that will be legible against the background in your slides.
- In the Advance Slides area, if you've added slide timings, you can decide to use them or to advance slides manually.
- In the Multiple Monitors area, if your computer supports using multiple monitors, you can decide to display the slide show on one of the monitors.
- In the Performance area, when the Use Hardware Graphics Acceleration check box is selected, PowerPoint will attempt to use hardware acceleration to improve performance. If performance is degraded, clear this check box.

(1) Open the presentation, and choose Set Up Show from the Slide Show menu.

(3) In the Show Slides area, specify which slides you want to include in the show. You can click Custom Show if you have created one or more custom shows.

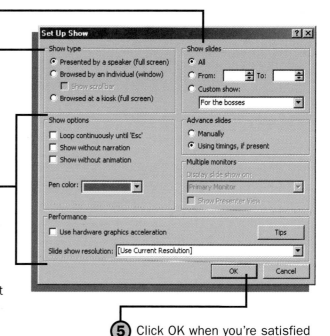

(5) Click OK when you're satisfied with the settings.

> **CAUTION:** To use dual-monitor support with a desktop computer, you must have two video cards installed—one for each monitor; and you must turn on dual monitor support in the Display settings in the Windows Control Panel. Laptop computers do not require a second video card, but check with the manufacturer about dual-monitor support—not all versions of Microsoft Windows support multiple monitors on laptop computers.

Rehearsing and Timing a Presentation

Delivering a PowerPoint presentation is where all your hard work pays off—or doesn't. The best slide show in the world is no good if your delivery is rough, if you run over, or, perhaps worst of all, if you're distracted by completely avoidable technical problems.

You can rehearse your presentation manually by advancing the slides as you practice what you'll say. But you can also have PowerPoint keep track of the time you spend on each slide, so you can later see how much time you're actually spending on each one, adjust the times if you want, and then use them to make PowerPoint advance the slides automatically during your presentation.

Rehearse a Presentation

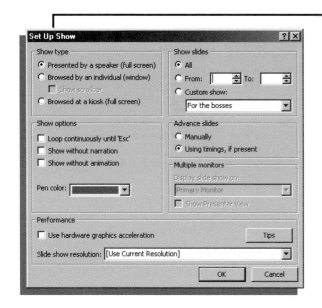

(1) To check your slide show settings, choose Set Up Show from the Slide Show menu. Make sure you set the following options:

● In the Show Type area, click Presented By A Speaker (Full Screen).

● In the Show Slides area, if you're using a subset of the slides or a custom slide show, type in the slide range or click Custom Show.

● In the Advanced Slides area, click Using Timings, If Present.

(2) Click OK.

(3) Choose Rehearse Timings from the Slide Show menu.

(4) When the slide show appears, practice what you will say for each slide. As you practice, click the buttons on the Rehearsal bar to move to the next slide, pause the show, or restart timing for the current slide.

(5) To save slide timings, click Yes.

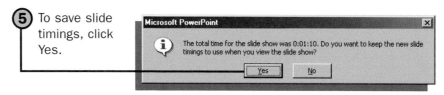

Review and Adjust Slide Timing

(1) Choose the Slide Sorter from the View menu.

(2) Choose Slide Transition from the Slide Show menu.

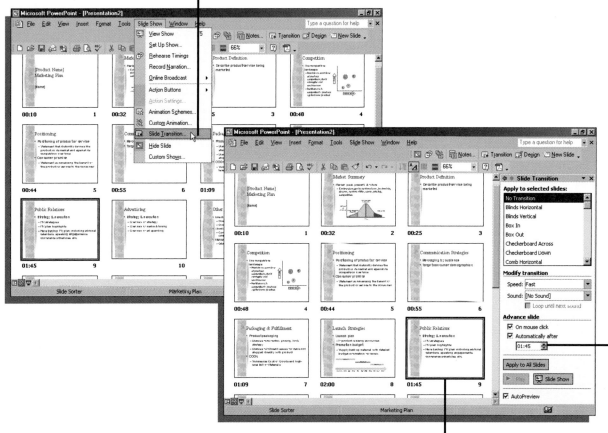

(4) Adjust the duration of the slide by typing a new duration; or, to remove automatic advancement for that slide, clear the Automatically After check box.

(3) Click a slide in the Slide Sorter.

Presenting a Slide Show

After you've built your presentation and practiced delivering it, eventually you'll deliver it in front of an audience. It's not unlikely that you'll deliver it using a projection system, which can be as simple as plugging the system into the external monitor port of your portable or desktop computer. If you're not using your own computer to do the presentation, PowerPoint's Pack And Go Wizard packages up everything you need to view the presentation on virtually any Windows computer—even if it doesn't have PowerPoint installed on it.

Deliver a Presentation

1) Press the F5 key to start the slide show.

2) Click to advance to each slide. (If you've added slide timings, you need not click.)

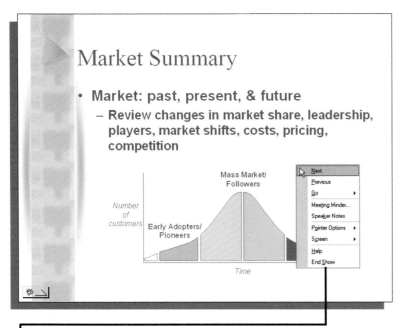

3) Optionally, you can right-click, and then click the commands on the shortcut menu to control the slide show in other ways.

Shortcut Menu Commands

Command	What it does
Next	Moves slide show forward one slide.
Previous	Moves slide show back one slide.
Go	Submenu options let you move to any slide by name or by opening the Slide Navigator; switch to a custom show; or switch to the last slide viewed.
Meeting Minder	Allows you to quickly take meeting notes and assign action items without leaving the presentation.
Speaker Notes	Allows you to quickly add a speaker note without leaving the presentation; the note will appear on the Notes page when you next edit it.
Pointer Options	Submenu options let you switch the pointer between the familiar arrow, an invisible arrow, or a pen to mark up the slides during the presentation.
Screen	Submenu options let you pause and resume the presentation (if it is a timed presentation), black out the screen, and remove any markings on the screen.
Help	Displays a list of shortcuts for presenting slide shows.
End Show	Ends the show and returns you to the PowerPoint window.

Package a Slide Show for Another Computer

(1) Open the presentation.

(2) Choose Pack And Go from the File menu.

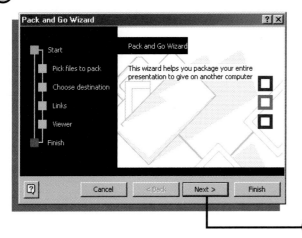

(3) Follow the instructions in the Pack And Go Wizard, clicking Next to proceed through each step in the wizard.

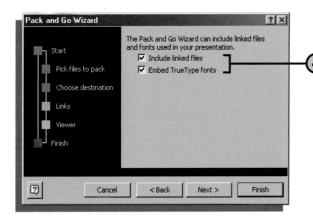

(4) On the Links page of the wizard, make sure that both the Include Linked Files and Embed TrueType Fonts check boxes are selected.

(!) TIP: Test the Pack And Go feature before you're under a deadline crunch. Use the wizard to package your presentation, and then try it out on another computer. In particular, make sure the fonts are correct (Pack And Go can't package some copyrighted fonts), and make sure that your package includes the Viewer, which the wizard prompts you to include.

Broadcasting a Presentation

Broadcasting a presentation live to distant viewers over the Internet or an intranet, or recording a broadcast so others can view it at any time, is a great way to share a presentation from the comfort of your own desk.

Understanding your options as you set up an online broadcast may be a little daunting: you'll have to make decisions about audio and video, whether the files are archived, and how people log in to view the presentation. If you plan to record your narration, you'll need to have a microphone and, optionally, a camera (such as a Web camera) installed and working on your computer. Additionally, if you plan to broadcast to more than 10 computers, you'll need to have Microsoft Windows Media Services installed on your network server—particularly if you broadcast video of the presenter (that's you) along with the slides. Preparing for an online broadcast is definitely not something to be left to the last minute—or to the last hour, or even day. If you've never done an online broadcast, make sure all your technical "ducks" are in a row before you advertise the event.

That said, online broadcasting—whether you do live events or just record for later viewing—can be an extremely useful, cost-effective way of disseminating information. Office XP provides detailed instructions for helping you get over the learning curve. It's easy to make use of these instructions: click in the Ask A Question box, type **broadcast a presentation**, and press the Enter key. When a topic menu appears, two topics listed are particularly helpful: "About Presentation Broadcasting," which provides a great overview of the process, and "Broadcast a Live Presentation," which provides the specific steps you'll need to follow.

Beyond this online assistance, it's helpful to have a sense of your options and why you might want to choose them. You start any of these tasks by pointing to Online Broadcast on the Slide Show menu and then clicking a command on the submenu that appears. As you work your way through the setup process, be sure to investigate the options for audio, video, and delivery.

Settings: Choose whether to include audio, video, or both. Note: if you include audio *and* video, performance might suffer unless you're using a Windows Media Server, even if you're delivering the broadcast to 10 or fewer people. If you want audio in the presentation but aren't using a Windows Media server, consider recording narration for each slide in the show rather than delivering live audio as you present the show. For more information about recording narration, see "Recording Narration for a Presentation" on page 232.

Schedule a Live Broadcast: PowerPoint helps you with the task of inviting others to your online presentation, notifying them via an e-mail meeting invitation, and providing a link that they can simply click to view your broadcast. For more information about meeting invitations, see "Scheduling Appointments, Meetings, and Events" on page 168.

Record and Save a Broadcast: Recording a broadcast for later viewing may be how you use PowerPoint's broadcast feature most. It's just like broadcasting a presentation, except you don't schedule an audience, send reminders, or create a chat or lobby page.

Getting Started Using an Access Database

If your organization needs to track large quantities of information, consider using Microsoft Access, a flexible database management system. If you aren't quite sure what a database is, think of it as an organized collection of information. Most of us accumulate job-critical information, which ends up in a variety of places. For example, a paper filing system might store valuable customer information, while customer addresses are filed in an electronic address book, and invoices are tracked in spreadsheets. An Access database can consolidate critical information in a way that's easier to maintain and retrieve in the long run than multiple files and documents.

However, the big advantage of a database is the way you can use it to look at your information from a variety of angles. Suppose you want to create an address list of the customers who purchased products during a special promotion. You could manually cross-reference your spreadsheets of invoices with your address file, but an Access database provides a better method. In Access, you can request a list of exactly the information you want, sorted according to criteria that you specify. Moreover, you can specify the format in which Access delivers the information to you. Access even includes wizards that help you perform many tasks, from setting up a working database to creating reports that reveal relationships among disparate pieces of information.

Although databases can be a complex and abstract subject, this section focuses on practical, simple ways to take advantage of the powerful data management tools in Access.

What Is a Database?

Access databases store names and addresses, organize numbers and text into columns and rows, perform calculations, and create reports based on those columns and rows of information—all of which sounds a lot like what Microsoft Outlook and Microsoft Excel do. So why use Access? Frankly, a database program packs more power for storing information. Suppose you do use Outlook to store names and addresses and Excel to catalog part numbers, tally receipts, and estimate costs. What if you want to see the name and address of the person who purchased a particular part and find out what they paid for it, and then create a list of all the names and addresses of people who purchased the same part? That's when you want the unique capabilities of a database.

> **! TIP: Microsoft Access Help provides valuable information for newcomers to the database world. Click in the Ask A Question box in the upper right corner of the window. Type** database concepts, **and then press the Enter key. Click Ways To Get Started If You're Using A Database For The First Time in the list.**

What Access can do that Excel cannot is provide different views of your information so that you can see correlations that might not otherwise be clear. In fact, an Access database is what's called a *relational database*, which is a rather abstract way of saying that you can use Access to define the relationships among the information (or data) that you store. With Access, you can store information in one place but access it from multiple places. For example, you can type employee names into a database in one location, but use those names in one place with address information and in another place with salary details.

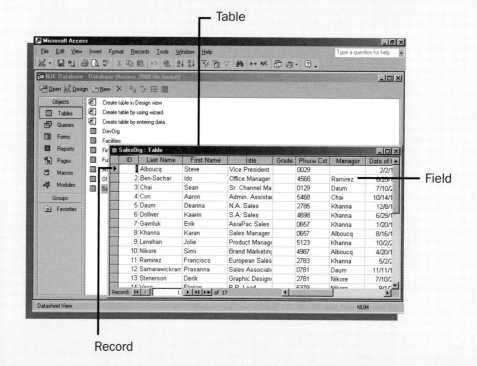

Table

Field

Record

The way a database does all this is by breaking down information into discrete pieces, much as an atom breaks down into protons and neutrons. At the atomic level of a database, then, you have the following:

- **Fields.** A field contains a single piece of information, such as a name, telephone number, or street address. In spreadsheet terms, a field is like one cell that can store information.

- **Records.** A record contains two or more related fields. For example, an Employee record might contain the Name, Title, and Salary fields. In spreadsheet terms, a record is like one row or column.

- **Tables.** A table stores a collection of records much as a single spreadsheet stores a collection of rows and columns. For example, a business database might include one table for employee details, another for customer contacts, and a third for product descriptions.

The easiest way to get information into a database is to type in a *form*, which displays one record at a time. In Access, you can design attractive forms that make it clear what to type. For example, a form might show one employee record. In the Last Name and First Name fields, you would type a person's name, such as Ido Ben-Sachar. In the Title field, you would type his job title, such as Office Manager. In the Date Of Hire field, you would type a date, such as 6/25/1997.

This Access form shows one employee record with eight fields that you can type in to add information to a database.

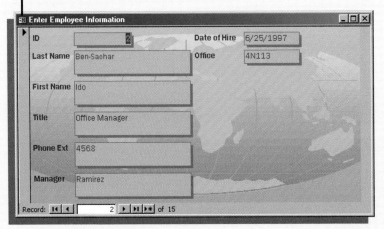

One way to get information out of a database in the format you want is to create a *report*. A report can show you the relationships among the records in different tables. For example, a report could show which sales employees have generated customer contacts for a given product.

Although database development is admittedly a professional specialty, Access makes powerful data management tools available to any business computer user. After you grasp the fundamental database concepts—fields, records, and tables—you can jump-start your database project by starting with the Northwind sample database that Access provides.

Using a Wizard to Start a Database

The task of creating a new database from scratch might look daunting until you know that Access provides several wizards that can help you. The 10 database wizards help you create common types of databases for tracking assets, orders, inventory, contacts, time and billing, expenses, schedules, events, contacts, and service calls. For example, the Order Entry Database Wizard creates a database with tables for customer information, order information, order details, payment information, product information, and company information.

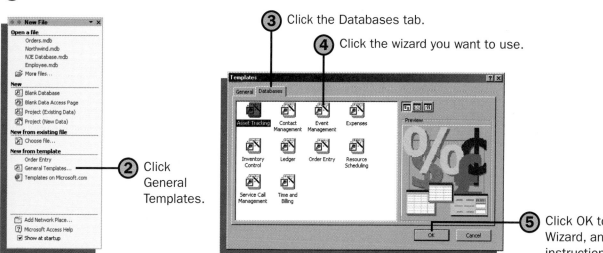

> **TRY THIS:** To learn more about how Access works, start by creating a database of your contacts. Click Contact Management on the Databases tab, and then click OK to start the Database Wizard, which prompts you for information about the people you contact and the calls you make.

Start the Database Wizard

1 Choose New from the File menu.

3 Click the Databases tab.

4 Click the wizard you want to use.

2 Click General Templates.

5 Click OK to start the Database Wizard, and follow the instructions on the screen.

> **TIP:** If you do nothing more than click Next on every screen of the Database Wizard, you'll create a fully functioning database that you can use to enter the information you want.

Learning by Example from the Northwind Database

If you're a database novice, you might prefer to learn how Access works by example. Fortunately, Access provides that example in the Northwind database, which includes employee, product, and ordering information for a fictitious company, Northwind Traders, that imports and exports specialty food. To open the sample database, point to Sample Databases on the Help menu, and then click Northwind Sample Database.

CAUTION: The sample databases that Access includes might not be installed on your system. If you choose a database from the menu and Access prompts you to install it, click Yes to install it now. You will need to insert your Microsoft Office XP CD into the CD-ROM drive. If you don't see a list of databases when you choose the Sample Databases command from the Help menu, you can install them all by running the Office XP Setup program.

In the Database window, you can see that the Northwind database contains eight tables.

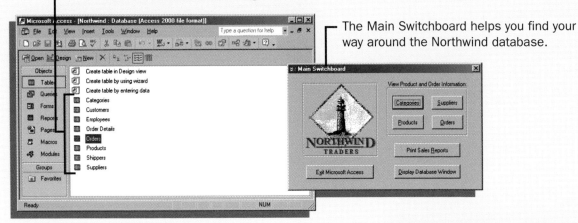

The Main Switchboard helps you find your way around the Northwind database.

The Northwind database provides two views into the contents of the database. The Main Switchboard provides quick access to reports and to the forms you use to add data to different tables of the database. Everything you can do in the Main Switchboard you can also do in the Database window, which is described in more detail on the following page.

TRY THIS: A report provides one way to retrieve information from a database. In the Main Switchboard of the Northwind database, click Print Sales Reports to experiment with the reports in this sample database.

Viewing Database Objects in the Database Window

Your main view into a database is the Database window, which shows you everything that your database contains. You can think of the Database window as a dashboard with all the controls you need to operate a database. Each type of control is a *database object*, an Access term that refers to a type of information that you can create. For example, a table is one type of database object.

You use the Database window to create and open each type of object that a database contains. The Objects bar on the left side of the Database window displays each type: Tables, Queries, Forms, Reports, Pages, Macros, and Modules. This section focuses on the first four database objects. For more information about pages, macros, and modules, which are more advanced database concepts, refer to Microsoft Access Help.

> **! TIP:** For more information about using objects to design a database, click in the Ask A Question box in the upper right corner of the window. Type database objects, and then press the Enter key. Click About Designing A Database in the list.

Open Objects in the Database Window

1 Click an object type on the Objects bar.

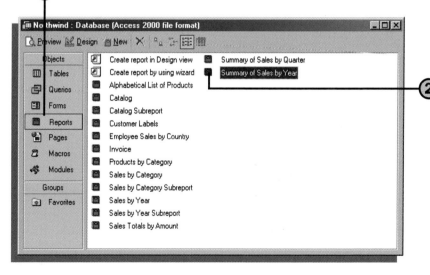

2 Double-click the object you want to open.

> **! TIP:** When you use a wizard to create a new database, Access creates a Main Switchboard that you might find easier to use than the Database window. However, every database includes the Database window, so this section focuses on how to use it to create and work with the objects in a database.

Display Object Details

(1) Click the Details button on the Database toolbar.

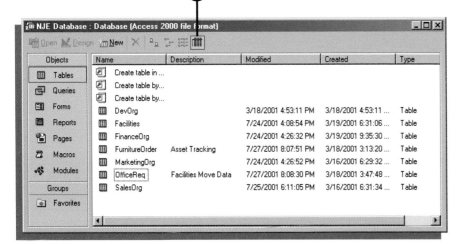

TRY THIS: To add a description that appears in the Description column when viewing object details in the Database window, right-click an object, and click Properties. Type the description text in the Description box on the General tab, and then click OK.

TIP: To sort the objects in the Database window, point to Arrange Icons on the View menu, and then click one of the following: By Name, By Type, By Created, or By Modified.

Add a Database Object

(2) Click New.

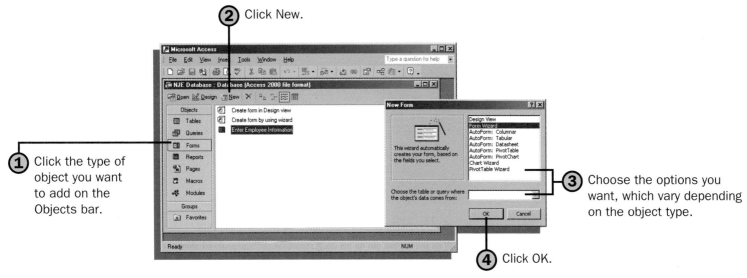

(1) Click the type of object you want to add on the Objects bar.

(3) Choose the options you want, which vary depending on the object type.

(4) Click OK.

Opening and Editing a Database Table

Access can display a table's records and fields in several different ways, called views. The easiest one to use is Datasheet view, which displays the records and fields like the rows and columns of a spread-sheet. For this reason, Datasheet view will look familiar to anyone who has used Excel. Here's how the information is organized:

- A record looks like one row in the datasheet.

- A field looks like one column in the datasheet. In fact, "field" and "column" are used interchangeably in the database world.

When you work with tables in Datasheet view, you can add and remove fields and records and add data for a specific record (as explained on the next page). In short, you can make sure that the table is collecting the type of information you want.

Open a Table in Datasheet View

1 Click Tables on the Objects bar.

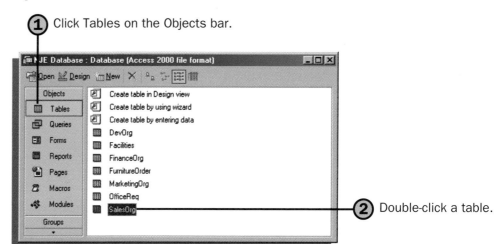

2 Double-click a table.

> **TRY THIS: If you're working in the Northwind database, you can use the Main Switchboard to open a table. In the Main Switchboard window, click Display Database Window, and then follow the steps in "Open a Table in Datasheet View."**

> **TIP: For more information about designing a database table, click in the Ask A Question box in the upper right corner of the window. Type** design view, **and then press the Enter key.**

Add a Field

(1) In Datasheet view, click a column heading to the right of where you want to insert a new field.

(2) Choose Column from the Insert menu.

(3) Double-click the new column's name, type a new name, and press the Enter key.

Add a New Record

(2) Type the information you want.

(1) In Datasheet view, click the New Record button.

Adding Data

So far, this section has covered all the structural parts of a database—the two-by-fours that define the rooms. When you add data, it's like you're putting furniture in the rooms. For example, an employee record is just an empty set of fields. Adding data makes the record useful because you fill in the details, such as a real person's name, title, and so on. Adding data is the same thing as typing in a field.

There are a couple of different ways to add data in Access. The friendliest-looking view for adding data is Forms view, where you are presented with one record at a time, formatted with attractive colors and fonts that make it easy to see what to type where. You can also add data to fields in Datasheet view, which is more like working in Excel—you click in a cell and type.

Add Data to a Record in Datasheet View

(1) In Datasheet view, open a table.

(2) Click in a cell, and type the data you want.

TRY THIS: To make text easier to read as you type in Datasheet view, you can format the font. Drag across one or more columns to select the cells you want to format, and choose Font from the Format menu. Choose the font, style, and size you want, and then click OK.

TIP: When you move to another record in Datasheet view, Access saves your changes automatically.

TRY THIS: To move from one field to another, either use the mouse, press the Tab key, or press Shift+Tab.

TIP: If you make a mistake while typing, you can do any of the following: press the Backspace key to back up and type again, press the Esc key to cancel your changes in the record, or click the Undo button on the Datasheet toolbar.

Add Data to a Record in Forms View

(1) Click Forms on the Objects bar.

(2) Double-click the form you want.

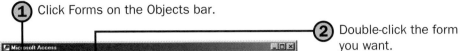

(3) Click the Previous Record or Next Record button to scroll through the records until the one you want is displayed.

(4) Click in a field, and type the data you want to add.

New Record button

> **! TIP:** Like Datasheet view, Forms view includes a New Record button at the bottom of the window that you can click to insert a new record.

Delete a Record in Forms View

(1) Click the Next Record button until the record you want is displayed, or type a record number.

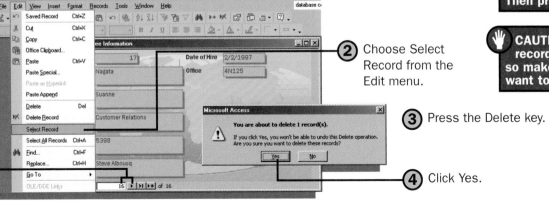

(2) Choose Select Record from the Edit menu.

(3) Press the Delete key.

(4) Click Yes.

> **TRY THIS:** To delete a record in Datasheet view, select a record by clicking in the leftmost column for the row you want. This column looks like a plain, gray button. Access highlights the selected record. Then press the Delete key.

> **✋ CAUTION:** After you delete a record, you can't restore the data, so make sure this is the action you want to take.

Asking a Database Question

The information in a database is useful to the extent that you can retrieve it. One way to retrieve information is to create a *query*, which is how you ask a question of a database. With a query, you can look at data in a table based on criteria that you define. For example, you can create a query that lists employees and their date of hire so that you see who was hired after a particular date.

Access includes the Simple Query Wizard to help you select the fields you want to include in a query. Like a table, the query you create is saved with a name that appears in the Database window.

> **TRY THIS:** After you complete the Simple Query Wizard, Access displays your query in a datasheet. To sort the information, right-click a column heading, and then click **Sort Ascending** or **Sort Descending**.

> **TIP:** For more query wizards, click **Queries** on the Objects bar, and then click **New** on the Database toolbar. The New Queries dialog box lists several wizards for creating specific types of queries.

Create a Query

1 Click Queries on the Objects bar.

2 Double-click Create Query By Using Wizard.

3 In the Tables/Queries list, click the table containing the fields you want to query.

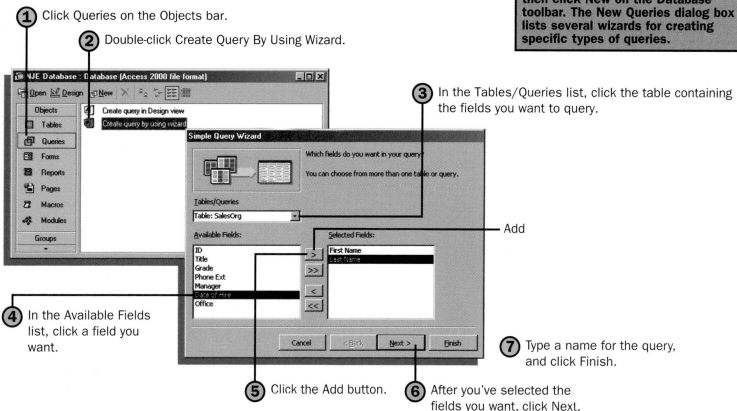

Add

4 In the Available Fields list, click a field you want.

7 Type a name for the query, and click Finish.

5 Click the Add button.

6 After you've selected the fields you want, click Next.

Creating a Report

To create an attractive version of your data that's suitable for printing, you can create a report. A report is yet another way to retrieve information from your database. You choose the fields you want to see from either tables or queries that you have created, and then select the appropriate layout for viewing the data, such as a tabular or columnar format. Access can even apply an AutoFormat, which is a premade design that changes the look of headings and colors in the report. The simplest way to create a report is to use the Report Wizard, which walks you through all the required steps.

> **! TIP:** To print a report, first open the report you want by double-clicking the report name in the Database window and then choosing Print from the File menu.

Create a Report Using a Wizard

1 Click Reports on the Objects bar.

2 Click New.

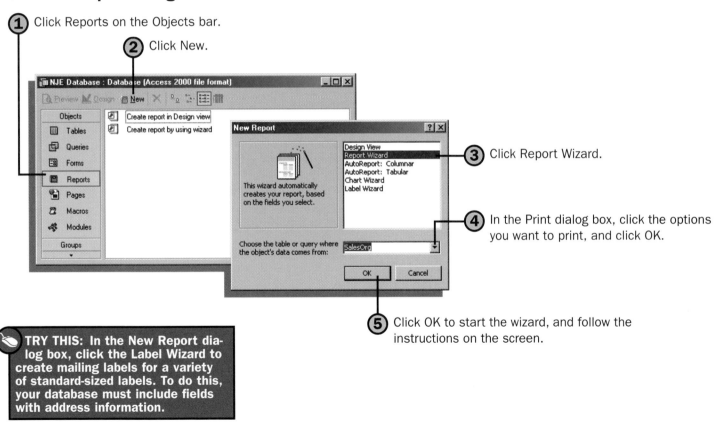

3 Click Report Wizard.

4 In the Print dialog box, click the options you want to print, and click OK.

5 Click OK to start the wizard, and follow the instructions on the screen.

> **TRY THIS:** In the New Report dialog box, click the Label Wizard to create mailing labels for a variety of standard-sized labels. To do this, your database must include fields with address information.

Printing from Access

In Access, you can print any database object, including reports, queries, forms, and tables. The only tricky part to printing is to make sure the view you want to print is displayed before you choose the Print command.

🖱️ **TRY THIS:** To see what the object looks like before you print it, click the Print Preview button on the Database toolbar.

Print an Object from a Database

① Click an object on the Objects bar.

② Double-click the object you want to print.

③ Choose Print from the File menu.

④ In the Print dialog box, click the options you want to print, and click OK.

18 Using FrontPage

M icrosoft FrontPage brings full-featured Web development tools to your desktop—and you don't need to know a thing about writing code. If you've browsed the Internet, you know that a Web site is a great way to advertise, publicize, and inform. In the past, creating a Web site was the province of programmers. Today, FrontPage makes it easy for anyone to create and maintain a Web site, from a simple résumé site to a more complex business site that includes a product catalog, order forms, and customer feedback pages.

If you're new to Web site development, you can lean on FrontPage as much or as little as you like. FrontPage can supply the basic text and graphics for an entire Web site as well as the navigation links that connect those pages. Templates and wizards in FrontPage help you jump-start your Web project so that you can focus on *content*—that is, the text, pictures, and other information that make up your site.

In this section, you'll see that you can rely on FrontPage to take care of the structural work while you focus on the creative side. FrontPage includes many task-specific tools that you can use to automate the process of creating entire Web sites. You'll learn how to set up a new Web site, customize the content to suit your needs, and then preview and publish your site.

What is a Web Site?

Most people are familiar with the colorful world of the Internet. When you browse a Web site, what you see might look like a magazine, a catalog, a book, a photo album, or something else entirely. Most Web sites are a collection of Web pages, which are documents written in Hypertext Markup Language (HTML). Microsoft Office has made HTML its native language, so any document you create in an Office program can become a Web page. If that's the case, why use FrontPage? Why not just use Microsoft Word or whichever Office program you're most comfortable with?

Web sites, as it happens, are something more than merely a collection of pages. FrontPage is uniquely set up to help you manage both the entirety of a site and each individual component that makes up a Web site. Although a Web page is typically one file, it can contain images in the form of pictures, photos, and button and bullet graphics, which are stored in separate files. A Web page might also feature multimedia elements, such as sound or video, which are stored in yet more files. One Web page might represent dozens of files! You could say that FrontPage knows how to keep all the files together that make up a Web site.

FrontPage can also create a *navigation structure*, which is the way a site's viewers get around in the Web site. Anyone who has created a Web site from scratch can tell you that one of the most time-consuming tasks is setting up the navigation structure, *link bars*, and *hyperlinks*. FrontPage takes care of this for you. To help viewers navigate your site, FrontPage adds link bars to your pages, which look like rows of buttons or text along the top, bottom, or sides of a Web page. Link bars contain hyperlinks to the other pages in a site. A hyperlink is the item you click—typically, a button or underlined text—to navigate in a Web site.

In many ways, working in FrontPage is like working in other Office programs. You can type and format text, insert pictures, and change the overall look of your pages in FrontPage using many of the same commands you use in other Office programs. In addition, if you have existing documents or publications that contain information you want to use in your Web site, you can easily copy text and graphics from other Office programs and paste them in FrontPage. What about Web pages that you created in other Office programs? You can add those as well to your FrontPage-based Web site by inserting a hyperlink to that page.

A final word about HTML: don't be intimidated! HTML is simply a set of *tags*. A tag looks like a word enclosed in angle brackets and tells a *browser* how to format and display a Web page. A browser is simply a program, such as Microsoft Internet Explorer, that can display Web pages. FrontPage inserts all the correct HTML tags for you. Although it isn't necessary to know HTML to use FrontPage, it's useful to understand roughly what it does. After you've acquainted yourself with FrontPage, you can start learning more about HTML by viewing the tags that FrontPage creates.

 SEE ALSO: For more information about creating Web pages in other Office programs, see "Creating Web Pages," on page 282.

TRY THIS: You can view the HTML code that FrontPage inserts—an interesting way to learn more about how HTML formats information. In much the same way that Word has the Normal, Web Layout, and Outline views, FrontPage has Page, HTML, and Preview views that provide alternative ways of viewing your Web pages, To view the HTML that makes up your Web page, click the HTML tab that appears at the bottom of the FrontPage window when you display a page.

Creating a New Web Site Using a Wizard

FrontPage offers a convenient set of wizards that you can use to start a new Web site. The Web site wizards prompt you for the information needed to set up a complete site and add placeholder text that you can replace. Most importantly, wizards set up the navigation structure of a Web site—that is, the way your site's viewers will jump from page to page.

FrontPage includes the following Web site wizards:

- **Corporate Presence.** This wizard helps you set up a standard corporate site with pages such as What's New, Products or Services, a feedback form, and a Search form.

- **Database Interface.** This wizard helps you connect to an existing database, such as a product or e-commerce database, which is used to provide content for a Web site.

- **Discussion Web.** This wizard helps you set up a Web discussion forum for the topic of your choice.

- **Import Web.** This wizard imports existing files from a local or network directory to set up a Web site for you.

Use a Web Site Wizard

① Point to New on the File menu, and click Page Or Web.

② Click Web Site Templates.

③ Click the wizard you want to use.

④ Click the Specify The Location Of The New Web down arrow, and click the location you want.

TIP: You can download more templates from the Office Web site. In the New Page Or Web task pane, under New From Template, click Templates On Microsoft.com. If you don't see the task pane, choose New from the File menu, and then click Page Or Web.

⑤ Click OK, and follow the wizard's instructions.

SEE ALSO: For information about how to use FrontPage to customize a team Web site based on Microsoft SharePoint Team Services, see "Editing the SharePoint Team Web Site in FrontPage" on page 332.

Opening and Closing a Web Site

When you browse a Web site on the Internet, most of the time you are viewing a series of Web pages. In FrontPage, you can open all the pages associated with a Web site, which makes it easy to update and modify the site's content. FrontPage calls this opening a *Web*. A FrontPage-based Web is really just a folder that includes all the text, images, and multimedia files that make up an entire Web site. When you open a Web, FrontPage opens all of these files at once so that you can make changes. When you finish modifying Web pages, you can close the Web, which closes all the files.

You can create and open either a *disk-based* or a *server-based* Web site. A disk-based Web site is one you create on your local computer, and then publish to a Web server later. A server-based (also called *Web-based*) site is one you create online.

> **!** **TIP: When FrontPage opens, a message box prompts you to make FrontPage your default Web page (HTML) editor. If you click Yes, you can then open any Web page by double-clicking the file in Microsoft Windows Explorer.**

Open a FrontPage-based Web

① Choose Open Web from the File menu.

② Click the Look In down arrow, and click the folder or Web server that contains your Web site files.

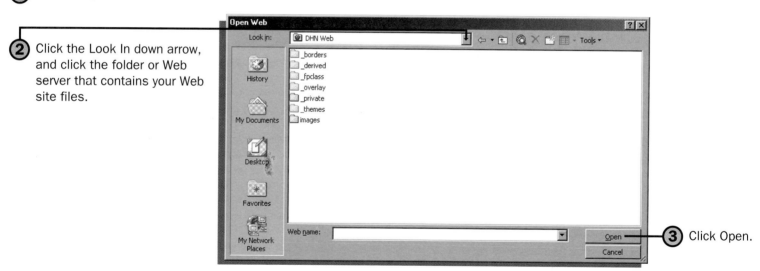

③ Click Open.

Close a FrontPage-based Web

① Choose Close Web from the File menu.

Listing Web Pages and Images Using Folders

When you want to manage the files associated with a Web site, you can use Folders view in FrontPage. A Web site typically includes several folders, each containing a set of files associated with the site. For example, FrontPage creates an images folder and uses it to save the pictures, clip art, and photographs that are used on your Web page. Folders view includes a list of all the folders in a Web site. When you click a folder, FrontPage lists each file by name and displays its page title, size, file type, and the date the file was last modified and by whom. In short, Folders view is similar to Windows Explorer and gives you another perspective on your site. You can even view comments associated with files.

> **TIP:** If the Folder List is not visible, click the Toggle Pane down arrow on the Standard toolbar, and then click Folder List.

Display a Web Site's Folders and Files

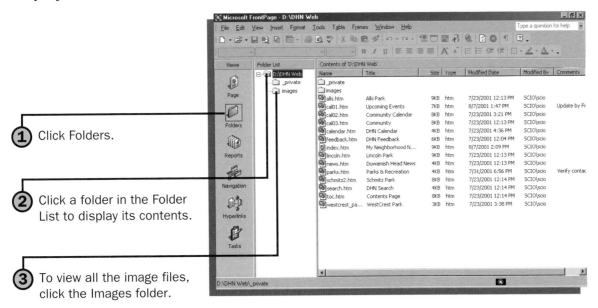

1. Click Folders.

2. Click a folder in the Folder List to display its contents.

3. To view all the image files, click the Images folder.

Editing Web Pages

When you use a wizard to set up a Web site in FrontPage, it's like redecorating a room rather than building the room from the ground up. FrontPage inserts structural and formatting elements for all the basic pages you specified in the wizard and adds placeholder text for page titles, articles, forms, and other textual information. All you have to do is redecorate—that is, replace the wizard-generated text and graphics with the content you want to use. In FrontPage, Page view is the place to edit a Web page.

> **⚠ TIP:** To edit the link bars so that the correct text appears throughout your site, change the page name in the Folder List or Navigation Pane. To do this, right-click a page, and then click Rename.

Customize a Web Page Created by a Wizard

(5) To replace the placeholder picture or logo, select it, and choose Picture from the Insert menu to replace the section with a graphic file, clip art image, photo gallery image, or other picture.

(1) Click Page.

(2) Double-click the page you want to customize.

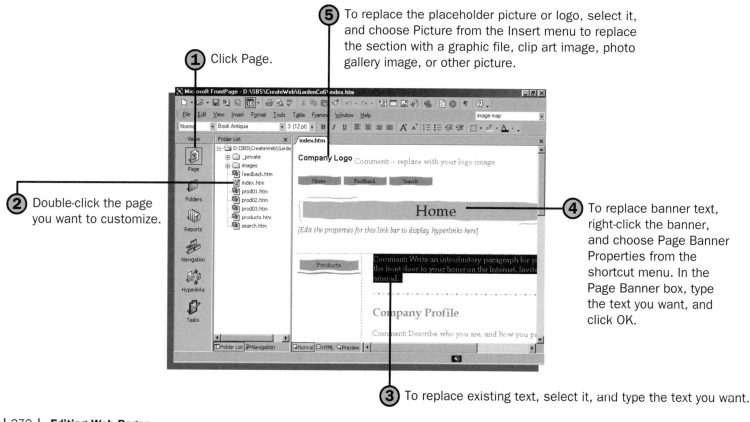

(4) To replace banner text, right-click the banner, and choose Page Banner Properties from the shortcut menu. In the Page Banner box, type the text you want, and click OK.

(3) To replace existing text, select it, and type the text you want.

Changing the Look of a Web Site ⊛ NEW FEATURE

Like other Office programs, FrontPage features a quick way to change the overall look of your work. Use the Theme command on the Format menu to apply a *theme*, which is a coordinated set of colors, text formats, bullet styles, and button graphics. FrontPage includes dozens of themes from formal and businesslike to casual and artistic. You can choose the right look for your site or use a theme to change the look of just a single page. You can also use a theme as the basis of a new theme that you create. The Themes dialog box previews each theme so that you can see what it looks like before applying it to your Web pages.

> ⓘ **TIP:** Many Web sites use a *cascading style sheet* (CSS), which is a file that stores the style and formatting information used throughout a Web site. A cascading style sheet helps maintain a consistent look for a site. For more information about using cascading style sheets in FrontPage, click in the Ask A Question box in the upper right corner of the window. **Type** cascading style sheet, **and then press the Enter key.**

Apply a Design Theme

① Choose Theme from the Format menu.

② Click All Pages.

③ Click the theme you want.

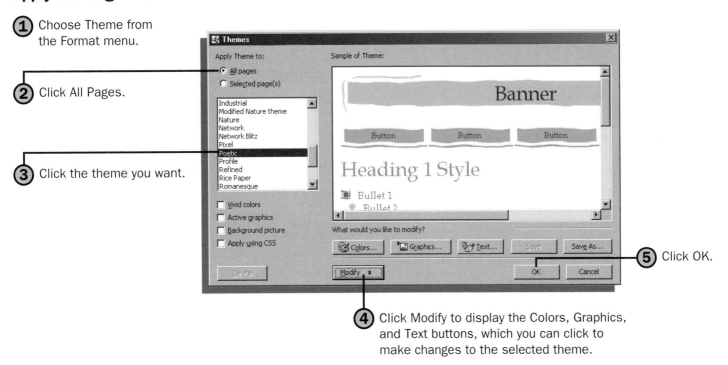

⑤ Click OK.

④ Click Modify to display the Colors, Graphics, and Text buttons, which you can click to make changes to the selected theme.

Checking and Fixing Hyperlinks in a Web Site

All the pages of a Web site are connected by the site's navigation structure, which depends on hyperlinks. The wizards in FrontPage create the hyperlinks needed for your Web site's navigation structure. In addition, FrontPage provides several tools that you can use to create, test, and manage all the hyperlinks in a Web site.

You create and modify a hyperlink in FrontPage the same way you do in any Office program—by using the Hyperlink command on the Insert menu. When you use one of the Web site wizards to create a new Web site, FrontPage inserts all the hyperlinks for you. As you change the placeholder titles and text on the pages, FrontPage updates the hyperlinks so that the correct labels are dis-

played. When you move or rename a page, FrontPage checks to see whether there are any hyperlinks to or from the page. If so, the hyperlinks are updated automatically.

To see the way the hyperlinks form a site's navigation structure, you can display Hyperlinks view, which shows you the hyperlinks to and from any file in your Web site.

> TIP: In Hyperlinks view, FrontPage displays different icons to represent different types of hyperlinks. For example, the home page hyperlink looks like a house, and the e-mail hyperlink looks like an envelope.

View the Hyperlinks in a Web

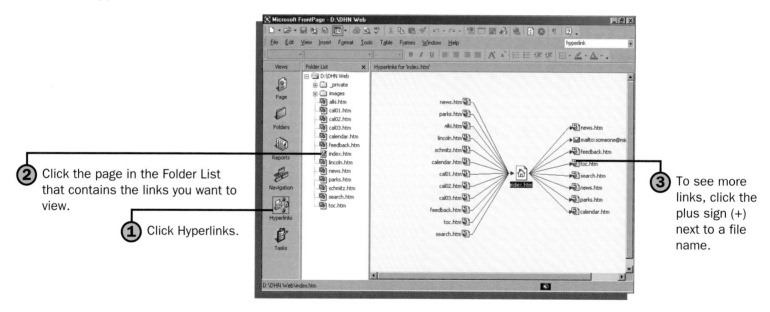

2 Click the page in the Folder List that contains the links you want to view.

1 Click Hyperlinks.

3 To see more links, click the plus sign (+) next to a file name.

List and Repair Broken Links

(1) Point to Reports on the View menu, point to Problems, and click Broken Hyperlinks.

(2) Double-click a broken hyperlink in the Status column.

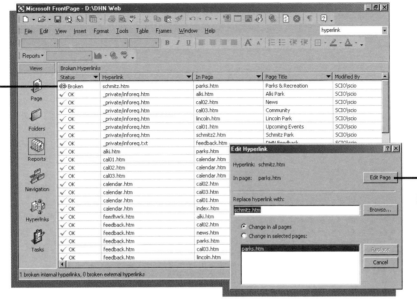

(3) To repair the link, do one of the following:

- Click Edit Page to display the page containing the broken link.

- Type the correct URL of the page you want to link to in the Replace Hyperlink With box.

- Click Browse, and locate the correct destination page or file in a Web site, file system, or on the World Wide Web.

TRY THIS: To modify a hyperlink while editing a Web page, right-click the link, and then click Hyperlink Properties.

TIP: If your site contains no broken links when you click Broken Hyperlinks on the Problems submenu, a message appears, telling you that there are no items to show.

TIP: For more information about repairing hyperlinks, click in the Ask A Question box in the upper right corner of the window. Type manage hyperlinks, and then press the Enter key. Click Manage Hyperlinks in the list.

Adding and Deleting Pages

As your Web site evolves, you'll want to add new pages of content and delete others. Adding and deleting Web pages is a little different than, say, adding pages to a Word document. Because a Web site connects pages with hyperlinks, you need to think about your site's navigation structure when you add or remove a page. That's why it's wise to add and remove pages in the Navigation Pane, because it shows you in a hierarchical list all the pages in a site.

When you remove a page, you have a choice: you can remove the page from the navigation structure of your site, which simply removes all links to and from that page. The page itself is saved in case you want to reuse it. You can also delete the page altogether, which removes it from the Web site and your computer.

> **TIP:** To rearrange pages in your Web site, click Navigation in the Views list, and then drag a page to a new position in the Navigation view window. You can add files to your Web site in a similar fashion—drag them from the Folder List into the Navigation view window to the appropriate location.

Insert a New Web Page

(2) Right-click a page, point to New, and click Page.

(1) To display the Navigation Pane, click Navigation.

Remove a Web Page

TIP: If the Navigation button is not visible, click the Toggle Pane down arrow on the Standard toolbar, and then click Navigation Pane.

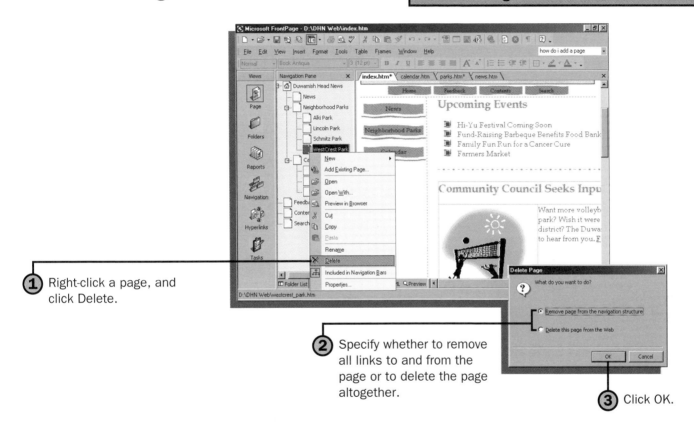

1 Right-click a page, and click Delete.

2 Specify whether to remove all links to and from the page or to delete the page altogether.

3 Click OK.

NEW FEATURE: If you want to include a number of pictures on your Web site in a photo gallery style, use the Web Component command on the Insert menu. FrontPage creates the *thumbnails* (that is, miniature versions of the pictures) for you, and then you add captions and descrip-

TRY THIS: Create a *private page*—that is, a page that site visitors can't view. For example, you can create a page to advertise a special promotion but make it available only at certain times. To do this, display Folders view, hold down the Ctrl key, and then click the pages you want to hide. Drag the selected pages to the _Private folder.

Adding Hyperlinks to Pictures

If you've ever browsed a Web site containing photographs that you could enlarge by clicking the picture, you've experienced a picture hyperlink. In FrontPage, you can add a hyperlink to a picture just as you can add one to text by using the Hyperlink command on the Insert menu. The Hyperlink command makes the entire picture clickable. However, you can also designate specific areas on the picture that can be clicked, called *hotspots*. A picture with hotspots is called an *image map*, which is an especially useful way to provide a number of links in a unique design. Each hotspot can link to a different part of the Web site. For example, a logo graphic on the home page can be an image map with hotspots that link to each of the site's top sections.

Create an Image Map

(1) Click a graphic in the Page view window.

(2) Click one of the following buttons on the Pictures toolbar:

- Click the Rectangular Hotspot button to create a hotspot shaped like a rectangle.
- Click the Circular Hotspot button to create a hotspot shaped like a circle.
- Click the Polygonal Hotspot button to create a hotspot with edges that you define.

(3) Draw a rectangle, circle, or a polygon in the location you want. When you release the mouse, the Insert Hyperlink dialog box appears.

(4) Click the destination for the hotspot.

(5) Click OK.

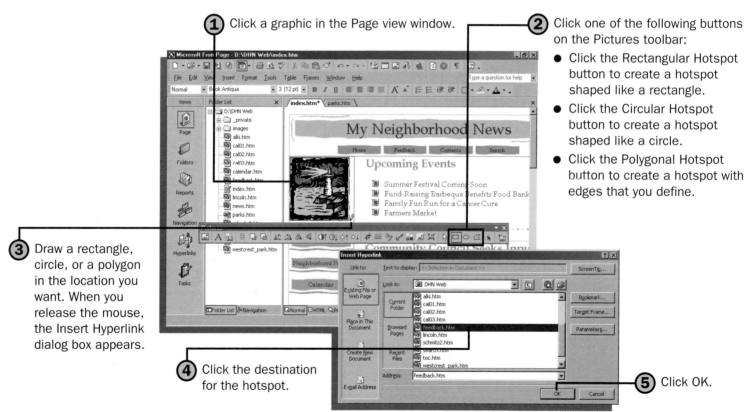

Previewing Web Pages

As you refine your Web site in FrontPage, you can preview pages to see what they'll look like to your site's viewers. Previewing a Web page displays the page as it will look in a Web browser. FrontPage previews a page based on the browser that was installed on your computer at the time you installed FrontPage. However, not all Web browsers are alike in what they can display, and your site's viewers might not have the same Web browser or display settings that you do. Before you publish a site, it's a good idea to test it using several different types and versions of browsers.

Preview a Web Page

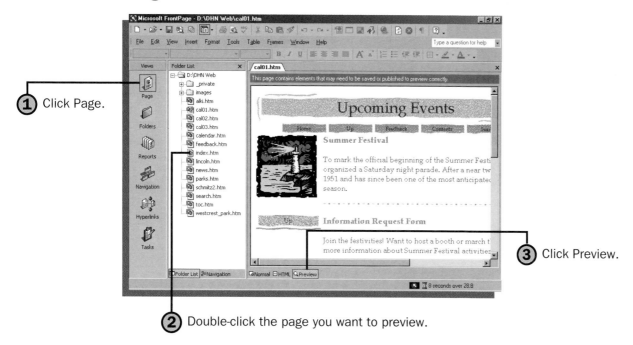

1 Click Page.

2 Double-click the page you want to preview.

3 Click Preview.

TIP: If you install a browser after installing FrontPage, you can add it to the list of browsers that you can use to preview a Web page. Choose Preview In Browser from the File menu, and then click Add.

TIP: For more information about how different browsers display a Web site, click in the Ask A Question box in the upper right corner of the window. Type browser, and then press the Enter key. Click About Browser Compatibility in the list.

Printing from FrontPage

One way to preview your Web site before you publish it is to print all or parts of it. FrontPage includes some unique printing features that help you manage your Web pages. You can print a Web page as it appears in Page view or you can print the HTML version of your page to make sure the page is coded properly. In addition, you can print just the navigation structure of your Web site so that you can make sure pages are linked as you want.

> **TIP:** To print the HTML code for a Web page, follow steps 1 and 2 in "Print a Web Page." In step 3, click the HTML button instead of the Normal button, and then continue the procedure.

Print a Web Page

④ Choose Print from the File menu.

① Click Page.

② Double-click the page you want to print.

⑤ Click the options you want.

⑥ Click OK.

③ To ensure the correct view is printed, click Normal.

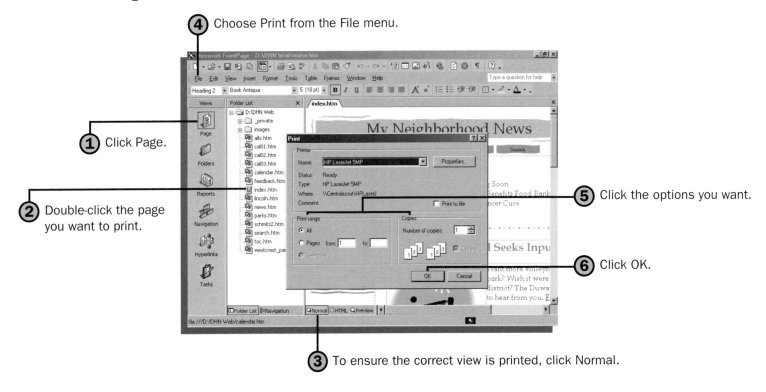

Print a Web Site's Navigation Structure

(2) Choose Print from the File menu.

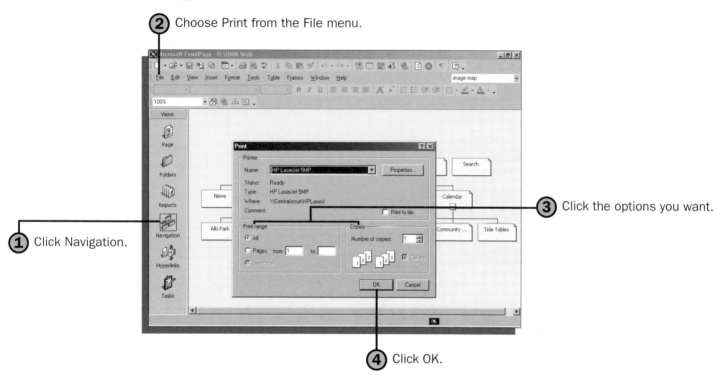

(1) Click Navigation.

(3) Click the options you want.

(4) Click OK.

TRY THIS: To fit a Web site with many pages onto one printed page, use the Zoom box on the Navigation toolbar before you print. Click the Zoom down arrow, click a size (such as 50%) that reduces the view so that all pages are visible, and then choose Print from the File menu.

CAUTION: If your Web site extends off the page in Navigation view, the printed version will probably look the same. To remedy this before you print, click the Portrait/Landscape button on the Navigation toolbar to switch the orientation of the layout that is displayed.

Opening and Navigating Web Pages

What will your site's visitors see when they view your Web site? To find out, you can open your Web site in a browser and navigate among the pages. You don't have to publish your site first. If you've been creating a disk-based Web site—that is, a site whose pages are stored on your computer—you can open the local copy of your Web site in a browser. That way, you can test how well the navigation structure works and see whether information is easy to find. The best way to open a Web site in a browser when you want to test the navigation structure is to open the home page first. FrontPage typically names this page "index.htm."

> **! TIP:** If you have a browser other than Internet Explorer, see your browser's online help for information about opening Web pages.

Open a Web Site and Test Links in a Browser

(1) Open your Web browser.

(2) Type the complete path and file name for your site's home page.

(3) Click Go.

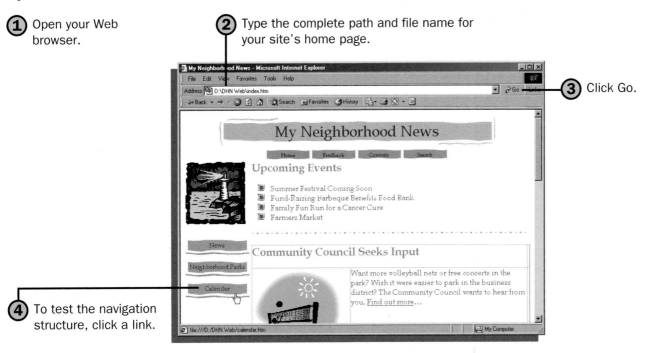

(4) To test the navigation structure, click a link.

> **! TIP:** If you can't recall the complete path and file name to type in the Address box, type just the drive letter and a colon (C:, for example), and click Go. Then you can browse through your folders to locate the file you want.

19 Publishing Web Pages in Office

The Internet has changed the way people communicate. Many businesses and organizations today share information among employees on *intranets*, internal Web sites that only employees can access. For example, personnel procedures, organization charts, and departmental processes are common intranet materials. Other information, such as details about a company and its products or services, is published on a public Web site for anyone to view. Whether the information appears on an intranet or on the Internet, it must be up-to-date. Fortunately, all of the Microsoft Office XP programs feature built-in tools for publishing your documents on a Web site.

Creating a Web page in Office is no different from creating a regular presentation, a spreadsheet, or other document. You simply save your work in Web page format. The result is typically a set of files containing all the text and graphics needed to display the original document in Web format. You can even add *hyperlinks* to an Office document so that readers can click in order to jump between the Web pages or documents you want them to see. After you publish your Web page on an intranet or Internet site, anyone with a Web browser can display it.

This section focuses primarily on how to create Web pages from Microsoft Word, Microsoft Excel, Microsoft PowerPoint, or Microsoft Publisher documents. Because each program has unique strengths, they differ slightly in their Web options, as this section discusses.

Creating Web Pages

You can use a special program, such as Microsoft FrontPage, to create an entire Web site with multiple pages linked together by navigation bars along the top, side, or bottom of every page. But what if you just want to take something you've created in Word, Excel, or PowerPoint and publish it in a location that everyone has access to? If you don't need the full power of a Web development tool like FrontPage, or if you create Web pages only occasionally, you can create Web pages from any Office document.

A *Web page* is a component of a Web site that displays one screen of information (although you might have to scroll to see the entire page). A *Web site* is a collection of Web pages linked together by some type of navigation element, which often looks like a row of buttons or text. Most Web sites use a consistent style of navigation that appears along the top, side, or bottom of each Web page in the site. Word and Publisher include wizards that help you set up a Web site complete with navigation. Excel and PowerPoint include features that are useful when you save your worksheet or presentation as a Web page, but you typically wouldn't use either program to create a Web site.

The program you use to display Web pages is called a *browser*. For example, Microsoft Internet Explorer is a browser. In Word, Excel, PowerPoint, and Publisher, you can save your work as a Web page, or series of pages, that can be displayed in a browser or added to an existing Web site. For example, you can save a Word document that lists a project's team members as a Web page that your webmaster can add to the team's intranet site. Or you can use PowerPoint to design a series of slides that reveal steps in a new departmental process. You can then save the slides as Web pages—each slide becomes one Web page—that can be added to a Web site.

For the most part, the Web page that you create looks just like the document you see in Word, Excel, PowerPoint, or Publisher. However, a Web page might not include everything that the original document can. For example, you can't track changes when you're editing a Web page as you can with a Word document, and you might not be able to use all the same kinds of formatting for a Web page as you can for a printed document.

Although an Office document is a single, self-contained file, the Save As Web Page command typically creates *several* files. The main body of your Web page is created as a file with the extension .htm or .html, both of which mean an HTML (Hypertext Markup Language) file. HTML is the language of Web pages, but you don't need to know anything about it to create a Web page from your Office document. If your document contains pictures, clip art, bullets, sound, animation, or video, the Save As Web Page command saves each individual item in a separate file. Links in the Web page indicate which graphic file to display in what location or which media file to play and when. Because the Save As Web Page command can create multiple files, it creates a new folder in which it stores all the files needed to display a page. To make your Web pages available to an intranet or Internet Web site, you must copy the entire folder to a Web server and then add links from existing pages to the new pages you created.

> **TRY THIS:** In Word, you can view the HTML code that makes up a Web page—a useful exercise if you want to learn more about how HTML formats information. HTML code includes *tags*, which appear in angle brackets and indicate how to format a Web page. To view the HTML that makes up your Web page, open the Web page file in Word, and choose HTML Source from the View menu. The HTML Source command is not available if the document is not a Web page.

Publishing Web Pages on the Internet

What does it mean to *publish* your Web site? Publishing in the Web world means to copy all the files associated with your Web pages to the appropriate folder on the computer that includes (or *hosts*) a Web server. A Web server enables a computer to retrieve information from and make information accessible to the Internet. A Web browser communicates with a Web server to display the information the server contains. Your Web pages become available to the Internet or your company's intranet when you publish them on a Web server.

If your computer has access to the Web server, you can publish your Web pages directly from Office. That is, when you use the Save As Web Page command, specify the network location of a folder on your Web server. Otherwise, you'll need to ask your Web hosting service, company webmaster, or network administrator about how to publish your Web pages.

To view your Web pages after they've been published, open your browser, and then type the address of the Web site. If you find an error or want to make a change, return to your original Web pages on your computer. Make the required change, save new copies of the Web pages, and then republish the pages you changed. To see the changes, make sure to refresh your browser next time you view the pages (press F5 in Internet Explorer).

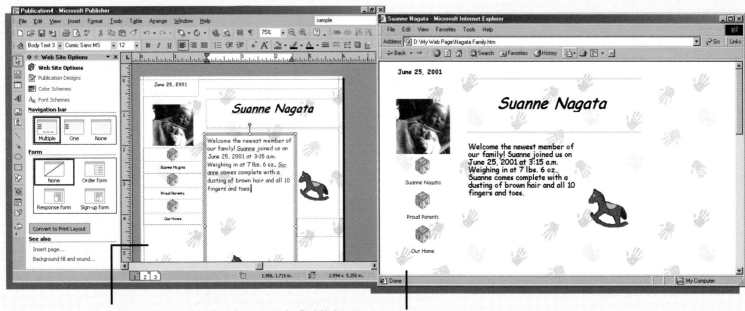

A Web site under development in Publisher

The Web site as it appears in the Internet Explorer browser

Starting Web Pages Using a Wizard

A quick way to set up a document that you intend to publish as a Web site is to use the Web Page Wizard. The wizard sets up design and navigation options for you, so all you need to do is add the text and graphics you want in Word. In the wizard, you choose the number of pages you want and then specify a layout for the *navigation frame* (also known as the navigation bar), which is a separate column, row, or page in your Web page that contains the hyperlinks used to jump from one page to another. You can even select a *visual theme*, a premade design that adds a consistent look to the visual elements on your pages.

Any Office document can be saved as a Web page—you don't need to start with the Web Page Wizard. In fact, if you plan to add your document to an existing Web site, it's best not to use the wizard, which adds navigation frames that would be redundant.

> **! TIP: Click No Visual Theme in the Web Page Wizard if your Web pages will be posted to an existing site that already has a design theme in place.**

> **TRY THIS: You can start the Web Page Wizard from Word. Choose New from the File menu to open the New Document task pane. In the New From Template area, click Web Page Wizard.**

Create a Web Site Using the Web Page Wizard

1 Click the Windows Start menu, and choose New Office Document.

2 Click the Web Pages tab, and double-click Web Page Wizard.

3 In the Web Page Wizard, click Next.

4 Type a title for your Web site, and click Next.

5 Click a layout style for the frame that will contain your navigation links, and click Next.

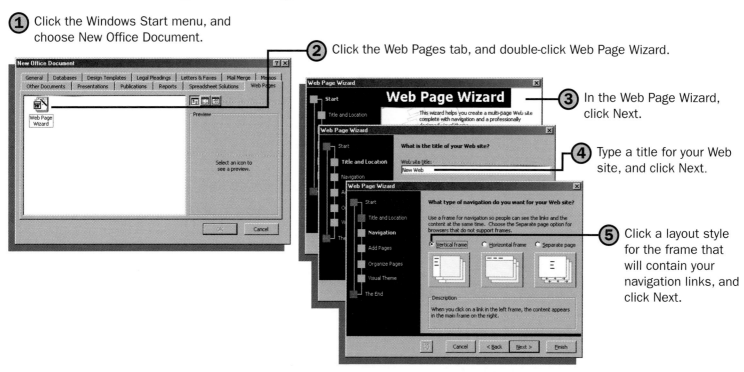

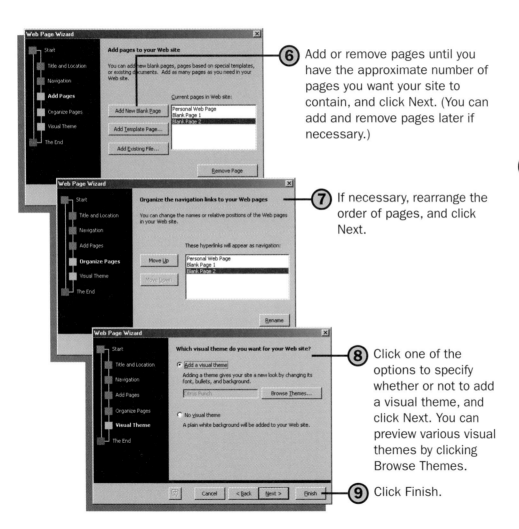

6 Add or remove pages until you have the approximate number of pages you want your site to contain, and click Next. (You can add and remove pages later if necessary.)

7 If necessary, rearrange the order of pages, and click Next.

8 Click one of the options to specify whether or not to add a visual theme, and click Next. You can preview various visual themes by clicking Browse Themes.

9 Click Finish.

CAUTION: The Web Page Wizard creates a site that uses frames for navigation. On a Web page, a *frame* is special type of structure—technically, a named *subwindow*—that divides the page area when viewed in a browser. Some older browsers cannot display frames, so make sure to test your Web pages by viewing them in the types of browsers you expect your audience will have.

TIP: Although you will be able to preview and use some of the visual themes, you might need to install the theme you want from your Office XP Professional with FrontPage disk if you did not originally install all of the features in Office.

SEE ALSO: For information about using a wizard in FrontPage to create a Web site, see "Starting Web Pages Using a Wizard" on page 284.

CAUTION: When you start a document with the Web Page Wizard, Word turns off certain features (columns, for example) that can't be displayed in your target browser.

Starting a Web Site in Publisher

Like the Office Web Page Wizard, the Web Sites Wizard in Publisher creates a series of pages that you can publish on the Web. Although you can save any Publisher document as a Web page, the Web Sites Wizard creates an entire Web site with pages linked by a *navigation bar*, which is an element that is repeated on each page and contains the links you click to jump from one page to the next. As you add pages to your publication, Publisher automatically adds links on the navigation bar for each page. The wizard also includes a wide variety of designs, from fun to formal, that ensure a consistent look for your Web site.

 SEE ALSO: For more information about working in Publisher, see "Creating a Publication with Publisher" on page 297.

Create a Web Site in Publisher ⊕ NEW FEATURE

1 Choose New from the File menu.

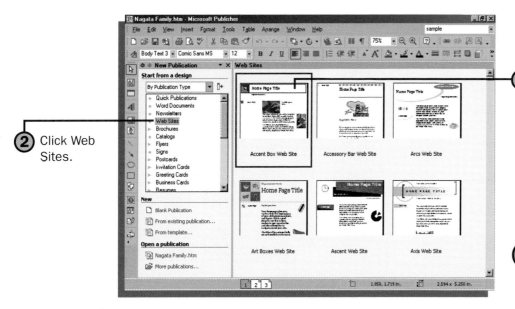

2 Click Web Sites.

3 Click the design you want to use to start a new Web site document.

TIP: You can add a visitor counter to a Web site you create in Publisher. A *visitor counter* is a box that appears on a Web page and automatically counts the number of people who visit your Web site. For more information, click in the Ask A Question box in the upper right corner of the window. Type visitor counter, and then press the Enter key.

Previewing a Web Page

You can easily preview what your Office document will look like as a Web page. Previewing your document opens your Web browser and displays your document as a Web page. That way, you can see your page exactly as your audience will see it and make sure the formats you've specified in the Office document look the way you want in a browser. For example, if you preview a Word document that contains blinking text animations and newspaper columns, you'll discover that these formats aren't preserved when you save your document as a Web page.

Preview an Office Document as a Web Page

① Open the document you want to preview.

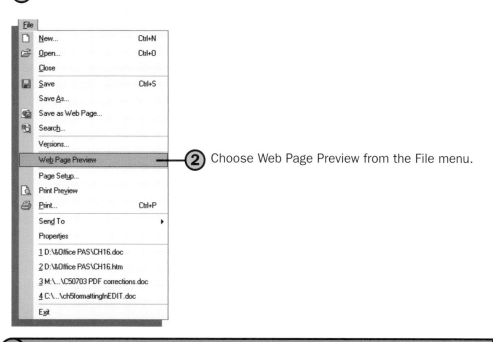

② Choose Web Page Preview from the File menu.

⚠ TIP: To switch between your browser program and Office so that you can make changes, press Alt+Tab. To update the view displayed in Internet Explorer, press the F5 key.

SEE ALSO: For more information about changing views in Word, see "Viewing a Document" on page 58.

TRY THIS: To preview a Word document in Web Layout view, which approximates the look of a Web page in a browser, choose Web Layout from the View menu.

⚠ TIP: When you use the Web Page Preview command in Publisher, a dialog box appears with options for displaying the entire site or one page of the site. Click an option, and then click OK to open the site or page in your browser.

Linking Pages Together

What makes Web pages particularly handy? Hyperlinks. These are commands you insert to create a link between pages so that you can "jump" from one Web page to another location on that page or to another Web page or document. You can create a hyperlink in any Office document whether or not you plan to save it as a Web page. In fact, you've probably created one before—whenever you type a Web or e-mail address, Office automatically turns your text into a hyperlink.

After you save your document as a Web page and then open it in a browser, the look of the linked object can change depending on the browser or the styles defined for a Web site. In most browsers, however, the mouse pointer changes to a pointing hand icon when you point to an object with a hyperlink. Then you click the link to display the document, Web page, or other item defined in the hyperlink.

> **!** **TIP: To create a ScreenTip when you insert a hyperlink, click the ScreenTip button in the Insert Hyperlink dialog box, type the text you want to appear (such as** Go to asset report**), and then click OK.**

Add a Hyperlink

(1) Select the text or object you want to link from.

(2) Choose Hyperlink from the Insert menu.

(3) In the Link To area, do one of the following:

- Click Existing File Or Web Page to display options for creating a hyperlink to a file, including multimedia files or Office documents, or to another Web page, such as www.microsoft.com.

- Click Place In This Document to display options for creating a hyperlink to another section, slide, or worksheet in the current document.

- Click Create New Document to display options for creating a hyperlink to a document that you want to create now.

- Click E-Mail Address to display options for creating a hyperlink that starts an e-mail message with an address.

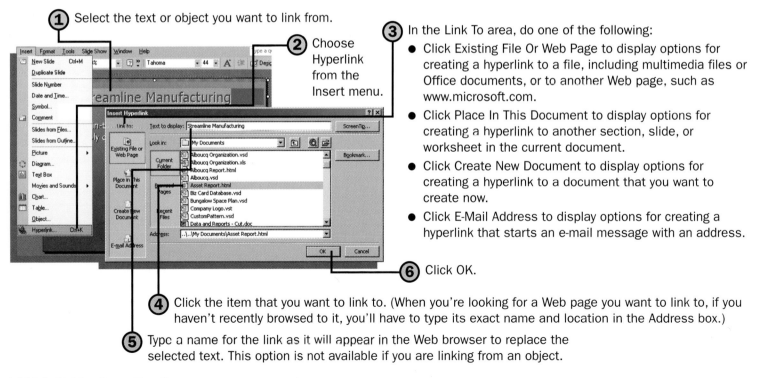

(6) Click OK.

(4) Click the item that you want to link to. (When you're looking for a Web page you want to link to, if you haven't recently browsed to it, you'll have to type its exact name and location in the Address box.)

(5) Type a name for the link as it will appear in the Web browser to replace the selected text. This option is not available if you are linking from an object.

Editing and Deleting Hyperlinks

After you define a hyperlink, you can change it easily. Maybe you want the link to go to a different page, or you want to change the text in a ScreenTip. Perhaps you linked to a Web page that is no longer available and you want to delete the hyperlink altogether.

When you delete a hyperlink, only the hyperlink itself is removed—not the text or object that contained the hyperlink.

Edit a Hyperlink

(1) Right-click the text or object that contains the hyperlink.

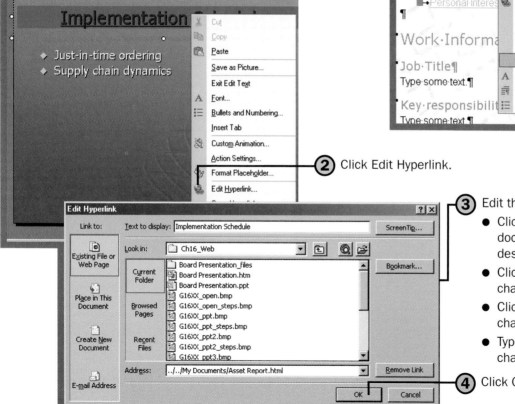

(2) Click Edit Hyperlink.

(3) Edit the hyperlink as follows:
- Click a new file, page, place in the document, or e-mail address to change the destination for the link.
- Click an option in the Link To area to change the type of link.
- Click the ScreenTip button to add or change the text of the ScreenTip.
- Type in the Text To Display box to add or change the title text.

(4) Click OK.

Delete a Hyperlink

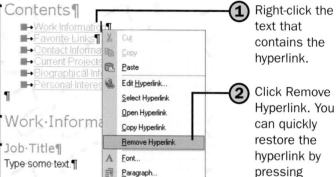

(1) Right-click the text that contains the hyperlink.

(2) Click Remove Hyperlink. You can quickly restore the hyperlink by pressing Ctrl+Z.

Changing the Look of a Web Page

When you start a Web site using the Web Page Wizard in Word or the Web Sites Wizard in Publisher, the wizard applies formatting to each Web page. You can quickly change the overall look of your Web site by applying a visual theme in Word or a new design in Publisher. Choose from a variety of coordinated sets of color and design elements such as fonts, decorative lines, and bullet characters.

If you're creating only Web pages in Word rather than an entire Web site, and you just want to add some color or texture, a background might be all you need. A background provides color and, if you like, a pattern or texture behind the text on the page to provide a more polished look when you save your document as a Web page.

Add a Visual Theme in Word

① Choose Theme from the Format menu.

② Click the theme you want.

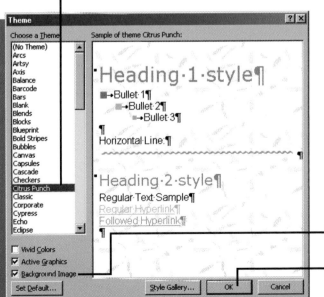

③ Select the Background Image check box.

④ Click OK.

Change a Design in Publisher

① In the Web Site Options task pane, click Publication Designs. If you don't see the Web Site Options task pane, choose Task Pane from the View menu.

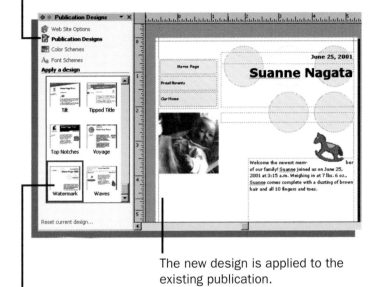

The new design is applied to the existing publication.

② Under Apply A Design, click the design you want to use.

> ✋ **CAUTION:** When you apply a new design to an existing Web site publication, Publisher changes the layout and inserts new clip art. You might need to move or resize the existing pictures and clip art to better suit the new design.

Saving a Word or Publisher Web Page

After you've finished adding text and pictures to your Word document or Publisher publication, you're ready to save it as a Web page—that is, in HTML format. You use the Save As Web Page command on the File menu, which saves any Word or Publisher document, including those you started with a Web wizard, as one or more Web pages and creates a new folder in which to store the supporting graphics and media files.

If you started your document using the Web Page Wizard in Word, the Save As Web Page command suggests the name "default.htm" for the home page of your Web site. (It's common practice in Web publishing to name the home page file "default.htm" or "index.htm.") A home page is the first page you want your site's visitors to display. Publisher names this page "Publication*n*.htm," where *n* is a number. You can rename the home page if you want.

Save a Document as a Web Page

1 Choose Save As Web Page from the File menu.

2 Click the Save In down arrow, and click a location for the file and its associated Web folder.

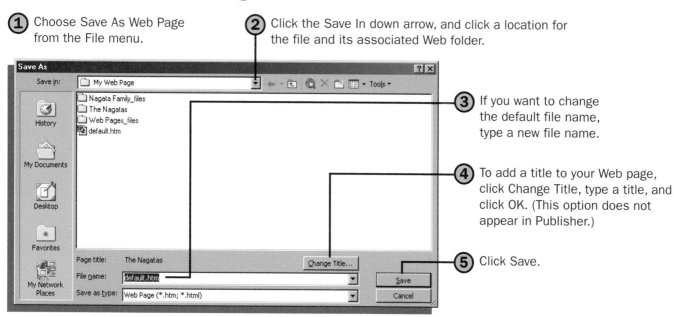

3 If you want to change the default file name, type a new file name.

4 To add a title to your Web page, click Change Title, type a title, and click OK. (This option does not appear in Publisher.)

5 Click Save.

> **TIP:** Before saving your Office document as a Web page, save a copy in the original file format (.doc, .xls, .ppt, for example). That way, you'll have a backup to revise in case the Web page format doesn't include everything in the original document.

> **CAUTION:** When you create a Web page from a Word document, some formatting features—such as borders, shading, and columns—might not be compatible with a particular browser. To turn off features that may not appear in some Web browsers, choose Options from the Tools menu. Then click Web Options on the General tab, and select the Disable Features Not Supported By These Browsers check box.

Saving a Worksheet as a Web Page ⊕ NEW FEATURE

Suppose you have a budget worksheet or an interest rate calculator that you want to share with others on a Web site. You can save your Excel worksheet as a Web page in two different ways:

- You can save a snapshot of your worksheet as a noninteractive Web page that displays the sheet's data exactly as it appeared when you use the Save As Web Page command.

- You can save an Excel worksheet as an interactive Web page that can be edited in a Web browser. For example, suppose you save an interest rate calculator as an interactive Web page. When viewed in a browser, the worksheet is interactive, and users can perform calculations with different values.

When you use the Save As Web Page command in Excel, you can specify whether to save the entire workbook or only a portion of it. You can also save a new version of an Excel workbook as a Web page every time you save your changes to the original document. This option, called Auto Republish, ensures that your Web page stays up-to-date. Some features and formatting might not appear when the page is displayed in a browser. For example, cell comments do not appear

in a Web page. For a list of features that are not retained when you use the Save As Web Page command, click in the Ask A Question box in the upper right corner of the window. Type **web limitations**, and then press the Enter key.

> **!** TIP: To customize an Excel worksheet for publication on the Web, choose Options from the Tools menu, and then click Web Options on the General tab.

Save an Excel Worksheet as a Web Page

1 Choose Save As Web Page from the File menu.

2 Click the Save In down arrow, and click a location for the file and its associated Web folder.

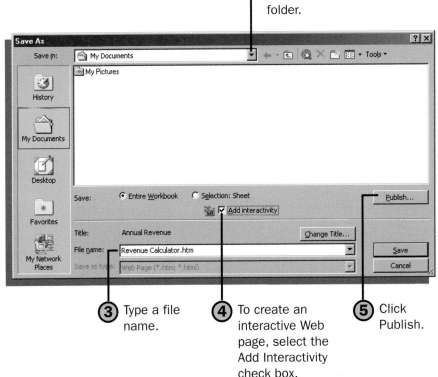

3 Type a file name.

4 To create an interactive Web page, select the Add Interactivity check box.

5 Click Publish.

CAUTION: To work with interactive Excel data on a Web page, you must have Microsoft Office Web Components, an appropriate Office XP license, and Internet Explorer version 4.01 or later.

SEE ALSO: For more information about creating worksheets, see "Naming, Adding, and Moving Worksheets" on page 116.

TIP: When you perform calculations in your Web page workbook in a Web browser, your changes are not saved. The next time you display the Web page, you'll see the same figures that were saved when you created the Web page.

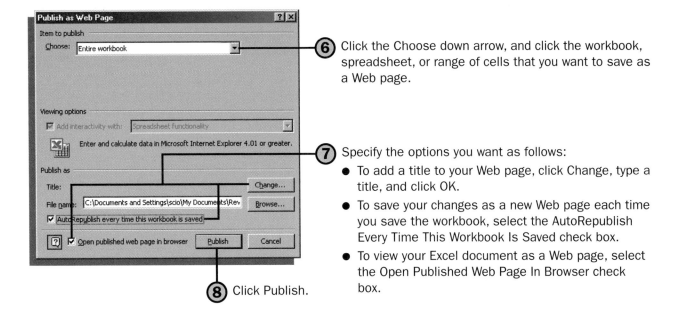

(6) Click the Choose down arrow, and click the workbook, spreadsheet, or range of cells that you want to save as a Web page.

(7) Specify the options you want as follows:

- To add a title to your Web page, click Change, type a title, and click OK.

- To save your changes as a new Web page each time you save the workbook, select the AutoRepublish Every Time This Workbook Is Saved check box.

- To view your Excel document as a Web page, select the Open Published Web Page In Browser check box.

(8) Click Publish.

Saving a Presentation as a Web Page

When you save a PowerPoint presentation as a Web page, anyone who has a Web browser can view your slides whether or not they have PowerPoint. You can save an entire presentation as Web pages or only a range of slides.

In addition to slides, a presentation often includes speaker notes and an outline, as well as special formatting such as slide transitions. The Save As Web Page command automatically includes these features and formatting. The Web pages include a *navigation frame*, which includes the outline of the presentation, a *slide frame*, which displays the slide, and *browser controls*, which appear below the slide frame and allow you to hide and show the other frames and navigate between slides.

Publish Web Pages in PowerPoint

(1) Choose Save As Web Page from the File menu.

(2) Click the Save In down arrow, and click a location for the file and its associated Web folder.

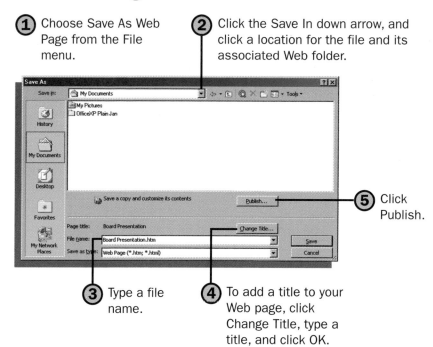

(5) Click Publish.

(3) Type a file name.

(4) To add a title to your Web page, click Change Title, type a title, and click OK.

SEE ALSO: For more information about designing presentations, see "Creating a PowerPoint Presentation" on page 211.

TIP: For more Web-specific PowerPoint options, choose Options from the Tools menu, and then click Web Options on the General tab.

SEE ALSO: For more information about delivering a PowerPoint presentation, see "Delivering a PowerPoint Presentation" on page 239.

6 Specify which portion of the presentation you want to save as a Web page.

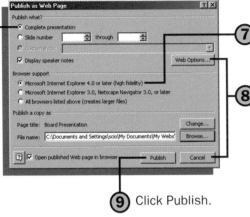

7 Click the browser support option that best matches your audience's Web browsers.

8 Specify the other options you want as follows:

- To display the presentation's speaker notes as a frame on your Web pages, select the Display Speaker Notes check box.

- To add a title to your Web page, click Change, type a title, and click OK.

- To view your PowerPoint document as a Web page, select the Open Published Web Page In Browser check box.

9 Click Publish.

TIP: When you open a Web page in a browser, the speaker notes and outline are displayed in panes. To prevent these panes from appearing, click Web Options in the Publish As Web Page dialog box, and then clear the Add Slide Navigation Controls check box on the General tab.

Creating a Web Archive to Send in an E-mail Message ⊛ NEW FEATURE

Office has a new option that greatly simplifies the task of publishing your Web pages. Instead of saving a document as a Web page, you can create a Web *archive,* which is a type of file that contains all the contents of your Web pages so that you can easily send the archive as an e-mail attachment. For example, you can send a Web archive to your local webmaster to publish on an intranet site or send the archive to team members who need to review the pages' contents.

By contrast, the Save As Web Page command creates multiple files in a separate folder that contains all the text and graphic files associated with your Web pages. You can create a Web archive file format in Word, Excel, PowerPoint, and Publisher.

Save a Document as a Web Archive

1 Choose Save As Web Page from the File menu.

2 Click the Save In down arrow, and click a location for the archive file.

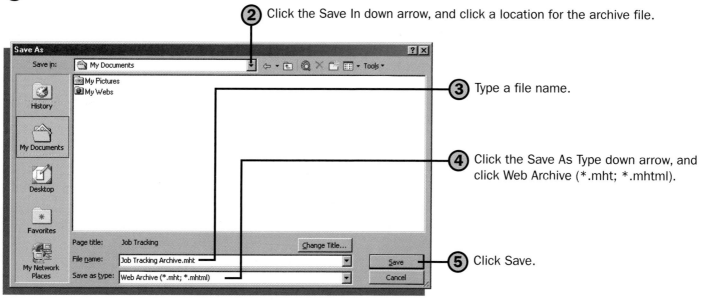

3 Type a file name.

4 Click the Save As Type down arrow, and click Web Archive (*.mht; *.mhtml).

5 Click Save.

SEE ALSO: For more information about using the Save As Web Page command, see "Creating Web Pages" on page 282.

CAUTION: Create a Web archive only if you and your audience have Internet Explorer 4 or later. Earlier versions do not support the Web archive format.

Creating a Publication with Publisher

Microsoft Publisher makes building a professional-looking publication not only easy, but fun. But why use Publisher? Why not stick with Microsoft Word?

If your documents are mostly text, adorned with little more than a page number and headings and perhaps punctuated by a picture or two, Word is your tool of choice. But if you plan a more elaborate layout that requires arranging text, pictures, and such elements as headlines or captions, Publisher will help you deliver your message with style and punch.

Publisher builds design assistance into the software with wizards that stand at the ready to help you build your publication from the ground up—lay it out, choose color and font sets, and add other embellishments such as mini-calendars, reply forms, and coupons. In this section, you'll learn the fine points of how Publisher handles text, particularly long blocks of text, and pick up the basics of adding and manipulating pictures—spin them on their axes, stack them, and wrap text around them—along with some advice about printing your publication.

Creating a Specific Type of Publication

We've featured two ways to begin: pick a publication type from among the seemingly endless list of newsletters, flyers, brochures, business papers, calendars, invitations, and so forth. Or start with the image you want your business to project, and *then* pick a publication type.

If you take the first route, you'll begin by picking a design from Publisher's repertoire. Then, experiment with the layout (Page Content), color and font schemes, and add other elements such as an ad or a coupon to the publication. (You can return later to tinker with any of these elements.) Now you're ready to fill the frames with your own content—pictures, stories, captions, and the like.

> **TRY THIS:** Of course you can design and build a publication on your own with Publisher's thorough Help System at your side. To do so, choose New from the File menu. Click the Start From A Design down arrow, and then click By Blank Publications. Click the type of publication you want to build—full page, index card, poster, and so on—and you're ready to go. If you need guidance, click in the Ask A Question box in the upper right corner of the window. Type your question, and then press the Enter key.

Start a Specific Type of Publication

1 Choose New from the File menu.

2 Click a publication type in the list.
If you don't see this list, click the down arrow, and then click By Publication Type.

3 To see your options, either scroll through the thumbnail sketches or click a category on the left and browse from there.

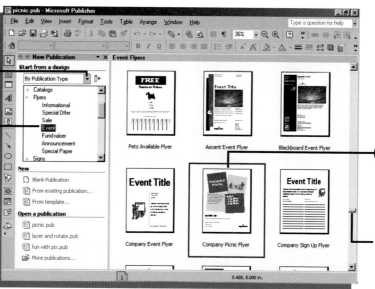

4 Click the design you want. (If Publisher asks, fill in the Personal Information dialog box.)

Scroll through these thumbnail sketches to see your options.

TRY THIS: You can use Publisher to transform ordinary reports into handsome publications. Start with step 1 in "Start a Specific Type of Publication." Then in step 2, click Word Documents as the publication type, and pick a design you like. Publisher prompts you to find your file, and the wizard adds as many pages as needed to hold it. Add a title page, adjust the number of columns, and you're ready to go.

TIP: To edit your personal information, choose Personal Information from the Edit menu. Note that although you can format the logo or change it any way you want, you can't remove it from your personal information set—even the placeholder logo Publisher provides. You can, however, delete the logo from each publication.

(5) Click to browse through different color and font schemes until you find the ones you want.

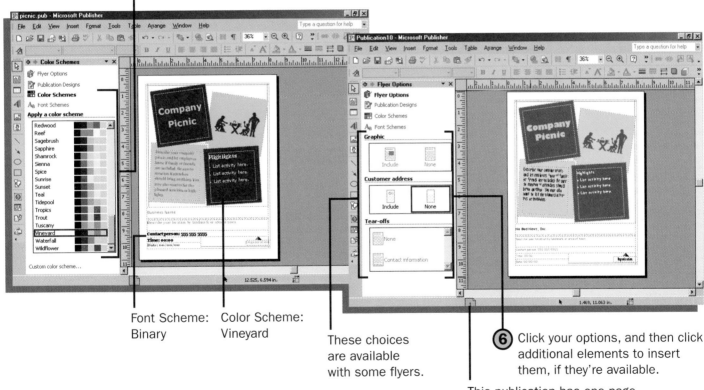

Font Scheme: Binary

Color Scheme: Vineyard

These choices are available with some flyers.

(6) Click your options, and then click additional elements to insert them, if they're available.

This publication has one page.

Publisher in a Nutshell

Using a word processor is like stringing beads: you can combine different sizes and colors, but basically the elements go together in only one way—in a line. Using a desktop publisher is more like creating a collage: the only limit to the possible arrangements of elements on the page is your imagination (and time). We've simmered Publisher's approach and requirements down to the four covered in the following paragraphs.

First, each element in a publication goes in a box (or *frame*)—a picture in a picture frame, text in a text box, and so on for tables, WordArt, and clip art. When objects are grouped together—captions and photographs, a company logo and address, and so on—they're also contained in a box. As in a collage, you simply drag these boxes around on the page, changing their sizes, and layering them to get the effect you want.

Use of the scratch area is also unique to Publisher and reflects its page-by-page orientation. Pages lie atop the scratch area like papers on your desk. And just like your desktop, you can use the scratch area to store elements— pictures, shards of text, and the like—awaiting inclusion or under consideration for use on other pages.

In addition, wizards can automate virtually every task you do. After a wizard helps you create a publication, a wizard will help you pick an entire font or color scheme or change the entire design; add a caption and a wizard helps you modify it. Wizards work in the background, too, checking your design for flaws or helping you ready your publication for a commercial printer.

In almost every other Microsoft Office program, printing is the culmination of a job well done. However, to get the same results on paper as you see on the screen depends entirely on the printer you're using. Because you go to such pains to polish every detail, in Publisher you choose the printer for your finished piece *before* you add any content to your publication—particularly if you intend to use a commercial printing service.

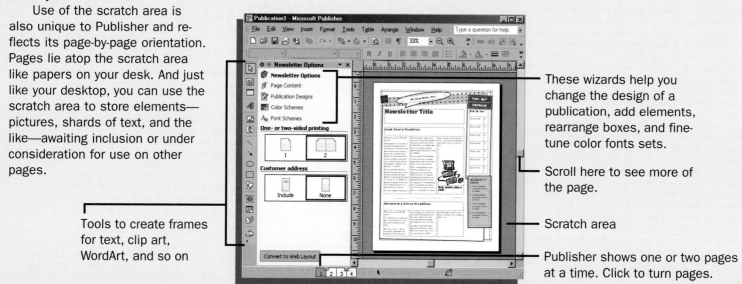

These wizards help you change the design of a publication, add elements, rearrange boxes, and fine-tune color fonts sets.

Scroll here to see more of the page.

Scratch area

Publisher shows one or two pages at a time. Click to turn pages.

Tools to create frames for text, clip art, WordArt, and so on

Creating a Publication with a Special "Look"

When you're building on a unique look—whether for your business or for yourself—you start by choosing a design from one of Publisher's Design Sets. Your choices of Publisher's Design Sets range from light-hearted "Bubbles," and conservative "Refined," to hip "Capsules."

After you've settled on the look you want, *then* you choose the type of publication. For example, if you've chosen "Bubbles" as the look for all your publications, you'd choose a publication type from the list of Bubbles options.

You can also pick a single design for special events or holidays, and build a set of publications around that theme.

> **CAUTION:** When you create a publication based on one of Publisher's design sets, tweak font and color schemes thoughtfully so you don't disturb the carefully co-ordinated look and feel created by Publisher's professional designers. This goes for adding elements, too—pick them by design wherever possible to match the established look.

Start a Publication with a Special "Look" or Purpose

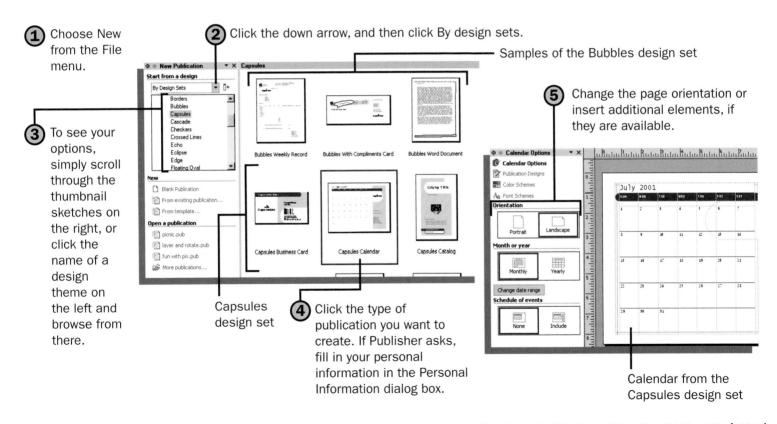

① Choose New from the File menu.

② Click the down arrow, and then click By design sets.

Samples of the Bubbles design set

③ To see your options, simply scroll through the thumbnail sketches on the right, or click the name of a design theme on the left and browse from there.

Capsules design set

④ Click the type of publication you want to create. If Publisher asks, fill in your personal information in the Personal Information dialog box.

⑤ Change the page orientation or insert additional elements, if they are available.

Calendar from the Capsules design set

Adding Calendars, Stars, and Other Elements to a Page

Publisher's designers understood the drive for individual expression. Even with hundreds of publication designs to choose from, they built two libraries, AutoShapes and Design Gallery Objects, overflowing with elements you can add to any publication.

The AutoShapes Library includes diagram arrows, starbursts, and cartoon balloons. (They're called AutoShapes because in most cases, when you draw a rectangle, Publisher draws the shape.)

The Design Gallery includes caption styles for pictures, mini-calendars, coupons, and even logos. You can hunt for Design Gallery Objects in two ways. Browse by category—reply forms, logos, and so on. Or, to maintain visual consistency with other publications, start with the design—say "Bubbles" or "Refined"—and *then* choose the object from that design.

> **SEE ALSO:** For information about how to rotate shapes, see "Layering, Grouping, and Rotating Pictures" on page 314.

Add an AutoShape

1 Click the AutoShapes button.

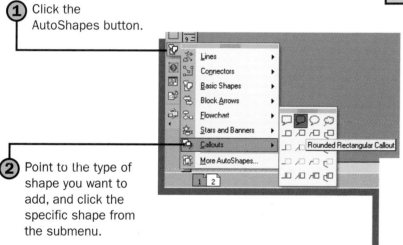

2 Point to the type of shape you want to add, and click the specific shape from the submenu.

3 Using the crosshair pointer, click and drag to draw a box or line until the shape or line is the size or length you want.

> **NEW FEATURE:** To nudge frames one pixel at a time, point to Nudge on the Arrange menu. A submenu appears—Up, Down, Left, Right. Move your mouse pointer over the gray bar at the top of the submenu, and drag the Nudge toolbar onto the page. To nudge a frame into place, click the frame, and keep clicking the appropriate arrow until the frame is in place.

Add a Design Gallery Object

(1) Go to the page where you want to add the object.

(2) Click the Design Gallery Object button.

(3) Click a tab depending on how you want to add the object:
- Click Objects By Category to look for different types of objects.
- Click Objects By Design to track down objects that match the look of other publications.

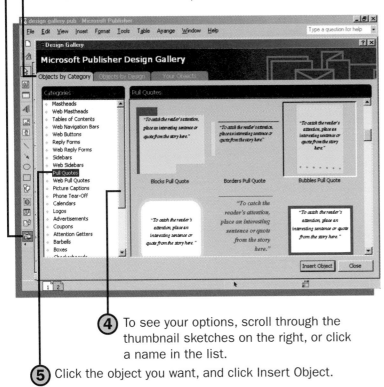

(4) To see your options, scroll through the thumbnail sketches on the right, or click a name in the list.

(5) Click the object you want, and click Insert Object.

(6) Drag the object into position, and adjust its size if you want.

(7) If you want to change the look of the object, click the Wizard button to display your choices in the task pane.

Adding and Deleting Pages

You can add as many pages as you want at a time, but you can delete pages only one or two (if you're in two-page view) at a time. You can add completely blank pages or ones with a single text frame, useful if you have a lengthy piece of text to place. Or, for those instances when the page you want to add is more similar to another page than not, add a page that copies every object—contents and all—to the new page. This has the added benefit of ensuring design consistency across pages.

Add Pages

(1) Go to the page that will come either before or after the page(s) you want to add.

(2) Choose Page from the Insert menu.

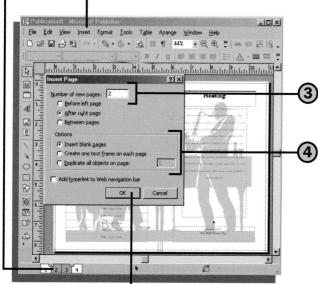

(5) Click OK.

> **TIP:** If your publication is a newsletter, Publisher lets you change certain design elements before you add pages. After step 2 in "Add Pages," click the Left-Hand Page down arrow, and click the element you want to add. (To keep the new page as shown in the preview, make sure the Story option is selected.) After you click the Left-Hand Page down arrow, Publisher displays a drop-down lists of elements to add. Then click More Options, and resume following the instructions in "Add Pages," starting with step 3.

> **CAUTION:** When you're adding pages in the *middle* of a booklet, newsletter, or other document where you expect to be looking at two pages at a time, you'll run into fewer design problems if you always add an even number of pages.

(3) Type the number of pages you want to add, and indicate where to add them.

(4) Do one of the following to specify what kind of page to add:

- Click Insert Blank Pages to add pages with nothing at all in them.
- Click Create One Text Frame On Each Page to create a page filled with a single text frame.
- Click Duplicate All Objects On Page to copy any page you specify, contents and all.

Delete a Page

② Choose Delete Page from the Edit menu.

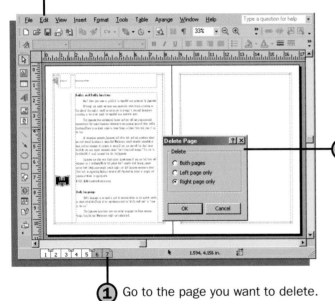

③ Follow the directions on your screen:

- If you're looking at a single page, a message appears, asking if you're sure you want to delete the page. Click OK.

- If you're in two-page view, in the Delete Pages dialog box, click the page or pages you want to delete, and then click OK.

① Go to the page you want to delete.

Changing Your Page View

You can see the pages of your work in different ways, depending on the task. Zoom in to magnify the page, so you can do precision work, such as nudging pictures or text. Zoom out for a bird's-eye view of the whole page—a kind of working print preview—where you can see how all the parts of the page work together. Or, if you're working on a publication in which your reader will see two pages at a time (a *two-page spread*), you can switch to a two-page view.

Zoom In or Out

① Click the Zoom Out button to get a page overview.

② Click the Zoom In button to magnify the page.

Zoom down arrow

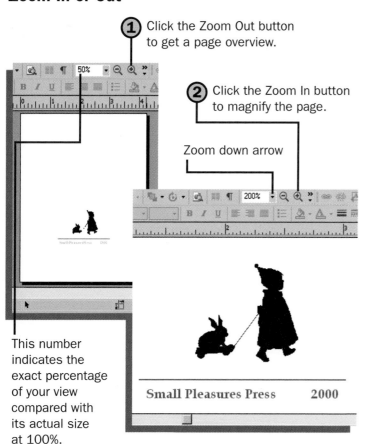

This number indicates the exact percentage of your view compared with its actual size at 100%.

Small Pleasures Press   2000

> ⚠ **TIP: To switch back and forth between your current view and the actual size (100 percent) of the publication, press the F9 key.**

Switch Between a One-Page and Two-Page View

① To switch between one-page and two-page views, choose Two-Page Spread from the View menu.

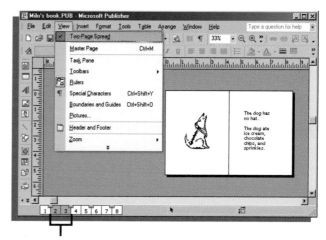

Click to change pages two at a time.

Working with Frames for Pictures and Text

Frames (or boxes) are basic to the way Publisher works: each picture and block of text goes in its own frame, and you use a unique tool to create each type of frame. To insert text, you draw a frame for text (called a "text box") using the Text Box tool; to insert pictures, you draw a picture frame using the Picture Frame tool, and so on.

These tools work in different ways. You click some tools, like the Text Box tool, to draw an empty frame and then add your own text. Others, like the WordArt tool, you click, and you start with design choices before entering text. Whatever tool you use, handling the frame is a lot like working with furniture: you can push a frame into just the spot you want, you can remove it, and you can refurbish it; unlike furniture, however, you can change a frame's size.

Create a Text, Picture, or Table Frame

(1) Click the Text Box, Insert Table, or Picture Frame tool.

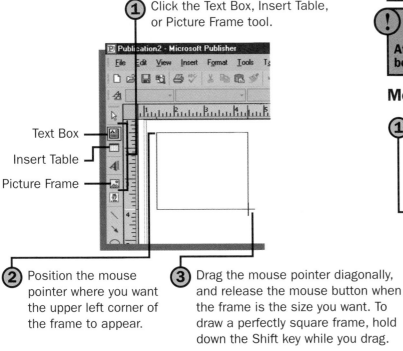

Text Box

Insert Table

Picture Frame

(2) Position the mouse pointer where you want the upper left corner of the frame to appear.

(3) Drag the mouse pointer diagonally, and release the mouse button when the frame is the size you want. To draw a perfectly square frame, hold down the Shift key while you drag.

Delete a Frame and Its Contents

(1) Right-click the frame, and click Delete Object on the short-cut menu.

SEE ALSO: For information about basic techniques for changing the size of a frame, see "Changing the Size, Placement, and Content of Pictures" on page 30.

TIP: After you draw a table frame, you specify the number of rows and columns before you see it on the page. After you draw a picture frame, you must insert a picture before you see it on the page.

Move a Frame

(1) Click the frame you want to move.

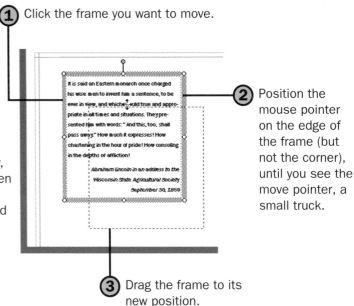

(2) Position the mouse pointer on the edge of the frame (but not the corner), until you see the move pointer, a small truck.

(3) Drag the frame to its new position.

Adding and Formatting Text

After you've created the frame, working with the text itself is a lot like working with text in Word—typing and editing, formatting, checking spelling, and so on.

But Publisher adds a couple of unique twists to this otherwise familiar territory. First, because the text box is finite in size, it can only display a certain amount of text; if Publisher can't fit all the text in the box, the text spills into an overflow area.

And second, a wizard helps you apply one of over two dozen sets of fonts (or schemes) that are carefully selected so that each font within the set harmonizes with the others. These font schemes dictate the look of all text in a publication—one font for headlines, another for body text, yet a third for captions—and protect those who are new to desktop publishing from making a common mistake, mingling incompatible fonts.

Enter Text in a Text Box

(1) If you don't already have a text box, draw one using the Text Box tool.

(2) Click in the text box where you want to add your text. This will be at the beginning if the text box is empty.

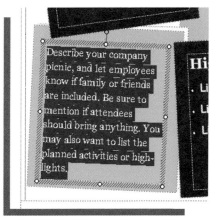

(3) Type the text you want to add, or paste it from another document. If you're replacing sample text, Publisher selects it and deletes it when you start typing.

SEE ALSO: For information about how to draw a text box, see "Working with Frames for Pictures and Text" on page 307.

TRY THIS: Instead of retyping a long document in Publisher, you can add it right from Word. Click in the text box where you want to add the document, and choose Text File from the Insert menu. (You might have to install a converter using the original Publisher disk.) In the Insert Text dialog box, browse to locate the file you want to import, and click OK. When Publisher asks if you want to use Autoflow, click No if you don't know how to do this. (When Publisher flows text automatically, it might put text in places you didn't intend, so it's safer to direct the text exactly where you want it later.)

SEE ALSO: For information about how to work with text that's too long to fit in a text frame, see "Fitting Text in Text Boxes" on page 310. For information about how to add text such as headlines, captions, and pull-quotes, see "Adding Calendars, Stars and Other Elements to a Page" on page 302.

Choose a Font Scheme

1 If the task pane isn't open, choose Task Pane from the View menu to open it.

2 Choose Font Schemes from the Format menu.

3 In the Font Schemes task pane, click font schemes until you find one that works.

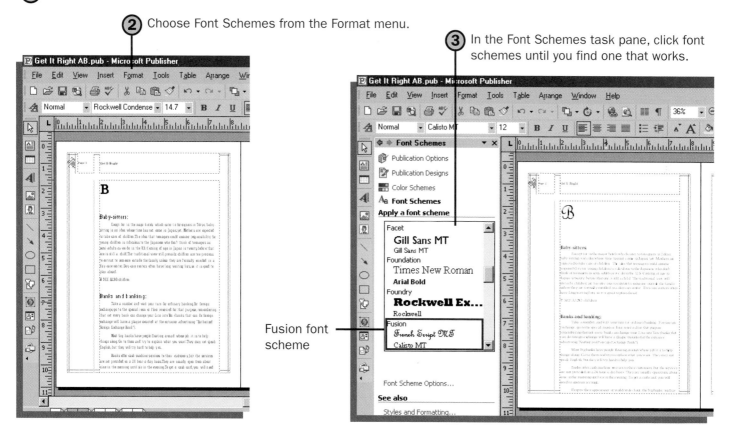

Fusion font scheme

TIP: If the fonts don't change in your document after you click a font scheme, click in the Ask A Question box in the upper right corner of the window. Type font schemes, and then press the Enter key. Click Troubleshoot Font Schemes in the list, and look for the problem that applies.

TRY THIS: If you have good design training or a keen eye, you can, of course, change the look of text on your own. Most of Publisher's choices—from font size and color to line spacing and drop caps—are available from the list when you right-click selected text, and click Change Text.

Fitting Text in Text Boxes

When you find that your text just doesn't fit in the box, don't worry. Publisher's designers have provided an army of strategies to help you fit—or *copyfit*—words into their assigned space. When text doesn't fit in its box, it goes into the overflow area where it can't be seen.

For minor fitting problems, you can change the size of the text, adjust the space between lines, or make the text box bigger. You can also, of course, edit the text to fit. Or you can direct Publisher to fit the copy for you using AutoFit. The AutoFit feature shrinks or increases the font size as you reduce or enlarge the text

box. In situations where you want the size of the text frame to remain steady, as with headlines, Publisher will shrink the font size as you add more text.

But what if you have a lengthy block of text that doesn't fit in the frame? In that case, you'll need to add more text boxes and connect them so that the text in one box flows into the next. The mouse pointer even changes into a pitcher so you "pour" words into connected frames to create what Publisher calls a *story*.

> **SEE ALSO:** For information about how to create another text box, see "Working with Frames for Pictures and Text" on page 307.

Fit Text in a Text Box Automatically

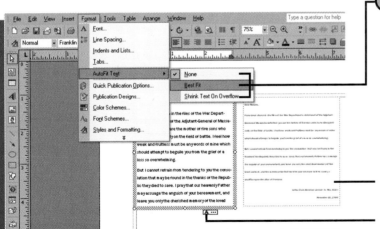

1 Click the text box to select it.

2 Point to AutoFit Text on the Format menu, and then do one of the following:
- Click None to keep the size of text constant, and have text that doesn't fit the frame disappear into the overflow area.
- Click Best Fit to shrink or enlarge the text when the size of the box might change.
- Click Shrink Text On Overflow to reduce the point size when you're trying to keep the size of the text box constant.

Publisher fits this text in the box.

Indicates that the text won't fit in the frame

Connect Text Boxes for a Long Story

① Make sure you have an empty text box in which to put the extra text.

② Click in the text box containing too much text.

③ Click the Create Text Box Link button.

④ Click in the text box where you want the story to continue and the words pour into it.

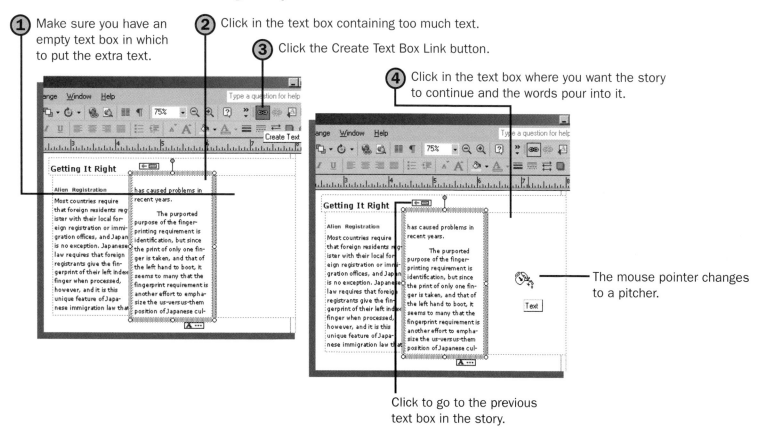

The mouse pointer changes to a pitcher.

Click to go to the previous text box in the story.

! **TIP:** When a story spills over to another page, it's not a bad idea to let your reader know that the story is "Continued on page x," or when they get there, to remind them that it was "Continued from page y." To do this, right-click the text box where you want to add the continued notice. (The text box must already be connected to the box that text is continued to or from.) Click Format Text Box, specify the type of continued notice you want, and then click OK. If you don't see the continued notice, you might not have connected the two text boxes, so Publisher doesn't know where to continue the story. Connect the two, and the continued notice should appear.

Adding Pictures

Most Publisher designs have a place in the design where you can drop in pictures—digital photos from your collection (stored on your computer's hard disk or on your camera), scanned images, or Publisher drawings and photos in the form of clip art, categorized and stored on the Microsoft Office Media CD.

Replace a Picture in an Existing Picture Frame

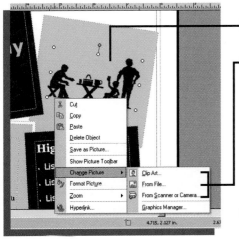

(1) Right-click in the picture or picture frame.

(2) Point to Change Picture, and specify the type of picture you want to add:

- Click Clip Art to add a ready-made image from the Office collection of drawings and sketches.
- Click From File to insert an image from your computer's hard disk.
- Click From Scanner Or Camera to add a picture directly if your computer is hooked up to either one.

(3) Follow the instructions in the dialog boxes that appear for each option you choose in step 2.

Add a Picture Without an Existing Picture Frame

(1) Use the Picture Frame tool to draw a picture frame.

(2) In the Insert Picture box, browse to find the picture you want to add, and then click Insert.

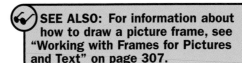

SEE ALSO: For information about adding clip art or inserting a picture file, and then cropping, resizing, organizing, and editing pictures, see "Enhancing Documents" on page 25.

SEE ALSO: For information about how to draw a picture frame, see "Working with Frames for Pictures and Text" on page 307.

TRY THIS: If your printer is slowed when you try to print a publication with many pictures, you can speed up the printing of drafts by printing empty boxes instead of the pictures themselves. Choose Print from the File menu, and click Advanced Print Settings. Then, in the Graphics area, click Do Not Print Any Graphics, and click OK.

Wrapping Text Around Pictures

Put a picture in a text frame and control how the text wraps (or flows) around either the picture frame or the picture itself. Text wrapping is a sticky business—if you replace an image, Publisher remembers the way text wrapped around the old picture.

Wrap Text Around the Shape of a Picture

1 If the Picture Toolbar isn't visible, right-click the picture you want to wrap text around, and click Show Picture Toolbar.

2 Click Text Wrapping on the Picture Toolbar.

3 Click Tight. If a dialog box appears, asking if you want to create a new wrap boundary, click Yes.

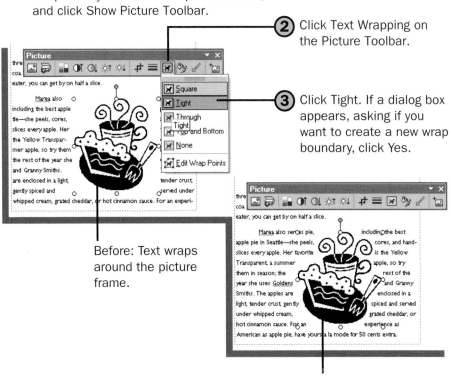

Before: Text wraps around the picture frame.

After: Text wraps around the shape of the picture.

> **TIP:** If you want text to wrap around the picture frame, follow the first two steps in "Wrapping Text Around the Shape of a Picture," and click Square.

> **TIP:** If the text doesn't wrap as you've directed—for example, it doesn't wrap around the shape or it appears on top of the picture or its margins—click in the Ask A Question box in the upper right corner of the window. Type text wrap, and then press the Enter key. Click Troubleshoot How Text Wraps in the list, and click the problem that applies.

> **TIP:** You can't wrap text in a table around a picture or other object; nor can you wrap text around a grouped object.

Layering, Grouping, and Rotating Pictures

Each Publisher page is built in layers. The invisible foundation is the Master page where elements repeated on every page reside, the Publisher equivalent of headers and footers in Word. Frames lie atop this foundation—some on one layer (the principle behind wrapping text around pictures) and some stacked.

Publisher lets you control where in the stack you put an object: move it up a bit (Bring Forward) or put it on top (Bring To Front). This works the same way for moving down (Send Backward) in the stack. And yes—a bigger object lying on top of a smaller one can obscure it.

Publisher also lets you group objects so you can work with them together—captions with photos, page numbers in calendars, and so on. Once grouped, they stay together until you split them up (*ungroup* them). Publisher also lets you flip objects horizontally or vertically, rotate them left or right, or spin them (*free rotate*) any which way.

> **! TIP:** To zoom in to a specific point on the page, right-click where you want to zoom to, point to Zoom, and click how close in or far out you want to zoom.

Layer Pictures and Other Objects

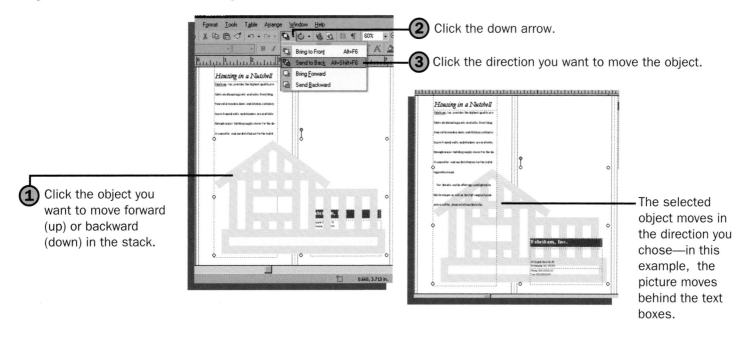

2 Click the down arrow.

3 Click the direction you want to move the object.

1 Click the object you want to move forward (up) or backward (down) in the stack.

The selected object moves in the direction you chose—in this example, the picture moves behind the text boxes.

Group Text, Pictures, and Other Objects

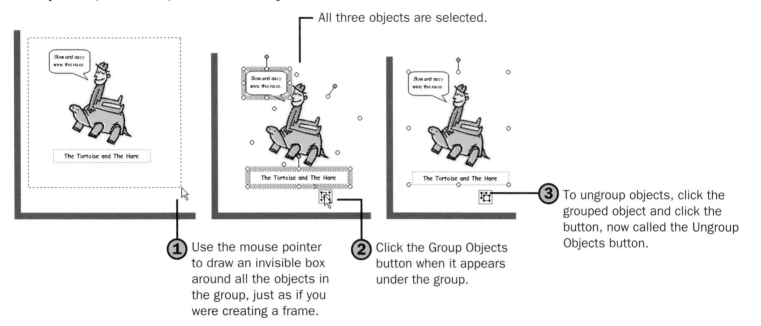

All three objects are selected.

1 Use the mouse pointer to draw an invisible box around all the objects in the group, just as if you were creating a frame.

2 Click the Group Objects button when it appears under the group.

3 To ungroup objects, click the grouped object and click the button, now called the Ungroup Objects button.

Rotate Pictures and Other Objects

1 Click the object you want to rotate.

2 Drag the Rotation handle in the direction you want to rotate the object.

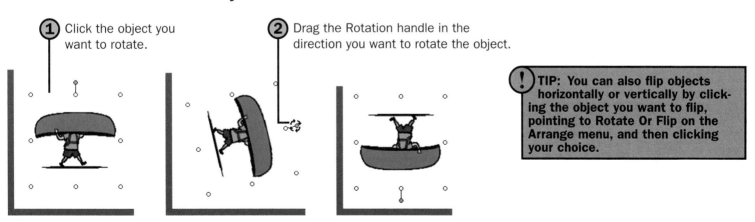

! TIP: You can also flip objects horizontally or vertically by clicking the object you want to flip, pointing to Rotate Or Flip on the Arrange menu, and then clicking your choice.

Checking and Printing a Publication

Publisher supports a wide range of print technologies that allow you to print from a desktop printer augmented by the services of a copy shop; to take your publication to a copy shop to print crisp, original output with quality that surpasses copies; or to take it to a commercial printer where you can get superior print quality and support for full color.

Contrary to usual practice, *before* you start work on your publication, make sure to set it up for the printer you'll use for the finished piece. Remember, getting the same results on paper as you see on the screen depends entirely on the printer you're using. The printer determines the fonts and styles available for text, the area of the page you can actually print on, the quality of output, and so on. You don't want to ruin a finely tuned publication at the last minute by switching printers.

If you decide to use an outside printing service, it's especially important to consult on your design up front. If you don't, you might need to make time-consuming and potentially costly design changes just before you print. Taking your publication to a commercial printer entails some extra work on your end. But Publisher's Pack And Go Wizard stands by to help you package files for just this purpose and ensure that the printing service has access to the graphics and fonts used in your publication.

Just before you print your publication, have Publisher's Design Checker scour your publication for problems—text in the overflow area, empty text frames, and objects in an area that won't print, for example. (Wait until the end, however; Design Checker is extremely thorough and takes time.) This is not a bad time to run the spelling checker as well.

Switch Printers

① Choose Print from the Format menu.

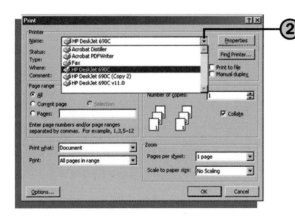

> **(!) TIP:** To set up a printer, click the Windows Start button (generally in the lower left corner of the window), point to Settings, and click Printers. Double-click Add Printer, and follow the instructions in the Add Printer Wizard.

② Click the Name down arrow, and click the name of the printer you want to use. If the printer's name is not on the list, it might not be set up.

> **(!) TIP:** Publisher has a lot of information built in to help you navigate through the details of printing a publication. To find it, click in the Ask A Question box in the upper right corner of the window. Type printing or commercial printing, and then press the Enter key. Browse through the topics that come up, and click to read (or print) the ones that are of interest.

Check Your Document Design

1 Choose Design Checker from
the Tools menu.

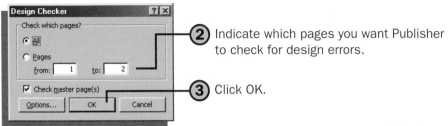

2 Indicate which pages you want Publisher
to check for design errors.

3 Click OK.

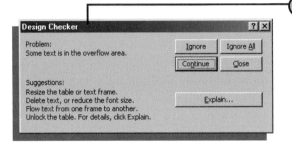

4 As Design Checker reports each
problem, decide how you want to solve
it, and do one of the following:

- Click Ignore to continue checking the
  design without fixing this problem.

- Click Ignore All to continue checking
  the design without fixing this problem
  or any other occurrence of it.

- Click Continue after you have fixed
  the problem and you are ready to find
  the next problem. (The dialog box will
  remain open while you fix it.)

- Click Close to stop checking the
  design and return to your publication.

- Click Explain to launch the Publisher
  Help pane, which offers an
  explanation of the problem and steps
  to solve it.

**TIP: To check the spelling in your
publication, click in any text box.
Point to Spelling on the Tools
menu, and click Spelling. In the
Check Spelling dialog box, select
the Check All Stories check box to
inspect your spelling in every text
frame in the publication. Then follow Publisher's directions.**

21 Creating and Working with a SharePoint Team Web Site

Microsoft SharePoint Team Services is a new feature in Microsoft Office XP designed to make working in the team environment simple for both administrators and users. But what can these services do to help your team produce better documents, and what do you need to know in order to start running a team Web site capable of being accessed via the Internet or your corporate intranet?

If you only send documents out to a few team members every once in a while, using e-mail to keep track of the process is fine, but if you're working on a big project with lots of collaborators, your need to keep track of content issues, document versions, and tasks becomes a lot more intense. A SharePoint team Web site can help you manage schedules, documents, and team members.

Creating and managing SharePoint team Web sites requires no HTML or programming knowledge. If you've got access to a Web server with SharePoint Team Services installed (check with your network administrator or Internet service provider), you can have a new team Web site up and running in a few minutes.

Using a Web browser, you can administer the team Web site, and your team members can create contact and task lists, event calendars, libraries for storing documents, and surveys. They can also create and participate in discussion lists, and sign up to receive updates through e-mail.

What Is a SharePoint Team Web Site?

In its simplest definition, a *team Web site* is a series of Web pages designed to organize and distribute information needed by a group, usually coworkers on a project. It can be a useful tool for project managers and team members alike, helping to sort out the often-complicated teamwork process. A team Web site can be as simple as a small list of schedules and critical documents or as complicated as any extensive corporate intranet.

SharePoint team Web sites take care of all the technical details involved in creating Web pages, administering file folders, and setting up lists. SharePoint Team Services, the application that manages your team Web sites, needs to be set up on a Microsoft Windows–based Web server by your network administrator or Internet service provider. You'll also need to have a user name and password for creating team Web sites set up on the server.

Once the server is properly configured, it will only take you a few steps to create new team Web sites. Within your new team Web site, you can organize documents, create schedules, maintain discussion groups, and provide contact information to your team members. As a creator or administrator of a SharePoint team Web site, you can set up your site using your browser. Adding and creating user accounts for your team members is easy and allows you to control who can read or add content to the site.

A Shared Documents folder allows your team members to access files from the team Web site, and you can organize these files in subfolders, or even search for them. Contact lists allow you to connect team members with each other and important people outside of the team. Discussion lists allow your team to communicate through publicly posted messages about important issues, scheduling, events, and tasks. SharePoint handles all the technical details, allowing you to think about the content that your team members need.

 SEE ALSO: For information about using Office to work with others, see "Collaborating Using Office" on page 195.

TIP: Check with your network administrator or Internet service provider to find out if your organization has SharePoint Team Services installed on one of their servers.

Creating a SharePoint Team Web Site

When you begin a project, you'll want to get organized right away. A team Web site can give you the structure you need to organize team members, whether they're in the same office or separated by oceans. Once you have access to a Web server with SharePoint Team Services installed, you can create a new team Web site in a few clicks using Microsoft FrontPage, giving your team members access to easily configurable lists, schedules, document folders, and discussions.

SEE ALSO: For information about creating Web sites using FrontPage, see "Using FrontPage" on page 265.

Use FrontPage to Create a Team Web Site

TIP: Check with your server administrator for details on the location of your SharePoint server.

① Point to New on the File menu, and click Page Or Web.

② Click Web Site Templates.

③ Click SharePoint-Based Team Web Site.

④ Type the Internet address of the team site you're creating.

⑤ Click OK.

⑥ Type your user name and password.

⑦ Click OK.

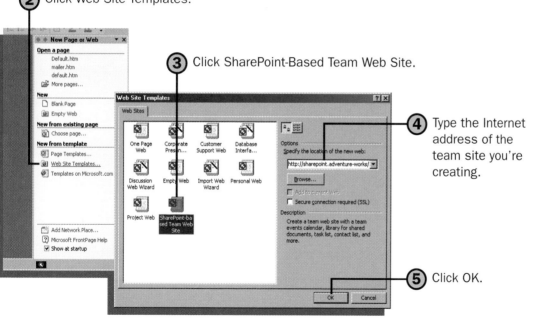
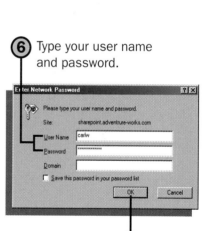

Adding Users to Your SharePoint Team Web Site

Once you've got your new team Web site up and running, you'll need to give other team members appropriate access to update tasks, upload files, post messages, and add any other information that other team members need to see. If you're administering the team Web site, you can use a Web browser to add and remove users, and assign and define *roles*, which control what parts of the site users have access to, and what type of information they can add.

Before you begin to add users, you'll need to specify that your site uses its own security settings, rather than the settings of any other sites on the server.

! **TIP: By default, new SharePoint Web sites inherit the user accounts of their parent sites (for example, sharepoint.adventure-works.com and sharepoint.adventure-works.com/mysite will share the same users by default). If all the Web sites on your SharePoint server share the same users in the same roles, there's no need to use unique security permissions.**

Set Unique User Accounts for Your Team Web Site

(1) Open your new Web site, and click Site Settings.

(2) Type your user name and password in the Enter Network Password dialog box, and click OK.

(3) Click the Change Permissions link under Web Administration on the Site Settings page.

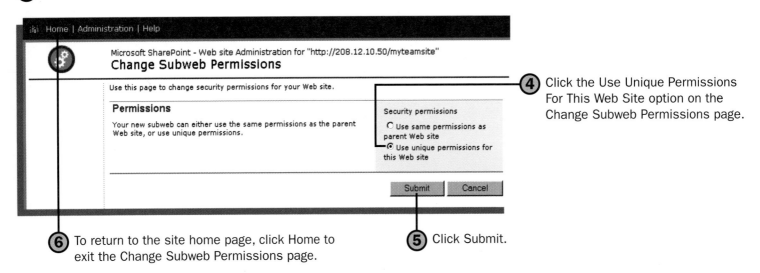

Home | Administration | Help

Microsoft SharePoint - Web site Administration for "http://208.12.10.50/myteamsite"
Change Subweb Permissions

Use this page to change security permissions for your Web site.

Permissions

Your new subweb can either use the same permissions as the parent Web site, or use unique permissions.

Security permissions

○ Use same permissions as parent Web site
⊙ Use unique permissions for this Web site

Submit   Cancel

(4) Click the Use Unique Permissions For This Web Site option on the Change Subweb Permissions page.

(6) To return to the site home page, click Home to exit the Change Subweb Permissions page.

(5) Click Submit.

Create a New User Account

① Open your new Web site, and click Site Settings.

② Type your user name and password in the Enter Network Password dialog box, and click OK.

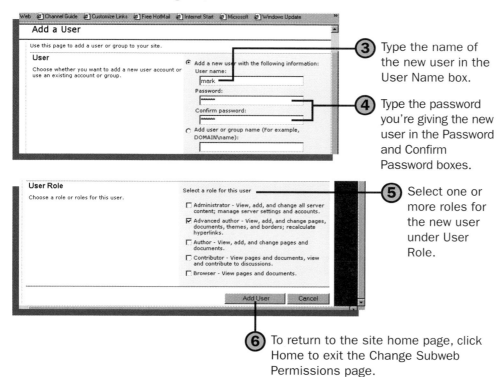

③ Type the name of the new user in the User Name box.

④ Type the password you're giving the new user in the Password and Confirm Password boxes.

⑤ Select one or more roles for the new user under User Role.

⑥ To return to the site home page, click Home to exit the Change Subweb Permissions page.

TRY THIS: If you've already created an account for a user on another SharePoint team Web site on the same server, click Add User Or Group Name, type their user name in the Add User Or Group Name box, and then select a role for them. Doing this allows your user to log on with the same name and password on both sites, while still allowing you to control their access.

TIP: Put some thought into what roles you give to your users. Having a clear hierarchy of who can change what in your site can save time and prevent individuals from making changes that adversely affect the rest of the team. You can also create and edit user roles in your browser by clicking the Go To Site Administration link on the Site Settings page, and then clicking Manage Roles under Users And Roles.

Storing Documents on a SharePoint Team Web Site

One of the most useful parts of a team Web site is its ability to store documents and other files in a central location that all of your team members can access. If you've got a new document draft that needs to be reviewed, or if you need to make a backup copy of a schedule, it only takes a few steps to send your files to the Shared Documents folder on your SharePoint team Web site. Whether uploading your files through a browser or saving them directly from Office, making your documents available through a SharePoint team Web site gives others in your group easy access to the files they need.

> **TRY THIS:** If you use Internet Explorer 5.0 or later, you can also view Shared Documents in Folder view, which allows you to navigate directories and deal with files just as you would in Windows Explorer. To do this, open your SharePoint site in your browser, and navigate to the Shared Documents page. Click the Folder View link on the left of the page, then enter your User Name and Password in the dialog box that appears. Double-click on the folders to open them in a new window.

Upload a Document to Your Team Web Site Through a Browser

(1) Click the Shared Documents link on the Home page (either on the Quick Launch taskbar or in one of the content columns).

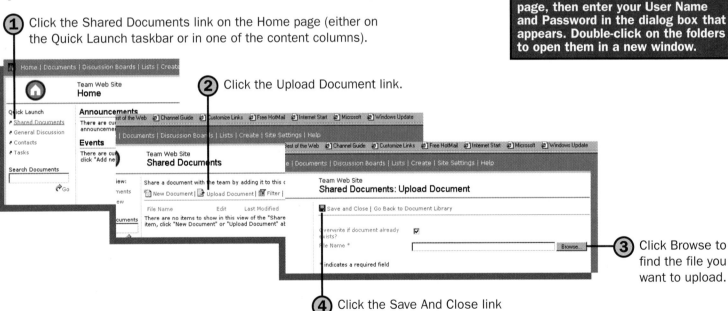

(2) Click the Upload Document link.

(3) Click Browse to find the file you want to upload.

(4) Click the Save And Close link

Save a Document to a SharePoint Team Web Site from Office

① Open the document you want to send to your team Web site, and choose Save As from the File menu.

② Click My Network Places (called Web Folders in Windows 98) in the Save As dialog box.

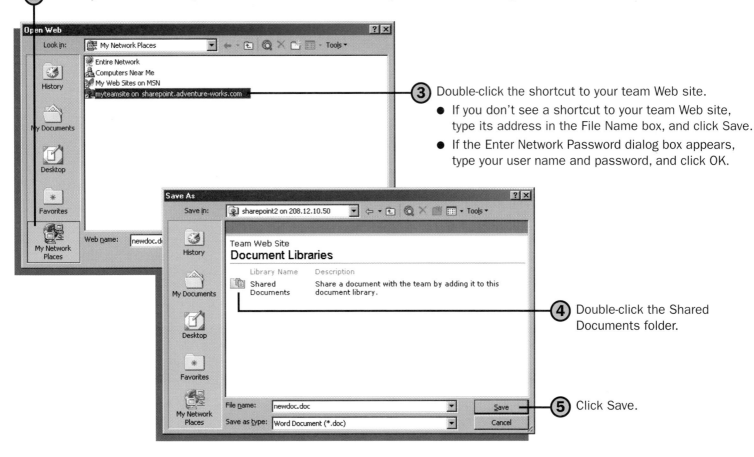

③ Double-click the shortcut to your team Web site.

- If you don't see a shortcut to your team Web site, type its address in the File Name box, and click Save.

- If the Enter Network Password dialog box appears, type your user name and password, and click OK.

④ Double-click the Shared Documents folder.

⑤ Click Save.

Organizing Documents on a SharePoint Team Web Site

The more files you've got stored in your Shared Documents folder, the more difficult it is to find a specific document. Creating subfolders for your documents is a simple fix, allowing you to organize your information just like you would on your own computer. SharePoint allows you to organize subfolders in your Shared Documents folder, and also search for documents stored on your site, all from within your Web browser.

Create a New Subfolder in the Shared Documents Folder

1 Click the Shared Documents link on the Home page.

2 Click the Folder View link.

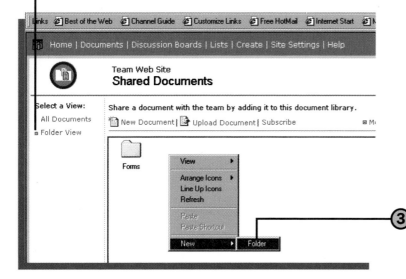

3 Right-click in the folder task pane (if you get a warning message, just click Yes to proceed), point to New, and click Folder.

> **TRY THIS:** You're not limited to just using the Shared Documents folder. If you need a separate storage area—for example, a place to store schedules aside from the normal document storage area—you can create a new shared folder in your site's Documents area. To create a new folder, click the Documents link, and then click New Document Library on the Document Libraries page.

> **TIP:** If the number of documents and files makes it difficult to find a shared document, use the Filter feature to narrow the list of items. From the Shared Documents page, click the Filter link. In the Modified By list, click the date the file was last edited or click the name of the person who last edited it. You see only items that match the filter selection.

Delete a File from the Shared Documents Folder

① Click the Shared Documents link on the Home page.

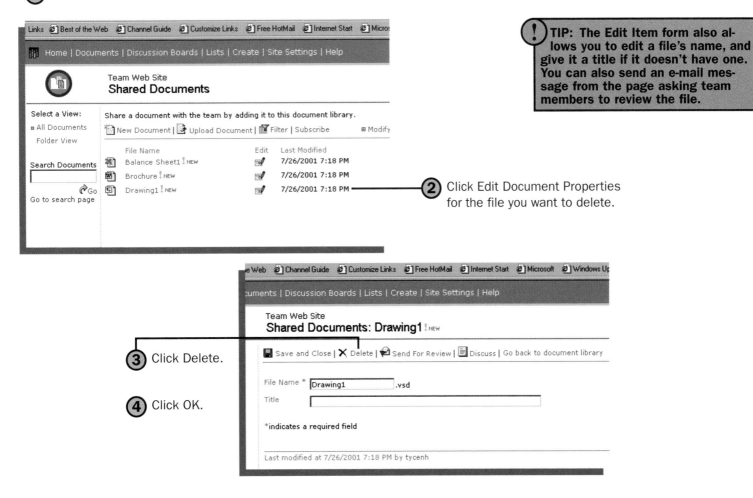

② Click Edit Document Properties for the file you want to delete.

③ Click Delete.

④ Click OK.

> **!** **TIP:** The Edit Item form also allows you to edit a file's name, and give it a title if it doesn't have one. You can also send an e-mail message from the page asking team members to review the file.

Scheduling Events for a Group

When working on a project, you'll need to set up meetings, milestones, and other events. Having a single place where you can post events is one of the key benefits of having a team Web site, and gives your team members a single up-to-date source for event information. SharePoint team Web sites allow you to enter event information in a few steps, creating entire schedules in just a few minutes.

Add an Event

TRY THIS: To view your events listed on a calendar, click the Calendar link on the Events page. The Events page also lets you view only events that you have created, events that happen today, or events that will happen in the next few days.

TIP: Click the Choose Date From Calendar buttons next to the Event Date and End Date boxes to quickly select a date.

(1) Click the Events link on the Home page.

(2) Click the New Item link on the Events page.

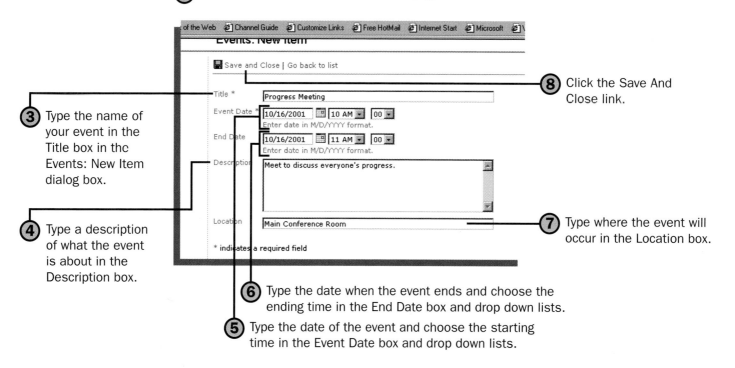

(3) Type the name of your event in the Title box in the Events: New Item dialog box.

(4) Type a description of what the event is about in the Description box.

(8) Click the Save And Close link.

(7) Type where the event will occur in the Location box.

(6) Type the date when the event ends and choose the ending time in the End Date box and drop down lists.

(5) Type the date of the event and choose the starting time in the Event Date box and drop down lists.

Setting Up a Contact List

In any project environment, you need a list of the people involved and how to reach them. In a publishing environment, for example, this list would include writers, editors, supervisors, experts, and anyone else involved with your team. Having a contact list on your team Web site means that even though you may not have access to your personal contact list, you can find that important phone number from anywhere as long as you have an Internet connection. A SharePoint team Web site allows you to add, manage, and remove contacts from within your browser.

TRY THIS: If you've already got the contacts you want in your Microsoft Outlook contact list, you can import them directly. To do this, click Import Contacts on the Contacts page. If the Choose Profile dialog box appears, select your account from that dialog box, and click OK. Then choose the contacts you want to import from the Select Users To Import dialog box.

Add a Contact

(1) Click the Contacts link on the Home page.

(2) Click New Item on the Contacts page.

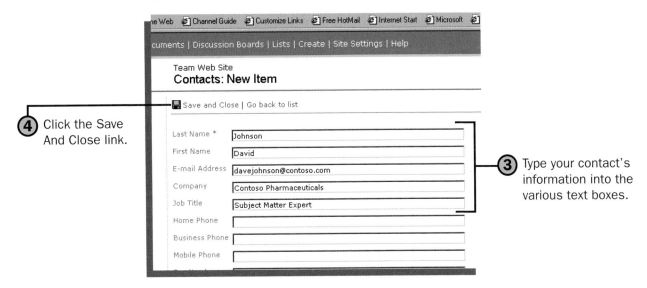

(4) Click the Save And Close link.

(3) Type your contact's information into the various text boxes.

Carrying On an Online Team Discussion

E-mail is a great way to discuss a document with your team members, but it isn't always the best way to carry on long conversations. Group e-mail messages can go to people who don't need them, needlessly filling up their inboxes, or—even worse—the people who really need information may accidentally be excluded from a mailing list. Discussion lists are often a better way to run online discussions. When posted on a team Web site, discussion lists allow team members to browse and post messages that are important to them. Using your Web browser to access a SharePoint team Web site, you can read, post, and organize messages with ease.

TRY THIS: If you need to know when somebody has replied to one of your messages, try using the Subscribe feature on the General Discussion page. When you subscribe to a discussion, you'll be sent an e-mail message telling you when a discussion changes. You can choose to receive this notice whenever there's a change, once every day, or once every week.

Post a Message to Your Team Web Site

1 Click the General Discussion link on the Home page.

2 Click New Discussion on the General Discussion page.

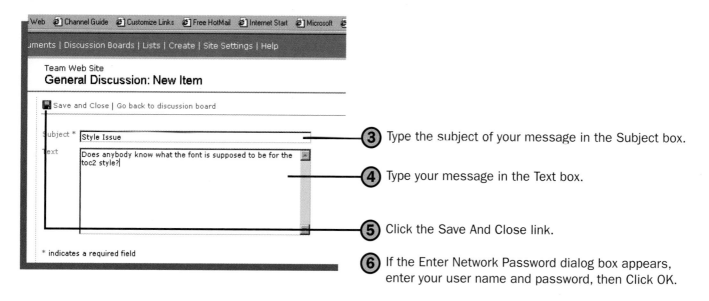

3 Type the subject of your message in the Subject box.

4 Type your message in the Text box.

5 Click the Save And Close link.

6 If the Enter Network Password dialog box appears, enter your user name and password, then Click OK.

Changing the Look of a SharePoint Team Web Site

Once you've created your SharePoint team Web site, you'll probably want to customize what information is displayed on your site's home page. Perhaps you want your newly updated task list to receive more attention from team members than the events list, or you want new announcements to be the only content that shows up when team members first visit the page. Using SharePoint Page Components you can specify what information gets displayed on your home page.

Reorganize Your Team Web Site's Home Page

> **TIP:** Aside from determining which content components go where on the home page, you can also set their placement in relation to each other by dragging. For instance, dragging the Events component above the Announcements component will cause the content of the Events component to be displayed above the content of the Announcements component on the home page.

① Click the Site Settings link on the Home page.

② Click the Customize Home Page Layout link under Web Site Settings on the Site Settings page.

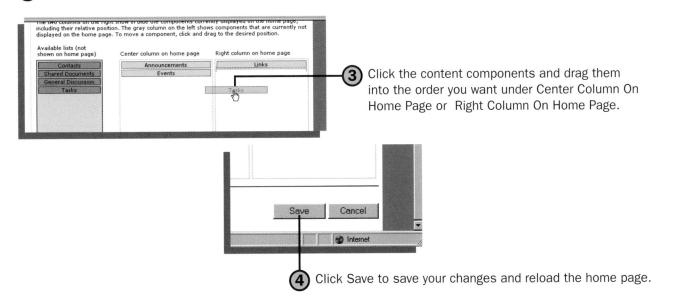

③ Click the content components and drag them into the order you want under Center Column On Home Page or Right Column On Home Page.

④ Click Save to save your changes and reload the home page.

Editing the SharePoint Team Web Site in FrontPage

One of the great hurdles in creating team Web sites in the past has been the need to know HTML or another programming language. Even if you know HTML, making small changes to a page (such as adding a picture to the site's home page) can be a frustrating process in a conventional site, involving server permissions, HTML editors, and transferring files back and forth. However, SharePoint sites are designed to work directly with FrontPage, allowing you to simply open the team Web site just as you would any other FrontPage Web, and edit it within FrontPage.

Once you've got your team Web site open in FrontPage, you can easily add graphics, text, and FrontPage themes to your sites.

SEE ALSO: For information about creating Web sites using FrontPage, see "Using FrontPage" on page 265.

Open a SharePoint Team Web Site in FrontPage

(1) In FrontPage, choose Open Web from the File menu.

(2) Click My Network Places (Web Folders in Windows 98) in the Open Web dialog box.

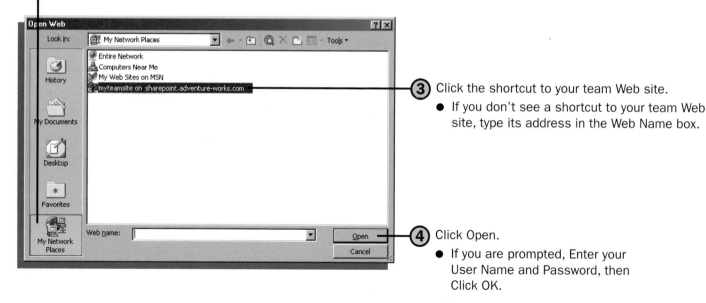

(3) Click the shortcut to your team Web site.
- If you don't see a shortcut to your team Web site, type its address in the Web Name box.

(4) Click Open.
- If you are prompted, Enter your User Name and Password, then Click OK.

Index

customizing
Outlook, 182
PowerPoint presentations, 228–38, 244
SharePoint team Web pages, 332
Web pages (FrontPage), 271
cutting and pasting. *See also* copying and
pasting
cells or ranges (Excel), 105
text, 42

D

data
adding to Access databases, 261–62
automating data entry (Excel), 133
displaying in an Excel chart, 140–47
hiding (Excel), 105
marker (Excel), 145
password-protecting, 211
preventing loss, 13
ranges (Excel), 141–43, 146
recovering after computer crash, 24
series (Excel), 144–45, 147
Database Interface Wizard (FrontPage), 268
database objects (Access), 257
Database Window (Access), 257
Database Wizard (Access), 255
databases. *See* Access databases
Datasheet view (Access), 259–60
date and time, inserting, 45–46
date formats, 107
day at a glance (Outlook), 181
decimal formatting (Excel data), 106
Decrease Decimal button (Excel), 106
Default Design template (PowerPoint), 213

default
margins (Word), 55
Web page editor, 269
defaults, restoring, 25
deleted files, restoring, 14
Deleted Items folder (Outlook), 165
deleting
Access records, 262
characters in Excel cells, 100
Excel cells, 103
Excel ranges, 103
Excel rows, 102
FrontPage Web pages, 275–76
hyperlinks, 290
Office XP files, 13–14
Outlook e-mail messages, 158, 165–66
Outlook folders, 165
Outlook notes, 191
Outlook tasks, 187
Publisher frames, 308
shared documents (SharePoint Web sites),
328
Design Checker (Publisher), 317–18
Design Gallery (Publisher), 303
Design Gallery Live Web site, 29
Design Gallery Objects (Publisher), 303–04
design
templates (PowerPoint), 214, 229–30
themes (Web site backgrounds), 272, 285–
86
designing publications. *See* Publisher
(Microsoft)
diagrams. *See* pictures
dialog box options, getting information about,
18
diary. *See* Outlook journal

digital
camera, adding pictures from, 28
images. *See* pictures
disaster recovery, 24
Discussion Web Wizard (FrontPage), 268
discussions
document review, 201–02
SharePoint team Web sites, 321, 331
disk-based Web sites, 269
distribution lists (Outlook), 183
docked toolbars, 19–20
Document Imaging (Office XP utility), 26
Document Libraries (SharePoint), 327
Document Scanning (Office XP utility), 26
documents. *See* Office XP documents; Word
documents
double-booking (Outlook), 170
double-clicking, 22
downloading files from FTP Web sites, 205
draft e-mail messages, 155
dragging items
Excel charts, 143
Outlook, 171–72, 176, 187
Publisher, 304
selected text, 42
SharePoint team Web pages, 332
toolbars, 20
Word tables, 79
drawings. *See* pictures
drop caps, 71
duplex (double-sided) printing, 61
duration of tasks (Outlook), 188

E

editing
  cells (Excel), 100
  charts (Excel), 143–47
  database tables (Access), 259–60
  hyperlinks, 290
  media files inserted in Office XP documents, 31–33
  multiple documents concurrently, 12
  undoing or redoing changes, 44
  Web pages (FrontPage), 271
  WordArt objects, 36
e-mail message. *See also* Outlook e-mail
  attaching a Web archive, 297
  attaching documents for review, 197, 328
  attaching files, 159
  blind carbon copy (Bcc) line, 155
  composing and sending, 155–56
  copying address from, 185
  deleting, 158, 165–66
  draft messages, 155–56
  forwarding, 159
  removing chevron (<<) marks, 50
  signing, 161–62
  translating, 97
  viruses, 157
e-mail servers, 154
embedding and linking information, 204, 209–10
Enhanced Metafiles, 204
enhancing
  documents with art and sound, 26–36
  PowerPoint presentations, 228–38
entire document, selecting (Word), 41
envelopes, addressing and printing, 55, 57–58

erasing contents of Excel cells or ranges, 103
error checking (Excel), 135
Events page (SharePoint), 329
events, scheduling. *See* Outlook Calendar; SharePoint team Web sites
Excel (Microsoft)
  AutoRepublish option, 293
  change tracking, enabling, 199
  changes, accepting or rejecting, 200
  charts. *See* Excel charts
  linking to other programs, 209–10
  lists. *See* Excel lists
  NetMeeting, accessing from, 207
  overview, 98
  password-protecting data, 211
  printing from, 119–22
  sharing documents via the Web, 205
  workbooks. *See* Excel workbooks
  worksheets. *See* Excel worksheets
Excel charts
  basic chart, creating, 141
  blank rows or columns, 142
  chart types, 141
  Chart Wizard, 141
  colors, 143–45
  data marker, 145
  Data Range tab, 141
  data ranges, copying, 146
  data ranges, multiple, 142
  data ranges, outlining in color, 143
  data ranges, reversing, 141
  data ranges, selecting, 146
  data series defined, 144
  data series, modifying, 145
  data series, removing, 147
  editing, 143–47
  Enhanced Metafile, 204

Excel charts, *continued*
  Excel Chart Object, 204
  formatting, 144–45
  grouping information, 142
  including more worksheet data, 146
  labels, 142–44
  legends, 141
  margins, 144
  organizing worksheet, 142
  pasting into Word documents, 204
  pie charts, 147
  plot area, 141
  previewing, 141
  text labels, 142–43
  titles, 141, 147
Excel lists
  averaging data, 151
  filtering data, 150
  header rows, 148
  separating, 148
  sorting data, 149
  subtotals, 151
  summarizing information, 148
Excel outlines, 217
Excel workbooks
  blank workbook, 99
  creating, 99, 115–16
  freezing and unfreezing panes, 137
  large workbooks, 137
  linking between, 132
  multiple, arranging on screen, 138
  New Workbook task pane, 99
  opening, 99
  recently used workbooks, opening, 99
  templates, 115–16
  tiling, 137

Internet, *continued*
   Web site development tools. *See* Microsoft
      FrontPage
intranet
   broadcasting PowerPoint presentations, 250
   publishing Web pages to, 282, 297
invitations, publishing. *See* Publisher
      (Microsoft)
ISP (Internet service provider), 153
italic text, 63

New Queries dialog box, 263
newsletters, publishing. *See* Publisher (Microsoft)
newspaper-style columns (Word), 69
nonadjacent areas, selecting (Excel), 101
non-breaking spaces, 45
non-contiguous text, selecting (Word), 41
non-Office files, opening in Word, 206
normal font, returning to (Word), 63
Normal template (Word), 73
Normal View, 59
Northwind sample database (Access), 256
notes
   Outlook, 191
   PowerPoint, 241–42
Notes Master Layout view (PowerPoint), 242
nudging frames (Publisher), 303
numbered lists (Word), 67
numbering pages, 53–54
numeric formats (Excel), 107

O

Objects By Design (Publisher), 304
Office XP (Microsoft). *See also* Office XP documents
   Access. *See* Access (Microsoft)
   clip art library, 29
   common tasks, 23
   double-clicking, 22
   embedding and linking data, 209–10
   Excel. *See* Excel (Microsoft)
   exiting programs, 16
   finding a file or text in a file, 10
   FrontPage. *See* FrontPage (Microsoft)
   Help resources, 17–18

Office XP (Microsoft), *continued*
   importing and exporting files, 206
   Internet Free/Busy Service, 161–62
   NetMeeting, 176, 207–08
   opening an existing file, 9
   Outlook. *See* Outlook (Microsoft)
   overview, 2–4, 6
   PowerPoint. *See* PowerPoint (Microsoft)
   printing in, 15
   Publisher. *See* Publisher (Microsoft)
   recently used files, opening, 9
   recovering files, 24
   repairing corrupted program files, 25
   Repeat key, 22
   restoring defaults, 25
   right-clicking, 22
   Save As feature, 13
   sharing information among applications, 204, 209–10
   Shortcut Bar. *See* Office XP Shortcut Bar
   speech recognition, 22
   starting an Office XP program, 7, 9
   switching between programs or documents, 11
   task panes, 19–20
   toolbars, 19–20, 22
   visual cues, 22
   Word. *See* Word (Microsoft)
Office XP Clipboard, 12, 42
Office XP documents. *See also* Word documents
   adding graphics, sound, and video, 26–36
   closing, 16
   collaborating on. *See* online collaboration
   deleting files, 13–14
   editing multiple documents, 12
   online collaboration, 196–211

Office XP documents, *continued*
   password-protecting, 211
   preventing data loss, 13
   previewing as Web pages, 288
   printing, 15, 61
   recovering, 24
   repairing, 24
   restoring deleted files, 14
   saving as Web archive files, 297
   saving as Web pages, 292
   saving files, 13–14
   saving to SharePoint team Web sites, 325–26
   scaling to fit paper size, 61
   searching for, 10
   storing on FTP Web sites, 205
   storing on SharePoint team Web sites, 325–28
   successive drafts, 13
   switching between, 11
   tiling multiple document windows, 11–12
   viewing, 59–60
   working in several programs at once, 11–12
Office XP Media Gallery, 26
Office XP Shortcut Bar
   buttons, hiding vs. deleting, 8
   displaying on Windows startup, 8
   installing, 7
   personalizing, 8
   starting Office XP programs from, 7
online address book. *See* Outlook contacts
online broadcasts (PowerPoint presentations), 250
online collaboration
   adding comments, 198
   change tracking, enabling, 199
   changes, accepting or rejecting, 200
   comments, merging and comparing, 203
   discussing documents online, 201–02

schedule
  information, sharing, 175
  overview (Outlook), 181
scheduling meetings and events
  Internet Free/Busy Service, 177–78
  live PowerPoint broadcasts, 250
  NetMeeting, 207
  Outlook, 169–72, 175–76, 186
  SharePoint team Web sites, 329
scheduling resources, 175
schematics. *See* pictures
scratch area (Publisher), 301, 306
ScreenTips, 18
searching
  for a file or text in a file, 10
  for clip art, 29
  for contact names in Microsoft Outlook, 183
  for Excel functions, 128
  for formatting, 77
  for text and replacing in Word documents,
    10, 49–50
  limiting searches, 10
  search parameters, 50
security
  password-protecting documents, 211
  SharePoint team Web sites, 323
selecting
  cell ranges (Excel), 101, 127, 137, 146
  functions (Excel), 127–28
  nonadjacent areas (Excel), 101
  text (Word), 41
sending
  attachments with e-mail messages, 159
  e-mail messages, 155–56
  out meeting invitations (Outlook), 175–76
sentences, selecting (Word), 41
sequential data, filling in (Excel), 133

server-based Web sites, 269
Set Transparent Color tool (FrontPage), 34
setting
  Outlook Today as home page, 182
  tab stops, 68
  up a PowerPoint slide show, 245
shaded backgrounds
  Excel cells, 111–12, 126
  Outlook e-mails, 162
  Word documents, 72
Shared Documents folder (SharePoint), 321,
  327–28
SharePoint Team Services (Microsoft)
  Events page, 329
  installing on Web server, 321
  overview, 320
  team Web sites. *See* SharePoint team Web
    sites
SharePoint team Web sites
  adding users, 323–24
  assigning roles to users, 323–24
  contact lists, 321, 330
  creating, 322
  customizing, 332
  definition and overview, 321
  discussion lists, 321
  Document Libraries, 327
  document management, 325–28
  editing using FrontPage, 333
  General Discussion page, 331
  importing Outlook contacts, 330
  online discussions, 331
  passwords, 324
  posting messages, 331
  removing users, 323
  scheduling events, 329
  security settings, 323

SharePoint team Web sites, *continued*
  Shared Documents folder, 321, 327–28
  SharePoint server location, 322
  user accounts, 323–24
sharing data between Office XP applications,
  204, 209–10
shifting cells (Excel), 104
shortcuts. *See also* keyboard shortcuts
  moving text, 42
  selecting text, 41
shrinking text to fit cell size (Excel), 108
signing e-mails automatically, 161–62
Simple Query Wizard (Access), 263
Slide Finder window (PowerPoint), 223
Slide Navigator window (PowerPoint), 225
slide shows. *See* PowerPoint presentations
Slide Sorter view (PowerPoint), 247
slide transitions, animating (PowerPoint), 231
smart tags
  AutoCorrect (Word text), 47
  copying formulas (Excel), 129
  error checking (Excel), 135
  formatting (Excel cells), 104
  formatting (Word text), 42
  overview, 22
sort order (Outlook items), 194
sorting and filtering
  Access data, 263
  documents on SharePoint team Web sites, 327
  Excel lists, 149–50
  Outlook journal entries, 189, 193–94
  undesirable e-mail, 167
sounds, adding to Office XP documents, 30
spacing between lines and paragraphs (Word),
  64
spam e-mail, 167
sparkling text, 63

speaker notes for PowerPoint presentations, 241–42
special effects
    PowerPoint presentations, 228–38
    text effects (Word), 71
speech recognition, 22
spell checking
    correcting typos automatically, 47–48
    Outlook e-mails, 156
    Publisher documents, 318
Spelling and Grammar dialog box (Word), 47
splitting
    cells within tables (Word), 83
    tables (Word), 82
    worksheets (Excel), 137
Start Menu, 7
starting Office XP programs, 7
static date and time, 45–46
sticky notes (Outlook), 191
stopping
    automatic correction of a word, 47
    printing, 15
storing documents on SharePoint team Web sites, 325–28
strikethrough text (Word), 63
styles
    FrontPage styles (cascading style sheets), 272
    Word styles, 73–76
Styles and Formatting button (Word), 76
subscript text (Word), 63
subtotals (Excel), 151
subwindows, 286
summarizing information (Excel), 148
superscript text (Word), 63

switching
    between programs or documents, 11
    between task panes, 20
    printers, 317
symbols, adding, 45
synonyms, finding, 51
system crash, preventing data loss due to, 13

T

tab stops, 68
table frames (Publisher), 308
table of contents (Word), 93
tables
    Access, 254, 259–60
    copying from Web into Excel, 114
    Word. *See* Word tables
Tables and Borders toolbar, 33, 83
tags
    FrontPage, 267
    smart tags. *See* smart tags
task panes, 19–20
tasks
    common (quick-find table), 23
    managing (Outlook), 186–88
team Web sites. *See* SharePoint team Web sites; online collaboration
teleconferencing, 176, 207–08, 331
telephone
    list (Outlook), 193
    numbers, formatting (Excel), 107
templates
    Excel, 115–16
    PowerPoint, 214, 229–30
    Word, 39, 73, 91–92
testing FrontPage Web sites with various browsers, 278

text
    adding to slides (PowerPoint), 224
    aligning (Excel), 108–09
    animating (PowerPoint), 235–36
    automatically correcting spelling, 47–48
    backgrounds and borders, 72
    boxes (Publisher), 309–12
    copying, 42
    cutting, 42
    finding and replacing, 49–50
    formatting (Excel), 100
    formatting (in Publisher text boxes), 309–11
    formatting (PowerPoint), 224
    formatting (Word), 62–73, 77
    inserting automatically (Word), 43–44
    labels (Excel), 100, 142
    lines around, 72
    moving, 42
    overflow area (Publisher), 309
    placement, controlling with tabs, 68
    searching for, in Office XP files, 10
    selecting, 41
    shrinking to fit cell (Excel), 108
    wrapping around pictures (Publisher), 314
    wrapping within cell (Excel), 108
Text Box tool (Publisher), 308
Text Effects tab (Word), 63
text-based chat (NetMeeting), 207
themes (Web site backgrounds), 272, 285–86, 291
thesaurus, 51
thumbnail
    pictures, FrontPage, 276
    pictures, PowerPoint, 213, 218
    sketches of publication types, 299, 304

About the Authors

Carol Brown has more than fifteen years of experience writing dozens of books and user manuals, online Help systems from the traditional to the revolutionary, training materials both computer-based and in print, and user interfaces from buttons to wizards. Before that she wrote the first guides to eating on the cheap in Seattle, served as a management and organizational consultant, taught high school math and science, created wearable art, and traveled the world.

Resources Online, and its founder and president Jim Larkin, has been creating and delivering content for companies and organizations via the Web, interactive CD-ROMs, traditional electronic media, and print for more than fifteen years. The company provides a range of services—broadcast-quality video production and digital post-production; streaming media; development of interactive Web sites and CD- and DVD-ROMs; print production; and creative services such as writing for books, instructional and marketing material, and video scripts.

The manuscript for this book was prepared and submitted to Microsoft Press in electronic form. Text files were prepared using Microsoft Word 2002. Pages were composed by Resources Online and Microsoft Press using Adobe PageMaker 6.52 for Windows, with text set in Times and display type in ITC Franklin Gothic. Composed pages were delivered to the printer as electronic prepress files.

Cover Graphic Designer

Tim Girvin Design

Interior Graphic Designers

Joel Panchot
James D. Kramer

Interior Graphic Artists

Kat Marriner
Laren Watson
Heidi Hackler
April Richards

Principal Compositor

Kat Marriner

Principal Proofreader/Copy Editor

Norreen Holmes

Indexer

Luke Celt

Get a **Free**
e-mail newsletter, updates,
special offers, links to related books,
and more when you
register on line!

Register your Microsoft Press® title on our Web site and you'll get a FREE subscription to our e-mail newsletter, *Microsoft Press Book Connections.* You'll find out about newly released and upcoming books and learning tools, online events, software downloads, special offers and coupons for Microsoft Press customers, and information about major Microsoft® product releases. You can also read useful additional information about all the titles we publish, such as detailed book descriptions, tables of contents and indexes, sample chapters, links to related books and book series, author biographies, and reviews by other customers.

Registration is easy. Just visit this Web page and fill in your information:
http://www.microsoft.com/mspress/register

Microsoft®

- -